P9-CCR-525

The Tale of the Allergist's Wife and Other Plays

CHARLES BUSCH

The Tale of the Allergist's Wife and Other Plays

Vampire Lesbians of Sodom

Psycho Beach Party

The Lady in Question

Red Scare on Sunset

The Tale of the Allergist's Wife

Grove Press
New York

The collection copyright © 2001 by Charles Busch
Introduction copyright © 2000 by Charles Busch
Vampire Lesbians of Sodom © 1985 by Charles Busch
Psycho Beach Party © 1988 by Charles Busch
The Lady in Question © 1989 by Charles Busch
Red Scare on Sunset © 1991 by Charles Busch
The Tale of the Allergist's Wife © 1999 by Charles Busch

All rights reserved. No part of this book may be reproduced in any form or by any electronic or mechanical means, including information storage and retrieval systems, without permission in writing from the publisher, except by a reviewer, who may quote brief passages in a review. Any member of educational institutions wishing to photocopy part or all of the work for classroom use, or publishers who would like to obtain permission to include the work in an anthology, should send their inquiries to Grove/Atlantic, Inc., 841 Broadway, New York, NY 10003.

CAUTION: Professionals and amateurs are hereby warned that performances of *Vampire Lesbians of Sodom, Psycho Beach Party, The Lady in Question, Red Scare on Sunset,* and *The Tale of the Allergist's Wife* are subject to a royalty. They are fully protected under the copyright laws of the United States, Canada, United Kingdom, and all British Commonwealth countries, all countries covered by the International Copyright Union, the Pan-American Copyright Convention, the Universal Copyright Convention, and the Berne Convention, and all countries with which the United States has reciprocal copyright relations. All rights, including professional/amateur stage rights, motion picture, recitation, public reading, radio broadcasting, television, video or sound taping, all other forms of mechanical or electronic reproduction, such as CD-ROM, CD-I, DVD, information storage and retrieval systems and photocopying, and rights of translation into foreign languages, are strictly reserved. In their present form the plays are dedicated to the reading public only.

The stock and amateur live stage performance rights to *Vampire Lesbians of Sodom, Psycho Beach Party, The Lady in Question, Red Scare on Sunset,* and *The Tale of the Allergist's Wife* are controlled exclusively by Samuel French, Inc. No professional or nonprofessional performance of the play may be given without obtaining in advance the written permission of Samuel French, Inc., 45 West 25th Street, New York, NY 10010, and paying the requisite fee, whether the play is presented for charity or gain and whether or not admission is charged.

Stock and amateur royalty quoted on application to Samuel French, Inc.

First-class professional applications for permission to perform the plays in this volume, and for those other rights stated above, must be made in advance to Jeff Melnick/Marc H. Glick, c/o Glick and Weintraub, P.C., 1501 Broadway, Suite 2401, New York, NY 10036.

Published simultaneously in Canada
Printed in the United States of America

Library of Congress Cataloging-in-Publication Data

Busch, Charles.
The tale of the allergist's wife, and other plays / Charles Busch.
p. cm.
Contents: Vampire lesbians of Sodom—Psycho beach party—The lady in question—
Red scare on sunset—The tale of the allergist's wife.
ISBN 0-8021-3785-7
I. Title.
PS3552.U813 T3 2001
812'.54—dc21 00-048376

Grove Press
841 Broadway
New York, NY 10003

02 03 10 9 8 7 6 5 4 3

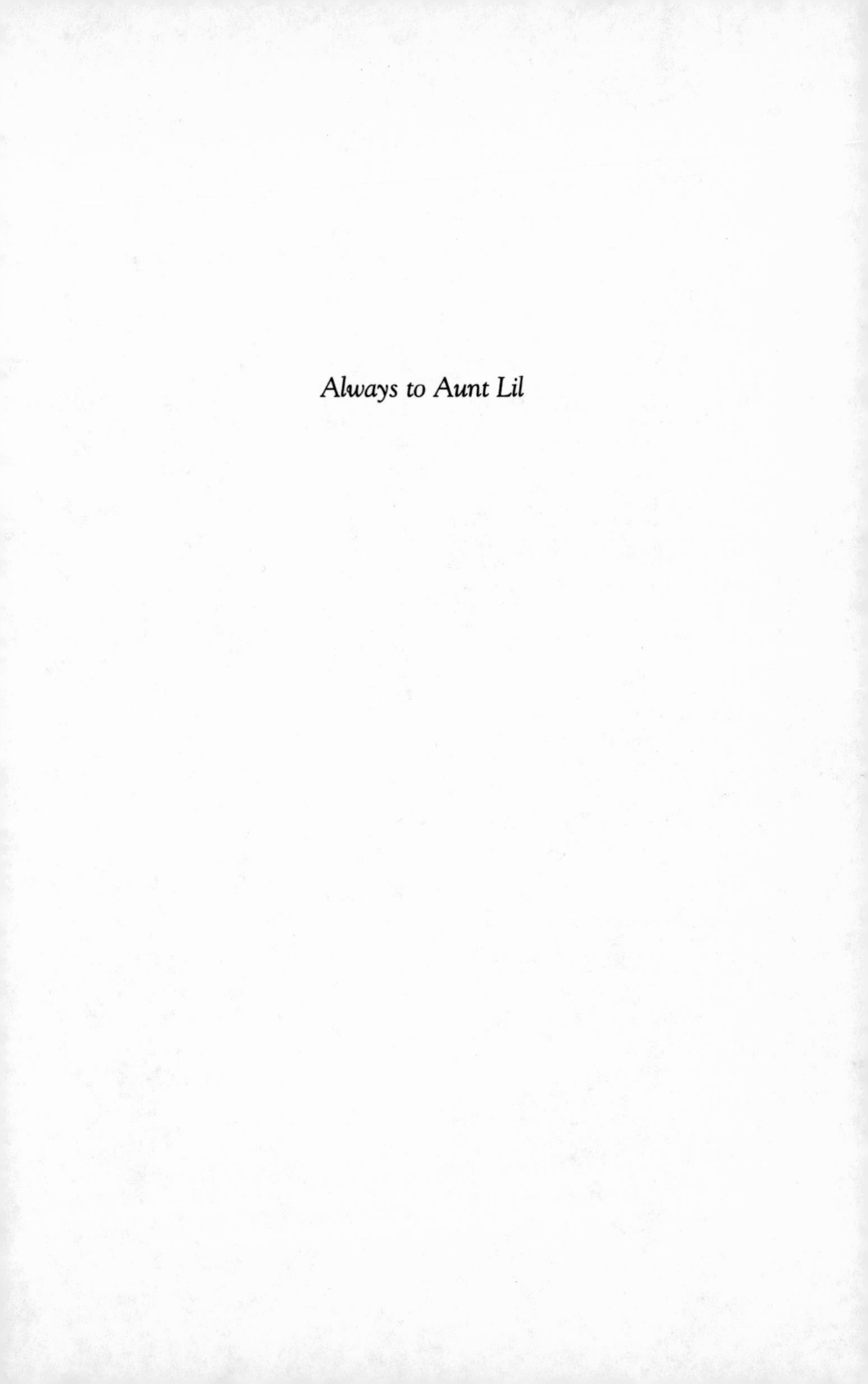

Always to Aunt Lil

Contents

Introduction

I was never in a school play, and for a good reason: I couldn't remember a line of dialogue. I nearly hyperventilated the moment I hit the stage. It was because I loved it too much. To be "up there" was almost too magical to imagine. Ever since the age of seven, when I was taken by my father to the old Metropolitan Opera House to see Joan Sutherland in *La Sonnambula,* I've been obsessed by the image of that magnificent redheaded lady drifting ethereally through a painted nineteenth-century landscape. It's not unfair to say that my entire career has been an attempt to re-create that first impression.

I was desperate to be a child star, only there was no one willing to exploit me. I went so far as to send a snapshot of myself to the producers of the film version of *Oliver,* offering my services for the title role. Growing up in Manhattan was helpful. Sometimes after school, I'd go to the Palace Theatre and persuade the stage doorman to let me go onstage. I can't even imagine what old "Pops" thought of this fragile twelve-year-old boy belting out "The Man That Got Away."

All but one of the plays in this volume were written to allow me to be "up there." I started out as a performer who needed lines to say and, through necessity, grew to be a writer. Along the way, I discovered that the pleasure I derived from writing nearly equaled the joy I received from being onstage. From 1984 through 1991, I was the leading lady and playwright-in-residence of "Theatre-in-Limbo." We were very much a throwback to the acting troupes of the nineteenth century. Considering that the group was assembled merely on the basis of who was available and willing to work for free, it was rather remarkable that each of us filled a very specific role in the traditional stock company. Arnie Kolodner was the handsome stalwart leading man. Ken Elliott, our director, played the effete villains. Theresa

Marlowe was always the ingenue. Andy Halliday was our character man, Julie Halston the comic soubrette, Bobby Carey the juvenile, Meghan Robinson the dark villainess—and I was the leading lady, a Sarah Bernhardt of Avenue C.

The advantage of writing play after play for an ensemble is that you're never facing a blank page. There are so many givens to constructing a plot. There must be a role for everyone in the company. The playwright has to take into consideration everyone's strengths and weaknesses. If an actor played a small role in the last play, he's owed a better opportunity in the next. In Theatre-in-Limbo, if an actor was in drag in the last play, he might feel the need to butch it up in the next. My early plays were Chinese puzzles constructed of promises and budgetary considerations. The style of the plays was dictated by our performing venue. The Limbo Lounge was an art gallery/after-hours bar (sans liquor license)/performance art space. There were actually two Limbo Lounges that we performed in. The first was a small floor-through on Tenth Street off First Avenue. Several months after our first show, the Limbo Lounge moved to a large garage on Ninth Street between Avenues B and C. It was impossible to store scenery or costumes in either place, so I wrote plays that required no set and collected shopping bags to schlep the costumes back and forth.

When I say "no set," I mean an empty stage, no furniture. These were "stand-up" plays. I learned a great deal about doling out exposition. In the first few lines of every scene, I had to make perfectly clear the location and time, and in an unobtrusive and entertaining manner. Our acting style was also affected by the venue. A large percentage of the audience was standing and drinking Rolling Rock beers. To command their attention, we had to be highly energized and emotionally intense. This fit perfectly with my perversely French fin de siècle melodramatic aesthetic. Indeed, two of our shows, *Theodora, She-Bitch of Byzantium* and *Pardon My Inquisition or Kiss the Blood Off My Castanets,* were directly inspired by the plays of Victorien Sardou, author of many of Bernhardt's greatest roles.

Vampire Lesbians of Sodom was the first play I wrote for Theatre-in-Limbo. I like to say I wrote it in four hours while working as a temp receptionist. In truth, I did a little rewriting the next day. But not too much. It really was meant to be just a sketch performed over one weekend. I had no idea it would become my calling card for years to come. The historical periods of the play were chosen because they lent themselves easily to cheap improvised costumes. Everyone knows that the women of Sodom and Gomorrah sauntered around town in G-strings and spike heels.

The three scenes that make up *Vampire Lesbians of Sodom* were written very much to showcase various characters and performance styles that I had been playing with for the previous eight years. The first scene, set in ancient Sodom, is written in the form of a burlesque sketch. The Succubus and the young virgin were played as aging strippers performing a bawdy scene between strip numbers. Scene Two, set in Hollywood in the early twenties, gave me the opportunity to play a theatrical grande dame on the order of Mrs. Patrick Campbell or Nazimova. The third and final scene, set in contemporary times, allowed me to create a world-weary, hard-boiled showbiz dame somewhere between Lucille Ball and Lauren Bacall.

For a long time I was embarrassed by what I considered to be the flimsiness of *Vampire Lesbians of Sodom*. Rereading it recently, I was struck by how entertaining a little sketch it is. Never meant to be considered a play at all, this little decadent dream achieved its goals quite well. It was created merely to entertain a late night crowd on a hot summer night in the East Village. The crazy miracle is that the play has had such an incredibly long life.

Each of us in our troupe had struggled long and hard for a place in the theatre—and with little success. How extraordinary it was for us to see the campy little *Vampire Lesbians of Sodom* develop such an intense cult following. Lines formed hours early in the crack-infested neighborhood. Once inside, people would be seated on top of the ice machine, crammed into the corners, and sometimes standing in the hallway, where they could only *hear* the play. On the heels of such hoopla, we tried to find a commercial producer to move the play to a real theatre. No one would touch it. My director, Ken Elliott, decided that we should produce the play ourselves. With herculean effort, we raised what was to us the astronomical sum of $55,000 and opened at the historic Provincetown Playhouse on Macdougal Street on June 19,

1985. After the opening-night performance, all of our friends jammed downstairs into the Green Room just in time for the early edition of *The New York Times* to be read aloud. It was an incredible rave that left no one out. I slipped away from the crowd and retreated to my dressing room, shut the door, and wept. I knew at that moment that I could finally achieve my hard-won goal, which was to earn my living in the theatre.

Vampire Lesbians of Sodom went on to run five years and is one of the longest-running plays in Off-Broadway history. Apart from a pretty fantastic title, one of the reasons for its longevity was, oddly enough, a sweet innocence that made people feel good. The two ladies of the title bitch and compete against each other for two thousand years, but at the end realize that the intensity of their relationship is what has sustained them. They belong to each other. I like to think the sweet innocence of our original company and our affection for each other played a great part in the show's success. We were an old-fashioned troupe of players.

Very early on, Ken Elliott and I decided to create the Pirandellian conceit that our East Village audience was actually watching a slightly faded theatrical star on tour with her somewhat seedy stock company. I was always, in effect, Charles Busch *playing* an aging actress playing the vampiress Madeleine Astarté or whatever the current role in her vast repertoire was. We heightened this concept through the use of footlights, a show curtain decorated with the titles of our many plays, a delayed star entrance, elaborately staged curtain calls, and lastly, the curtain speech. It was a curtain speech that inspired *Psycho Beach Party*.

After each performance, still in my "actress" persona, I'd make a curtain speech graciously imploring the audience to sign our mailing list. To make my pitch more entertaining, I'd improvise the titles of future plays they might see. One night, the title *Gidget Goes Psychotic* popped into my feverish brain. It got a big laugh and I used it as the punch line of my curtain speech for quite some time. Eventually, Ken said, "You know, we've been promoting this play for years. Maybe we *should* do a show called *Gidget Goes Psychotic.*" Initially, it didn't appeal to me at all. I found no glamour or fake grandeur in the Frankie and Annette beach party movies or in the film and television series *Gidget*. The shows I was writing for Theatre-in-Limbo were built on fantasies of who I'd like to play. A Byzantine empress, yes; a teenage surfer girl—I don't think so. Then it occurred to me that if Gidget were indeed psychotic, perhaps that would manifest itself in multiple personalities. These other selves, particularly her main alter ego, the dominatrix Ann Bowman, would give me the flamboyant acting opportunities I sought.

We originally performed *Gidget Goes Psychotic* as late shows at the Limbo Lounge while we were performing a full eight-show-a-week schedule of *Vampire Lesbians of Sodom* at the Provincetown Playhouse. As soon as the curtain came down on Macdougal Street, we'd jump into cabs and race across town. Our audience would be waiting outside the club before we got there. It was exhausting but exhilarating. The response was so overwhelming that we decided to transfer that play Off-Broadway as well.

There was some concern that there could be copyright problems with the title *Gidget Goes Psychotic* and that I should think of an alternate. Frankly, I was glad to retitle it *Psycho Beach Party*. What had begun as strictly a spoof of a specific movie and TV series had become a very personal piece of writing. I don't imagine I'm alone in having experienced as a young person a feeling of being a different person in each facet of my life. My heroine, Chicklet, learns that each of the various roles she plays in life are all part of one being, and that they only make her stronger. It was fascinating for me to realize that all creative writing is "personal." The campiest theatrical spoof full of movie references could be a revealing self-portrait that others might identify with.

In 1989, Ken Elliott and I met with Kyle Renick, the artistic director of the WPA Theatre, to discuss the possibility of doing a play there. There was never a question of doing an already-written play from my trunk. The trunk has always been empty, except perhaps for wigs, shoes, and corsets. I only wrote when I had an opening-night date set in my calendar. We were tossing around story ideas for possible plays when I remembered that I had a gorgeous 1940s gown gathering dust in the closet that had been made for me to wear at a charity benefit. It had always evoked for me Joan Crawford or Norma Shearer in an anti-Nazi war melodrama. I pitched that idea to Kyle and it turned out that he, too, had great affection for embattled heroines skiing to safety across the Alps. It was assumed that we would do this play in the same burlesque-sketch style and on the same bare stage as we had before. However, this would be my first opportunity to write a play to be specifically performed in a real theatre and not in a club. I felt free to write it in two rather leisurely acts. Though it was a film spoof, we were performing it on the stage, and so my frame of reference also ran to such stolid theatrical wartime fare as Lillian Hellman's *Watch on the Rhine* and Robert Sherwood's *There Shall Be No Night.*

Besides being a movie-genre satire, the play also had something to say about the New Age philosophy popular in the late eighties. I was very disturbed by the idea that everything that happens to us happens because we have somehow created it. While I certainly believe that we can affect our fates, this enlightened selfishness exhibits a dangerous lack of sympathy for those whom fate turns against, and has been the essence of many faddish religions, certainly from the mid nineteenth century onward. I had my myopic wartime heroine, Gertrude Garnet, falling under the sway of a somewhat suspect swami.

The genre we were satirizing was definitely not a B movie. It was a luxurious, star-driven vehicle and, now that I was no longer writing for the Limbo Lounge, I wanted a set. Indeed, I wanted a divan and a fireplace to dramatically lean against. The play being produced before us was Larry Kramer's *Just Say No,* which took place in an opulent Washington, D.C., town house. It had a lavish double-decker set complete with a massive staircase leading to the upper level. With some paint and a moose head, there was no reason why it couldn't be transformed into a Bavarian *Schloss.* I rewrote my play to accommodate all seven doors and a portrait hiding a safe. It may not sound like a lot, but it was a genuine thrill to finally be able to sit onstage.

I have such intense nostalgia for *The Lady In Question.* At the risk of sounding like one of my own pretentious heroines, I believe it to be the apotheosis of my years with Theatre-in-Limbo. Everyone was perfectly cast and working at a highly skilled level. I can't imagine any other production of that play being more definitive in its set, costumes, lighting, sound, direction, and performance.

We had established a great relationship with the WPA Theatre, which continued with my next play, *Red Scare on Sunset.* Once again,

I sold Kyle Renick with a one-line description of the plot: "I play a 1950s movie actress, filming a movie about Lady Godiva, who gets beaned on the head and dreams that she's back in medieval England." I suppose I found it comic fodder for me, a drag performer, to play a woman famous for being naked. As Ken Elliott and I developed the story, it became clear that he was more interested in the McCarthy-era framing device than the saga of Lady Godiva. Before I knew it, we'd concocted a 1950s red-scare melodrama with a short medieval dream sequence. I'm very grateful it turned out that way.

My plays up to this point had been strictly comic melodramas. As a student of nineteenth-century boulevard theatre and Hollywood film, I was intrigued that a contemporary audience could be swayed by the same melodramatic plot conventions that had slayed 'em in the balcony in days gone by—if they were leavened by parody and knowing laughter. In *Red Scare on Sunset,* I thought it would be interesting if the two leading characters we were led to root for—the lovable heroine and her wacky best friend—spouted ideologies reprehensible to our modern sensibility. I thought that would be a fascinating moral challenge to the audience. In writing a play about Hollywood during the McCarthy era, it seemed to me, the obvious story would be about a sympathetic leftist who is hounded out of his career. I thought it would be more outrageous to write the play as a mad right-wing nightmare. A very conservative movie actress discovers to her dismay that everyone in her circle is involved in a communist conspiracy to destroy the Hollywood star system. In this reversal of melodramatic convention, it is the lovely heroine who sanctimoniously "names names," who is revealed at the end to be the true horror.

The play dealt with the American fear of self-reflection, the fact that anyone who challenges the clichés of our Hollywood-inspired white-picket-fence fantasies is considered foreign, subversive, and dangerous. However liberal my own sympathies were, I thought it was important to show that radical extremists of both sides share ideological similarities—i.e., a fear of homosexuality, and the desire to deny the other side its freedom of speech. It required a well-developed sense of irony to traverse the morally askew territory of the play. I was taken by surprise at the number of critics and audience members who jumped to the odd conclusion that if I, the playwright, was playing a woman who "names names," somehow that implied that I was personally advocating blacklisting. It amazed me that anyone would take at face value what was, to me, clearly a satiric attack on radical conservatism.

By 1991, I felt that in writing play after play for myself in drag and for the same ensemble of actors, I was imposing too many limitations on myself as both writer and actor. I embarked on a decade of experimentation. I tried my hand at the novel, cabaret, musical revues, journalism, acting in other writers' plays, writing myself a noncomedic drag role, and, my God, even writing myself a male role. Some of these experiments were more successful than others, but it was all a journey to discover what I did best and what I enjoyed most. It wasn't difficult for me to see that my search for an artistic identity mirrored the quests for reinvention pursued by the heroines I played on the stage.

The protagonists of all of my plays are women who, in their struggle to find a place in the world, create a new persona that enables them to navigate life's rough waters. Eventually, they feel a terrible conflict between the false self and the girl they once were, and out of that conflict they emerge a stronger person. I never intend to tell that story, but it's always there: whether it's a virgin who evolves into a glamorous vampire, a teenage girl who requires a virago-like alter ego to feel complete, a honky-tonk piano player who streamlines herself into an elegant concert virtuoso, or an Indiana farm girl who becomes a popular movie star. I am my heroines. The Limbo Lounge transformed a skinny, confused performance artist into a parody grande dame of the theatre.

One of my projects in the nineties was writing the libretto to a musical entitled *The Green Heart.* The show, produced by Manhattan Theatre Club, wasn't terribly well received, but I established a wonderful rapport with Lynne Meadow, the artistic director of MTC. On opening night, when the reviews were less than stellar, she told me that she'd love Manhattan Theatre Club to be my artistic home and that she would produce and direct my next play. I was extremely touched by her gesture of faith.

Well, here we go again, I thought. I had no play to hand to her. Just as I had written *Vampire Lesbians of Sodom* for the Limbo Lounge, I set about writing a play for Manhattan Theatre Club. I wasn't starting from scratch. A few years before, I had performed a solo show called *Flipping My Wig*. One of the pieces in it was a six-minute monologue of a woman named Miriam Passman. Mrs. Passman was an emotionally intense Upper West Side matron who releases her long-pent-up creativity by performing a musical tribute to Edith Piaf at a Greenwich Village cabaret. That monologue was one of the few times I had tapped into the satirically-rich Suburban New York Jewish milieu that I'd grown up in. That lady was as much in my bones as my most arch movie-inspired heroines. For a long time, I'd wanted to write a play built around that bitterly raging character, but it was difficult coming up with a plot that didn't read like a TV sitcom episode. Spurred by Lynne Meadow's offer, I wondered what would happen if I placed Miriam (renamed Marjorie Taub) in a theatrical genre at odds with her manic New York attitudes. What if I flung her and her allergist husband into the middle of a very cryptic, enigmatic Pinter or Albee play? That concept forced me to take these comic urban characters onto foreign turf, which liberated my imagination and formed the essence of *The Tale of the Allergist's Wife*.

Marjorie suffers from the same feelings of dissatisfaction as my other heroines. However, this being a more naturalistic play, she doesn't abandon her family to become the world's most glamorous philosopher. She remains in her Riverside Drive apartment, raging in impotent frustration. Her only transformations lie in her frustrated fantasies. The character of her childhood friend Lee Green, née Lillian Greenblatt, bears a resemblance to my earlier ladies. A refugee from Bronx River Road, Lee has reinvented herself as a globe-trotting free spirit. I can't escape it.

The Tale of the Allergist's Wife was the first play of mine that wasn't a vehicle for me to perform in. That was never an option. One of my strengths as a performer is to play a female character with, one hopes, a psychological truth, but at the same time to add a layer that comments on the history of star acting. I find it an easy balancing act to play an emotionally honest scene while throwing in a dash of Susan Hayward's Brooklyn-inflected standard stage speech for satiric spice. The role of Marjorie Taub required none of that theatrical distancing. Though outrageously self-dramatizing, Marjorie has to be played for total reality. Early in the play's gestation, I went to see the play *Death Defying Acts*. I had long admired its star, Linda Lavin, but seeing her once more, I realized that she was the perfect actress to play Marjorie. I couldn't get her voice out of my head, and began to write every line for her. An important part of my life has been the worship of actresses, and I wanted the challenge of writing a very rich role for a great actress. It's difficult for me to express the thrill of hearing Linda read the role of Marjorie for the first time. Everything I hoped she'd be was there. I've relived that excitement at every performance of *The Tale of the Allergist's Wife* that I've seen her play.

Lynne Meadow's beautiful production of *The Tale of the Allergist's Wife* received glowing notices and prompted a Broadway transfer. Though it was pouring rain the first day the marquee went up at the Barrymore Theatre, nothing could have stopped me from gazing at it from every angle. The honky-tonk drag queen was now reinvented as a Broadway playwright. My overnight legitimacy was exciting, but like my self-created heroines, this new identity left me confused. It disturbed me when so many people kept telling me, "You must be so thrilled to finally be mainstream." I became very defensive and quipped, ad nauseam, "I always thought I *was* mainstream. I haven't performed in a bar for fifteen years. I don't think my audience has been composed of pinheads and carny folk." It bugged me that I was so prickly. Why couldn't I just shut up and be grateful? Was embracing the importance of being "mainstream" tantamount to a put-down of the work I'd done for the past twenty years? In truth, I didn't think my other plays *were* so on-the-fringe. Most of them had been commissioned by respected nonprofit theatres and transferred to commercial runs. They've been performed in theatres and colleges coast to coast. Is it that drag and plays deemed camp parody are never considered "mainstream," no matter how genteel their pedigree? Please forgive the chip on my shoulder. The first four plays in this volume have great emotional resonance for me and they represent collaborations that I found extraordinarily fruitful.

In my ongoing artistic trek, I envision a career where I can continue to grow as a writer and actor. To expand my horizons as a playwright will necessitate my writing plays that won't have to take into account the limitations of a very demanding drag actress. However, I'm still as hopelessly stagestruck as ever, and that means that the "actress" will continue to prosper.

Whenever she feels the great ache for a comeback, no doubt she will be provided with a vehicle perfectly suited to her peculiar charms. After all, she's sleeping with the playwright.

Charles Busch
New York City
September 2000

VAMPIRE LESBIANS
OF SODOM

Charles Busch in *Vampire Lesbians of Sodom*, Tokyo, 1990. Photo Credit: T. L. Boston.

The Cast

Vampire Lesbians of Sodom was originally produced at the Limbo Lounge in New York City in 1984. It moved to the Provincetown Playhouse, New York City, on June 19, 1985, and was produced by Kenneth Elliott and Gerald A. Davis. Directed by Kenneth Elliot, with set design by B. T. Whitehill; costumes, John Glaser; lighting, Vivien Leone; production stage manager and hair design, Elizabeth Katherine Carr; and choreography, Jeff Veazey, it was performed with the following cast, in order of appearance:

Ali .... Robert Carey
Hujar .... Arnie Kolodner
A virgin sacrifice .... Charles Busch
The Succubus .... Meghan Robinson
King Carlisle .... Kenneth Elliott
Etienne .... Andy Halliday
Renee Vain .... Theresa Marlowe
La Condesa .... Meghan Robinson
Madeleiné Astarté .... Charles Busch
Oatsie Carewe .... Tom Aulino
Zack .... Arnie Kolodner
P. J. .... Robert Carey
Danny .... Andy Halliday
Tracy .... Theresa Marlowe

The Characters

Ali .... a guard
Hujar .... a guard
A virgin sacrifice
The Succubus .... a monster
King Carlisle .... a silent movie idol
Etienne .... a butler
Renee Vain .... a starlet
La Condesa .... a silent screen vamp
Madeleiné Astarté .... a stage actress
Oatsie Carewe .... a gossip columnist
Zack .... a chorus boy
P. J. .... a chorus boy
Danny .... a chorus boy
Tracy .... an aspiring singer

Synopsis of Scenes

Scene 1: Sodom, in days of old. The entrance to a forbidding cave.

Scene 2: Hollywood, 1920. La Condesa's mansion.

Scene 3: Las Vegas today. A rehearsal hall.

VAMPIRE LESBIANS OF SODOM

PROLOGUE

Sodom in days of old. Two muscular, handsome GUARDS *are standing sentry before the entrance to a forbidding cave.*

ALI Who goes there?

HUJAR You needn't fear, Ali. No one ventures near this spot save for madmen and fools.

ALI Including you and me.

HUJAR Yes, but we are clever fools. For our deed today, we shall receive a kingly sum.

ALI If we live to spend it.

HUJAR The creature we guard desires nothing of the likes of you. The Succubus thrives upon the blood of young virgins.

ALI A rare delicacy, eh?

HUJAR You must be new to these parts. Where do your people hail from?

ALI I hail from Ishbar, in Asia Minor. You know, the fertile crescent.

HUJAR So what brings you to Sodom?

ALI Don't scoff, but I've come to seek my fortune.

HUJAR Then my friend, you've made a wise move. This city has everything. It never sleeps. Have you been to the bars?

ALI No, I'm living out in Gomorrah.

HUJAR Gomorrah?

ALI Hujar, I don't want to offend you but I'm really not into bars. I'm looking for a relationship.

HUJAR Then my man, you shouldn't have moved to the twin cities.

A cock crows.

HUJAR The cock has crowed. It's time to begin. The Succubus demands its breakfast.

ALI Have you ever seen the Succubus?

HUJAR No one has, except for the virgin sacrifice and obviously, they never live to tell. We had best begin. The sleeping potion will wear off; the virgin will awake and we'll have a lot of explaining to do. You wait here, I'll bring her in.

He exits. Hujar returns carrying in his arms the beautiful young VIRGIN.

HUJAR Quite a beauty, isn't she? A pity she is to be sacrificed.

ALI Hujar, she stirs.

HUJAR That cannot be. The potion should last an hour more. Damn the Gods, let's get out of here. (*The girl begins to wake in his arms.*)

GIRL No, Papa, I don't want to play. Please, don't make me. (*She awakes.*) Where am I? Who are you? Please sir, release me.

He puts her on her feet. The virgin is indeed beautjful but there is something about her costume and demeanor that suggests a stripper performing a burlesque sketch about vestal virgins. It could be the G-string and spike heels.

HUJAR We are soldiers under the command of the Governor.

GIRL My mind is such a jumble. I had such a strange dream. I dreamt there was a lottery to choose a sacrificial victim for the dreaded Succubus and I dreamed that I chose the black stone of death. You know, they say our dreams can be interpreted. They can tell us many things about ourselves. I wonder what this dream means.

HUJAR That was no dream, that was the truth. You are the virgin sacrifice.

GIRL (*Thinks they're joking.*) You couldn't be . . . but surely you . . . no, I . . . I couldn't . . . It's imposs . . . (*She realizes it's true and screams.*)

HUJAR (*Grabs her around the neck.*) Another peep out of you and we'll rip your tongue out.

ALI Hujar, be kind to the girl. These are her last moments on earth.

HUJAR And they shall be ours if her screams bring forth the Succubus.

Ali breaks Hujar's arm away.

GIRL Please sir, I beg of you. If there is any shred of pity or tenderness in your heart. Please, do not deliver me to the Succubus.

HUJAR We only follow our orders.

GIRL (*To Ali.*) You, you have the eyes of a poet. Surely you cannot see it just to send me to this most horrible of deaths.

ALI I wish there was something I could do.

HUJAR Soldier, control yourself. You are acting weak and womanish.

GIRL If having a kind heart is womanish, be proud of your womanhood. I implore you, sir, save me. My father has money. Aid my escape and all of his gold shall be yours.

HUJAR Child, you have been forsaken. Your father has publicly announced his pride in your selection as food for the Goddess.

GIRL I refuse to believe this.

ALI It's true. We have his sworn testimonial of acceptance.

GIRL Then it is true. I am truly alone. A mere child of fourteen. Friendless, parentless, damned to this most vile fate. Tell me, my good executioners, how much time do I have?

HUJAR But a few minutes more.

GIRL Then permit me a moment whilst I bid farewell to my girlhood. (*In a reverie.*) Goodbye youth. Adieu bubbling brook of joy, rosy hope of budding romance. I bid farewell to the frothy games of catching a whippoorwill and skipping to it's tune, lightning bugs parading their brilliance before the first evening stars. I wave goodbye to the beardless boys who breathlessly snatched a forbidden kiss and the silly girls who giggled at my follies. Goodbye dear friends. Farewell round orb.

ALI Is there nothing Ican do to ease your pain?

GIRL Yes, there is something you could do. Break my hymen. Rape me and I'll no longer be a virgin fit for sacrifice.

ALI But, I . . .

The girl rips off Ali's loincloth and chases him around screaming "Break my hymen, break my hymen!" Hujar pushes her to the ground.

HUJAR The child is mad. Away!

The two soldiers exit.

GIRL I beseech thee Isis, provide me with the courage to face my destruction.

The SUCCUBUS *enters in the form of a beautiful and very hardboiled dame. She is by turns very grand and also a bit cheap but most importantly, she has a very big chip on her shoulder.*

GIRL Run! Save yourself! The creature is about to emerge.

SUCCUBUS (*Irritated.*) Hey, hey, hey! Where are you going?

GIRL Woman, have you lost your senses?

SUCCUBUS Not that I'm aware of.

GIRL Who are you?

SUCCUBUS Give a guess.

GIRL An actress?

SUCCUBUS Guess again.

GIRL Are you a trollop?

SUCCUBUS I suppose you've never met a myth before.

GIRL (*Innocently.*) No. What can I do for you, myth?

SUCCUBUS Behold my magnificence, for I am the dreaded Succubus!

GIRL How can pure evil be embodied by such beauty?

SUCCUBUS How much easier to lure you into my arms. Come, child.

GIRL Vile thing, what right have you to demand my death?

SUCCUBUS (*Angrily.*) Do I not also have the right to life? As you need food and water so I need the pure unsullied blood of virgins.

GIRL What proof have you of my maidenhead? What if I told you I was the village slut, a repository for every man's seed in Sodom?

SUCCUBUS I'd say you were a big fat liar. Now get in that cave. I'm freezing my ass off in this draft.

GIRL I'm afraid to die.

SUCCUBUS (*With great self pity.*) That's nothing to be afraid of. Think how much crueler my fate, never to die, condemned to immortality. The perennial witness to the eternal passing parade. My cave is quite the lonely one.

GIRL Forgive me if I don't weep.

SUCCUBUS A spitfire, eh. But why should you pity me? I'm a goddess. You look around and see the glamorous way I live. My slaves, my riches, my dishware. But try throwing a dinner party for two pinheads and a cyclops. True, I have caskets full of sparkling jewels but where the fuck can I wear them. My life stinks. The only enjoyment I get is a vestal virgin now and then but time goes on and I survive. And how, how you may wonder do I face the prospect of a millenium of time on my hands? What keeps me going is a sense of humor. I giggle, I chuckle, I even guffaw but inside I weep. It's the age old story, laugh, Succubus, laugh.

GIRL (*Sarcastically.*) If you're so unhappy, why don't you leave Sodom?

SUCCUBUS And go where, pray tell, get married, have a couple of kids, turn my cave into a split level? The Gods owe me an answer. Deliver me an answer! I demand an answer!

GIRL Counseling. Seek good counsel from the High Priest and then hie thee hither, you bloodsucking old bag!

SUCCUBUS Child, I must say I am impressed by your fortitude. If you were a fellow Succubus, I might even be afraid of you. But you are not. You will look into my eyes and all thought of defiance shall vanish. Look into my eyes. Look into my eyes. Look into my eyes!

The girl is hypnotized by the Succubus.

SUCCUBUS You will come to me now. (*Very imperiously and most unseductively.*) Seek out my warmth. Suckle at my breast.

GIRL (*Crosses to the Succubus.*) Yes, yes, I shall suckle thy poisonous udder.

The Succubus lunges toward the girl and drinks her blood ravenously.

BLACKOUT

Scene 2

Hollywood, 1920. The drawing room of La Condesa's spectacular mansion high in the Hollywood hills. KING CARLISLE, *a handsome, young matinee idol is pacing back and forth.* ETIENNE, *La Condesa's extremely nervous butler enters.*

ETIENNE Young man, you will have to leave at once. Madame La Condesa is incommunicado.

KING You have kept me waiting for over an hour. I demand to see La Condesa. Why won't she see me?

ETIENNE Madame is ruled by her caprices.

KING This is intolerable. Sir, don't you know who I am?

ETIENNE Are you here to fix the victrola?

KING I take it you never go to the movies.

ETIENNE I only see Madame's films.

KING I am King Carlisle, the newest and biggest male star in silent pictures. She can't treat me this way.

ETIENNE My good man, only yesterday Madame received Winston Churchill, Monsieur Diaghilev and the King of Spain. King Carlisle? Small potatoes.

KING Well, Monsieur Le Butler, I consider your mistress even smaller potatoes. Furthermore, I am not impressed by her phoney title, Madame La Condesa Scrofula de Hoya, indeed. Surely she knows that the studio has brought the great stage actress, Madeleine Astarté out to Hollywood and is grooming her as Magda's rival.

ETIENNE Magda Legerdemain is a great artist with the divine spark, Madeleine Astarté: pure hambone.

KING You must help me. I have nothing against your mistress. I merely wish to save my fiancée Renee from her clutches. Renee is an innocent. She is new to Hollywood. She doesn't recognize corruption when she sees it. I must save her from La Condesa.

ETIENNE What have you to fear?

KING There are so many rumors surrounding Magda Legerdemain. Rumors that she's not only a vamp but . . . a vampire.

ETIENNE Excuse me, I must go. It's time to run Madame's leopards in Griffith Park.

He tries to leave. King stops him.

KING You're hiding something from me.

ETIENNE (*Screams.*) Don't touch me! I will tell you this. You have entered a mad household. This isn't hair on my head, these are nerve endings.

KING Then why do you work here?

ETIENNE Who else but Madame would employ me? You don't recognize me, do you?

KING No, who are you?

ETIENNE Suffering has changed my face as completely as a surgeon's scalpel. I will tell you this, Baby Kelly Ambrose lives!

KING Surely you're not Baby Kelly Ambrose, the hatchet wielding vaudeville child star.

ETIENNE (*Breaks into a timestep and swings an imaginary hatchet.*) I did them all in after a milk fund benefit in Kokomo. I dismembered all six of them and scattered their body parts along the entire Keith-Orpheum circuit. Only one person would aid my escape from the lunatic asylum and that was La Condesa and for her sake, I would gladly strike again.

KING Oh dear, I must remove Renee from this bedlam.

RENEE VAIN *runs on and speaks to Etienne. Renee is a lovely ingenue in the Mary Pickford mode but with the toughness of a Ma Barker.*

RENEE Etienne, La Condesa would like . . . (*Sees King.*) King, what on earth are you doing here?

KING My dearest darling, I'm here to talk some sense into you.

RENEE Please, go away. You don't understand.

KING I understand all too well.

RENEE (*With mad vitality.*) No, you don't. You want me to lead a quiet, dreary life as your wife. Well, that's not why I came to Hollywood. I want to live! I want to drive my roadster faster than anyone else on the road. I want to stay up all night, drinking whiskey and dancing on table tops. (*Laughs with wild abandon.*) I'm young, let me be reckless!

KING My darling, I fear for you.

RENEE Etienne, could you leave us alone for a moment?

ETIENNE If you think that's wise. (*He exits.*)

RENEE (*As tough as nails.*) King, you nincompoop, you're going to spoil everything. This dame's my entree to the big wigs in this burgh. She knows everyone. We had breakfast with Wallace Reid, lunch with Alma Rubens, tea with Clare Kimball Young and dinner with Rod La Rocque. This place is a social gold mine and I'm reaping in the nuggets. I got me three screen tests lined up for next week.

KING But I know people. I could help you.

RENEE (*Disdainfully.*) Oh, a lot of help you are. You got me tossed off the DeMille picture. You didn't think I knew that, did you?

KING The role was cheap and degrading.

RENEE Let me be cheap and degraded, I'm an actress! I've had enough of you butting into my career, you great big buddinsky!

He reaches for her.

RENEE Don't touch me. You repulse me. When I think of your feeble attempts to make love to me, I laugh. Do you hear me, I laugh. (*Explodes in hysterical laughter.*)

KING (*Shakes her violently.*) Stop it! Stop it! This isn't you, this isn't my Renee.

RENEE (*Suddenly lovely and vulnerable.*) King, I don't know what came over me. That was a different girl speaking. Some strange power overtook me and made me say those cruel words. Can you forgive me?

KING Of course darling. I must get you out of this mansion. Can't you smell the presence of evil?

LA CONDESA [*Condaysa*] *enters garbed in the barbaric excesses of silent screen vamps. She is of course the Succubus from Sodom looking not a day older.*

LA CONDESA Mr. Carlisle, you smell the presence of evil? Perhaps you are mistaking it for my perfume. If you are, it's expensive evil, fifty dollars an ounce. Now state your business.

KING I demand that you give up Renee.

LA CONDESA (*With flamboyant levity.*) Give her up? I see no handcuffs, I see no chains.

KING I believe she is under your spell. I've heard tales of the stream of young girls who pass through these portals. Young starlets who are never heard of again. Where are those starlets? You are an affront to everything that's good and decent in this country.

LA CONDESA Are you casting aspersions on my patriotism. I'll have you know, in the last war, I was a captain in the Medical

Corps, I had twenty nurses under me. Now Renee, would you inform Mister Carbunckle, I mean Mr. Carlisle, what terrible evil we're up to.

RENEE La Condesa is giving me acting lessons. Tonight, she's going to teach me how to play a passionate love scene.

KING I can't bear this torment. Don't you know what she is?

RENEE A very nice lady?

KING (*With self-righteous fury.*) This very nice lady drinks the blood of young virgins. Yes, I know the truth about you, Madame La Condesa. I know you had to flee Europe because of the rumors of your evil ways. And here you are corrupting every virgin in Hollywood.

LA CONDESA Slim pickings I must say. If I were interested in virgins, why the hell would I come to Hollywood? My friend, you've seen too many motion pictures.

KING I am not your friend. I spit on your friendship! (*He spits on the floor.*)

LA CONDESA (*Mad as a hornet.*) Spit on my friendship but not on my rug!

KING I will, I will if that will save my Renee. (*Spits several times.*)

LA CONDESA (*With great vulgarity.*) You clam one more time and there's gonna be hell to pay. Etienne! Clean up this mess.

Etienne runs in.

LA CONDESA Now look here you . . .

ETIENNE Madame, Miss Carewe from the Hearst newspapers will be here momentarily. Don't you think you should be composing yourself?

LA CONDESA Yes, I must compose myself before that nosy bitch arrives. Mr. Carlisle, the door is that way.

KING I am not leaving. I shall be here when Oatsie Carewe arrives and I shall provide her with some juicy gossip for her column.

RENEE (*Angrily.*) You wouldn't!

ETIENNE Madame, shall I call the police?

LA CONDESA No, let him stay. And let him repeat this slander. It shall only add fuel to my legend.

Doorbell rings.

LA CONDESA That must be Miss Carewe. Show her in, Etienne.

Etienne exits.

RENEE King, I wish you would get the point that you're not wanted here.

ETIENNE (*Enters.*) Madame Madeleine Astarté.

LA CONDESA (*Aghast.*) Astarté!

RENEE What's she doing here?

LA CONDESA Tell her to go away. Tell her I'm not receiving.

MADELEINÉ ASTARTÉ [*Astartay*] *enters in the grand manner. She is none other than the virgin from Sodom, now the dazzling grande dame of the New York stage.*

MADELEINE Balderdash, La Condesa. I've traveled all the way from New York just to see you.

LA CONDESA You must not flatter me. All Hollywood knows of your million dollar contract.

MADELEINE (*With gaiety.*) Million point five. The point five darlings is to keep me in mascara. (*Laughs and looks at Etienne next to her. She does a big burlesque double take at his deadpan expression.*)

LA CONDESA Madame Astarté, I would love to offer you tea but unfortunately I'm expecting Oatsie Carewe any minute for an in-depth profile.

MADELEINE Oh, I must stay for that. I do so want to get to know you better. Besides this will dispel all those awful rumors that we're rivals. How absurd, you and I rivals, we're entirely different. I'm sort of an elegant grande dame, perhaps a tad too aristocratic for my own good. But you have this marvelous, extraordinary vulgarity. An exhilarating streak of the gutter.

LA CONDESA (*Lightly bitchy.*) Thank you Madeleine and if I can be of any help to you because you know, acting for the screen is a special art. You can't be as hammy and grotesque as you've been on the stage.

MADELEINE I so appreciate your offer, Contessa.

LA CONDESA (*Cordially correcting her.*) Condesa [*Condaysa*] Dear, have they chosen your first vehicle?

MADELEINE Yes, I am to do the life of Madame DuBarry.

LA CONDESA You must be mistaken. I am to play DuBarry. My costumes are all made.

MADELEINE We had to take in the waist a little. Lay off the paté, Cunt-tessa.

LA CONDESA (*Angrily.*) Condesa! [*Condaysa*]

MADELEINE After the DuBarry picture, for a change of pace, I shall do the title role of *Peter Pan.* "Fly with me Wendy to the stars."

LA CONDESA But I was supposed to play that role. I *am* Peter Pan!!

MADELEINE Darling, you've been replaced. Studio wags have been saying your box office is sinking faster than your bustline.

LA CONDESA You conniving, manipulative . . .

MADELEINE The studio's been so kind. They gave me dressing room A.

LA CONDESA My dressing room?

MADELEINE And that divine dresser, Mamacita. She's such a . . .

LA CONDESA Not Mamacita.

MADELEINE And I found this adorable little pooch wandering lost on the back lot.

LA CONDESA (*Wildly.*) She stole my dog! The bitch stole my schnauzer! You won't get away with this treachery!

KING Madame Astarté, she has the devil on her side.

LA CONDESA I'll fix you, I'll fix you by all the powers that be!

RENEE What will you do?

LA CONDESA (*With intense frustration.*) I'm calling my agent! (*She exits.*)

ETIENNE Oh dear! (*Follows her out.*)

KING Madeleine, I fear for your life. You may think me mad but I have reason to believe La Condesa is one of the undead.

MADELEINE No darling, she just looks like death. (*To Renee.*) But you, my dear, you look much livelier. I don't believe we've met.

RENEE My name is Renee Vain. I'm a new contract player at the studio.

MADELEINE How perfectly divine. You have such a lovely face. Profile. Ah, yes.

KING We're engaged to be married.

MADELEINE Pish posh. An actress must be married to her art. Men, ugh. (*Shudders.*) Thespis shall be your lover.

RENEE That's what La Condesa says.

MADELEINE Does she? I suppose you and La Condesa are quite intimate.

RENEE I love her so much.

MADELEINE Yes, an older woman can be such a comfort to a young girl. I can tell you are a superb actress and we must play together. I know the perfect vehicle. I've just optioned a new book on an old subject. The story of Sappho. I play Sappho, a noble Greek woman, passionate, vibrant, a sexual revolutionary and you, my fair one, you shall play her lesbian lover . . . (*Searches for a name.*) Rusty.

RENEE Rusty?

MADELEINE I can see the scene. The cameraman lining up the shot. The director calls "Action," the off-screen violinist commences to play. Sappho sees Rusty coming out of the Parthenon, the wind tossing her hair away from her face. Sappho slips her arm around Rusty's waist and silently they . . .

RENEE But I don't . . .

MADELEINE I said silently, they walk down a dark winding street. It's the street where Sappho lives with her grandmother, um uh . . . Lillian. The street is empty. Everyone being at the Olympic games. They look into each other's eyes. Rusty finds herself yielding to the older woman's incandescent beauty. Cameras pan in for a tight shot. They kiss.

They kiss and then Astarté bites Renee's neck until the girl faints.

MADELEINE Kill the lights, call it a wrap.

KING (*In shock.*) You . . . you . . . you're a vampire!

MADELEINE I don't suppose you have a handkerchief.

KING She devil! Fiend! You've killed my Renee.

MADELEINE Nah, she'll come to, but let's say I've taken the bloom off the peach.

KING I'll expose you, I'll expose you as the monster you are.

MADELEINE (*Coolly.*) I wouldn't talk about exposing anyone if I were you.

KING What do you mean?

MADELEINE I happen to know King Carlisle's not your real name.

KING So, many stars change their names.

MADELEINE I happen to know your real name is Trixie Monahan and five years ago the coppers tossed you in the sex tank for impersonating a woman.

KING Drag is a perfectly legitimate theatrical tradition.

MADELEINE That may well be true but not on the corner of Hollywood and Vine.

KING I'd be ruined if anyone knew of my past. I'll be forced to kill myself.

MADELEINE There are other alternatives.

KING Such as?

MADELEINE You can be my personal slave.

KING What would you expect of me?

MADELEINE Lots of things. Escort me to premieres, wash my car, rinse out my dirty panties, but don't you dare let me catch you wearing them. I get plenty mad.

He collapses into despair. La Condesa enters.

LA CONDESA What is this? What have you done to her? Now you've really gone too far. You imagine yourself quite the cunning vixen. You have delusions that you can conquer me. Though I have always found you vulgar, I have never taken you for a fool, until now. Hollywood is my town. For centuries, you have been an albatross around my neck. First in Rome, I claimed as my bride, the most beautiful of Caligula's courtesans. She was mine until you stole her away to China. Then there was the nun in the dark ages who became my personal slave, stolen once again. We all know what treachery you conspired against me during the Spanish Inquisition but I triumphed. And did I plot revenge? No. Then in the sixteenth century, I had as my mistress, the most desired of Queen Elizabeth's ladies in waiting. You, the ever present vulture snatched her off to the colonies. Even then, did I choose revenge? No. And why? Because I am a great lady. I conduct myself with dignity and grandeur whilst you roll in the gutter, parading your twat onstage and calling it acting. You've got as much glamour as a common street whore and now madame, you have gone too far. I am the queen of vampires and I shall never, never relinquish my hold on Hollywood!

MADELEINE Are you through? As you desire to relive the past, shall we travel even further back in time. Many centuries ago, back in the days of the Bible, there was a young girl, a mere child of fourteen, a lovely girl, full of high spirits. A lottery was held to choose a sacrificial victim for the dreaded Succubus. As fate would have it, she chose the black stone of death. She was dragged by soldiers to the cave of the creature and there left to her desecration. The monster emerged and there under a Godless sky, the creature dug its teeth into the girl's fair flesh. Having gorged itself, the monster retired to its cave, leaving the girl's body to be pecked and devoured as carrion. But the girl did not die. The monster in its fury did not even notice that all the while it was sucking the girl's blood, the child herself had lodged her teeth into a vein of the monster. In her terror she drank. More and more she filled herself with the creature's fluid. And there on that bleached rocky point, left to rot like a piece of old meat, the girl did not die but was transformed, transformed into one of the undead, never to find eternal rest but to stalk the earth forever in search of a victim, forever alone, forever damned. Look at me, I am that girl! And I demand the death of the Succubus!

ETIENNE (*Enters.*) Miss Oatsie Carewe of the Hearst Newspapers.

OATSIE (*Enters—a middle-aged gossip columnist garbed in the matronly but bohemian manner of Madame Elinor Glyn.*) Darling! And Madeleine Astarté too. What a marvelous surprise. Who'd have thought you two gals would be chums. And they say Hollywood is a heartless town. Magda, I adore the dress. It does wonders for your figure, so concealing. And Madeleine, I just know that must be a Paris creation. I must have a description of it for my column.

LA CONDESA Oatsie darling, may I get you some tea?

OATSIE No, no, never touch the stuff. Okay girls, straight from the hip. My readers just gobble up movie star romance. Madeleine, love blooming anywhere?

MADELEINE As my dear friend Gertrude Stein says "My mystery is a mystery is a mystery."

OATSIE Hmmm. I wonder if any man has ever pierced your enigma.

MADELEINE (*Tough.*) Let him try.

OATSIE And you Magda, a man in your life?

LA CONDESA I still mourn my late husband, the Count Scrofula de Hoya. (*With a heavy castilian lisp.*) How I long for our life in Barthelona. A thity thaturated with thenuality.

OATSIE (*Sees King and Renee.*) What's this, King Carlisle, Renee Vain, two stars of tomorrow?

LA CONDESA Oatsie, we were having cocktails and these two lapped up the hootch like hogs at a trough. Look at them, out cold, stinko. I guess I've seen it all.

MADELEINE You certainly have. The poor dear's been around the block so many times, she's been mistaken for a taxi.

OATSIE Madeleine, I want to give you a real Hollywood welcome. I just insist you come to my house for dinner. I'm a demon in the kitchen and you come too, Magda, I insist. What shall I make? A goulash, a nice thick goulash, a native dish of Transylvania. Ever been there Magda?

LA CONDESA Can't say I have. No doubt, Madeleine has on one of her theatrical tours.

MADELEINE Not Transylvania. Pennsylvania. Played the Schubert in Altoona.

OATSIE I adore a good goulash, spiced with plenty of garlic. Either of you have an aversion to garlic?

LA CONDESA I must confess. I have a dreadful allergic reaction to garlic. Strictly *entre nous,* I get terrible chafing.

MADELEINE Indeed, when she lived in Spain, she couldn't keep her legs together for years.

OATSIE Ah Spain. The bullfights, the flamenco dancers, the magnificent cathedrals. One of my great passions is collecting models of the crucifixion. (*She takes out a cross.*) This, Condesa, is a Florentine cross, blessed by the brothers of Santa Giovanna.

The two vampires recoil and twitch with frenzy. Renee awakes.

KING Ah Renee, my precious.

RENEE I must have been dreaming. I dreamt I was being devoured by a horrid black bat. (*Sees Madeleine and screams.*) It was you, it was you!

MADELEINE Can't you shut her up?

OATSIE You can't shut out the truth.

MADELEINE What the . . .

She turns to Oatsie. Oatsie flashes the cross at her causing Madeleine's hips to bump like a burlesque stripper.

OATSIE I've studied your evil legends all my life, I know you both very well but you don't know me. Let me introduce myself. (*She flings her coat open and throws it to the floor, revealing a man's military jacket covered with medals and polkadotted boxer shorts. She throws off her hat and wig uncovering a shining bald pate. In a thick German dialect.*) I am Gregory Salazar, vampire hunter! God in all of his mercy has cast me in the role of avenging angel to rid the world of your filth.

LA CONDESA You silly little man, you have no power over us. You shall long be dust while we are forever young.

He shows her the cross and she too begins to twitch wildly.

SALAZAR At this very moment, the Los Angeles police are surrounding this mansion. The fire department is spraying the walls with holy water. We've got you cornered. Daughters of Lucifer, your reign of death is over. We shall hold you both in this room until the sun rises, the sun which will transform you both into ancient hags and then decaying skeletons and then dust. I will sweep the dust into the gutter with the rest of the swill. From there your remains will float down the pipes into the public sewer where no one will know the difference between your ashes and the rest of the waste products of the Greater Los Angeles Area.

MADELEINE La Condesa, have you the power to evoke the cry of the banshee?

LA CONDESA I know the ritual but I've never achieved it.

SALAZAR You do not frighten us with your primitive black magic.

LA CONDESA/MADELEINE
Flee from Hades, spirits rare.
We free you from your devils lair,
Paint our victims a deep blood red,
Banshees, phantoms, vampires dead.

SALAZAR Breathe your last, Brides of Beelzebub!

LA CONDESA/MADELEINE

Far, far into the night
Remove this enemy from our sight
Burn his flesh till it's black with char,
The vampire killer, Salazar!

Salazar's face grows grotesque as he writhes in agony.

KING Look at his face!

MADELEINE Flee, sister, flee!

The two Vampiresses exit as Renee unleashes a bloodcurdling scream.

SCENE 3

Las Vegas, today. A rehearsal room at Caesars Palace. Two chorus boys, ZACK *and* P.J. *enter in rehearsal clothes.*

ZACK Hey don't be nervous, man. Mellow out.

P.J. Mellow out? Easier said than done. I'm swallowing razor blades. You'd think I'd never been a chorus gypsy before. It's this town that's giving me the jitters.

ZACK P.J., you're gonna love Las Vegas. It's the greatest place on earth.

P.J. Besides Transylvania.

ZACK What do you mean by that?

P.J. Haven't you read in the papers about the string of vampire attacks on the Vegas strip?

ZACK Who hasn't? But hell, why should you worry? All the victims were young girls.

P.J. Vampires drink the blood of young virgins, right? As the song goes "Take Me Back to Manhattan."

ZACK Don't let this vampire thing get you down. Hey, give me a Vegas floor show any day over some tired Broadway trip. And this isn't any ordinary floor show. Do you know what the name Madeleine Andrews spells?

P.J. (*Spelling it out.*) M-A-D . . .

ZACK No doofus, it spells class. She's one hell of a lady.

P.J. But she hasn't made a movie since the sixties.

ZACK She did a TV movie two years ago where she played an insane millionairess who owns the Bermuda triangle and steals the shroud of Turin. It cleaned up in the Nielsens. Don't spread this around but she may be starring in a Broadway revival of "The Sound of Music." Play your cards right and you may be employed for a long, long time.

DANNY *enters.*

ZACK But take this tip, buddy, stay away from the queens in this company.

DANNY I heard that, Miss Zack. Stay away from the queens, indeed. Sweetie, has Miss Thing invited you to her dungeon room? Or did I arrive too soon?

ZACK Fuck off, Mary.

P.J. Hey guys, come on. Miss Andrews will be here any minute.

DANNY I hope she is. It's about time she discovered this one's true colors.

ZACK Jealousy, jealousy, jealousy.

DANNY If you're referring to the one night we slept together. I'd talk about your cock but I've got respect for the dead.

ZACK You goddamn . . .

Zack tries to attack Danny but P.J. stops them.

P.J. Hey guys, come on, can't you discuss this calmly?

DANNY I'll tell you what's going on. I've been dancing in Madeleine Andrews' Vegas act for five years. Before that I was a dancer on her TV Variety Show. I've paid my dues with that broad. My lover David has been with her just as long. Then Mata Hari here joins the company and tries to turn her against us.

ZACK First we have vampires on the strip, now I've got an hysterical faggot to deal with.

DANNY I wouldn't be worried about vampires, Whorina. Your ass is hardly virgin territory.

ZACK Don't give me your beads. Your boyfriend's a drunk, he missed a show and Madeleine fired him.

DANNY You didn't have to squeal on him.

ZACK Boo hoo.

P.J. Shh, Madeleine's going to hear you!

Madeleine Andrews enters. It is of course Astarté, now the epitome of the glacial, terrifying star of stage, screen, video and Vegas. She is not completely ageless. The centuries have left their mark. She appears now as a very hardboiled though grand legend in her fifties.

MADELEINE Hello boys, ready to throw the old girl around? It's nice to see everyone on time for a change.

ZACK Madeleine, this is P.J., the new dancer.

P.J. It's a real thrill working with you, Miss Andrews.

MADELEINE Call me Madeleine or we'll never get along. I love my boys and my boys love me, but there is one thing I will not tolerate and that is drinking or drugs. Is that clear?

P.J. Yes, Miss Andrews.

MADELEINE (*Laughingly.*) I told you to call me Madeleine. (*Slaps him.*) You're cute. Danny, aren't you going to say good morning?

DANNY Is that quite necessary, Madeleine?

MADELEINE You bet your sweet ass it is. Now Danny, I'm sure you're very upset that I was forced to fire David but where this show is concerned, I am ruthless. It's my reputation on the line. If Caesars Palace is willing to fork over fifty smackers a week, I better damn well be worth it and that goes for everyone in this clambake. Got me?

EVERYONE Yes, Madeleine.

MADELEINE I detest being a boss lady. It's so unattractive. Danny,

I'm very fond of you, I'd like to give you some good advice. You're better off without him.

DANNY Madeleine, I don't want to sound rude but . . .

MADELEINE Listen to Mama. You want to be a star?

DANNY (*Sullenly.*) Yeah.

MADELEINE Take this advice. You can't have it all. A long time ago, I made up my mind that there were certain things I had to give up on the road to fame. One of those things was personal happiness. Well, let's get to work. I want this new number in by tomorrow night. Think we can do it, Zack?

ZACK You bet.

MADELEINE I hope so. I'll freak if I have to go onstage one more time and do that "I'm Still Here" medley. Freddie, put on the playback.

They do a strenuous dance number, the chorus boys getting a tough workout while Madeleine barely moves and croaks out the lyrics. A CHAR WOMAN *enters mopping the floor. It is the Condesa fallen on hard times.*

MADELEINE Cut! Cut! Cut! Zack, would you tell the cleaning lady we're rehearsing.

ZACK (*To the Condesa.*) Miss, excuse me. We're rehearsing in here. You'll have to come back later.

LA CONDESA Look bub, I take my orders from Sol Weisenbloom.

ZACK You don't understand. Madeleine Andrews is rehearsing.

LA CONDESA Look kid, if I don't get this floor done, my ass will be in a sling.

MADELEINE Perhaps I can be of some assistance. I'm Madeleine Andrews. (*Madeleine walks over to the Condesa, recognizes her and screams in shock.*)

ZACK Madeleine, are you all right? You look as if you've seen a ghost.

MADELEINE (*Trying to compose herself.*) I believe I have. Zack, I'm not quite ready to rehearse.

ZACK Sure, Madeleine. Whatever you say. Hey guys, let's go get a diet coke.

The boys exit.

ZACK We'll be just outside.

MADELEINE (*With great phoniness.*) Zack, I love you.

Zack exits.

LA CONDESA La Astarté as I live and breathe. Looks like you're in the chips.

MADELEINE Can't complain. But what happened to your fortune?

LA CONDESA Bad investments.

MADELEINE What brings you here to Vegas?

LA CONDESA Showgirls. You know I was always a sucker for a shapely gam.

MADELEINE You've certainly been indiscreet. You've given the Vegas press vampires on the brain.

LA CONDESA What, have you suddenly switched to artificial plasma? With you it's always the same tune, I'm the monster, you're the victim. My head reels when I think what you did to that girl scout troupe in forty-two. You bounced Hitler off the front page that week.

MADELEINE Scandal rags. I learned my lesson from that one. Never again will I jeopardize my career. Now when I look for virgins I drive my jaguar beyond the city limits.

TRACY, *a very perky blonde aspiring singer enters.*

TRACY Madeleine, are you busy?

LA CONDESA Oh don't mind me, come right in. Are you a new addition to Madeleine's act?

TRACY Oh, I hope so. I'm Madeleine's latest protegé.

LA CONDESA Wherever did you two meet? Here in Vegas or beyond the city limits?

TRACY Oh right here in Vegas. I've been on tour with the Young Republican First Christian College Revue.

MADELEINE Tracy, what is it you wanted to ask me?

TRACY Which gymnastic feat do you think would give me the biggest climax? The Double Spread or the Flying Squat. And also, how long do I sing before you bite me on the neck?

LA CONDESA Please explain that bit of choreography.

TRACY It's a special Halloween extravaganza. Madeleine appears as a glamorous lady vampire and . . .

LA CONDESA I get the general idea. Madeleine, considering all the vampire business in the news, don't you think this could be construed as being in bad taste?

MADELEINE Darling, she may have a point, let's keep that part of the act to ourselves. Kind of like a surprise.

TRACY Sure thing. Well, I'll let you get back to your rehearsal. Tootles. (*Tracy exits.*)

LA CONDESA You lousy hypocrite. My blood simmers with hatred for you.

MADELEINE You're just full of venom, aren't you? Look at your face in the glass. For two thousand years you've worn the same expression. Do you know what that is? You're smelling shit. You always look like you're smelling shit. Everywhere you go, you smell shit. Lady, that's your problem. My kind always smells the roses.

LA CONDESA You don't smell too many roses in Siberia.

MADELEINE What are you flapping your gums about?

LA CONDESA 1952. You convinced me to take over your tour of "I Remember Mama." When we got to the Soviet Union, you had me arrested as a CIA spy.

MADELEINE I never.

LA CONDESA You did. While you were starting a new career in the movies, I was freezing my ass off in that Gulag.

MADELEINE 1964, I was top contender for the Oscar. Jimmy the Greek had me winning ten to one, yet I lost it. Don't think I don't know it was you who spread those filthy rumors that I was boffing Mahalia Jackson.

LA CONDESA Honey, you got it all wrong. You're the one who's been persecuting me. Me! You've been obsessed with me for two thousand years!

MADELEINE (*With intense emotion.*) Yes, I'm obsessed with you. You made me what I am. Do you think I can ever forgive you for turning me into this, this thing that has no human feeling, this creature who thinks of nothing but her own survival, clawing and attacking anyone who poses a threat to me? Yes, I'm at the top of my profession but I'm not so damn proud of it.

LA CONDESA Excuse me but I've got a floor to clean.

MADELEINE Last year, Liv Ullmann and I toured Africa for UNICEF. While I was in the Congo, I left Liv and visited a tribal witch doctor named Pooji Dung.

LA CONDESA (*Alarmed.*) Pooji Dung?

MADELEINE I see the name is familiar. He comes from an ancient line of jungle sorcerers. La Condesa, he has taught me all I need know to destroy you.

LA CONDESA So what do you expect me to do, scream, run around in circles? Do it, get out your voodoo dolls. This modern world stinks. Broadway's dead. My apartment is going co-op, you can't get a decent bialy. I've had it. Give me the jungle phase out. You'll be doing me a favor.

MADELEINE (*Chanting.*)
Neemy Tunka Seevy Ra.
Keemy Funga Lami Ga.

LA CONDESA But let me say this. When I'm gone, then will you be happy?

MADELEINE Feemy, feemy, feemy ragoola. Eemana, eemana, Kooray, ragu . . . ragu . . . (*On the verge of hysteria.*) Seemy nagu . . . (*Collapses to the floor.*) I can't! I can't kill you! Then I shall be truly alone. I've shed a tear. I feel something. Is it impossible that in this whole world, there is only you with whom I can travel through time?

LA CONDESA (*Tough.*) Save it for Valentines Day.

MADELEINE (*Simply*) I need you.

LA CONDESA (*Touched.*) You need me. Someone needs me?

MADELEINE In an odd way, your presence has always been a comfort.

LA CONDESA (*In reverie.*) You need me. I am needed.

MADELEINE Isn't that what life's all about? Funny. (*Trying to compose herself*) I'd better get back to rehearsal. What will you do now?

LA CONDESA I hear at the All Souls Mission they're handing out free grub.

MADELEINE Surely, you don't mean . . . Is there anything I can do?

LA CONDESA Nah.

MADELEINE No really. Anything. Anything I can do, ten dollars, a warm coat.

LA CONDESA Yeah, sure. I'd like to have one more shot at stardom. What can I say, I'm crazy for show business.

MADELEINE Then my girl, you shall be in show business.

LA CONDESA A comeback?

MADELEINE A spectacular comeback! Let me give that to you.

LA CONDESA But it's been so long. I haven't done anything since "Love American Style" in sixty-seven. I'd be terrified.

MADELEINE We'll do an act together and we'll break it in in Tahoe. From there we'll hit San Francisco, Los Angeles, Chicago, Boston, the Kennedy Center and then Broadway!

LA CONDESA Oh boy, the two of us singing and dancing up a storm. And we won't even think about the past.

MADELEINE What past? At this moment we are the youngest chorines in town.

LA CONDESA One more thing, dear, a small detail and something that really should be handled by lawyers and not us, nothing to get in the way of our deep friendship. But how do you see my billing in the act?

MADELEINE (*Laughing at the irony of it all.*) Dear heart, I can see it all. Glittering letters thirty feet high. Tonight on the great stage, Madeleine Andrews, Magda Legerdemain, the legendary, the notorious, love 'em or hate 'em, the Vampire Lesbians of Sodom!

The two ladies explode in laughter. The music swells covering their enthusiastic voices as they begin rehearsing a dance step for their new act.

CURTAIN

PSYCHO BEACH PARTY

Charles Busch in *Psycho Beach Party*. Photo Credit: Adam Newman.

The Cast

Theatre-in-Limbo, Kenneth Elliot, and Gerald A. Davis presented *Psycho Beach Party* on July 20, 1987, at the Players Theatre, New York City. The cast was as follows:

Yo-Yo .... Robert Carey
Dee Dee .... Judith Hansen
Nicky .... Mike Leitheed
Provoloney .... Andy Halliday
Star Cat .... Arnie Koldner
Chicklet .... Charles Busch
Kanaka .... Ralph Buckley
Berdine .... Becky London
Marvel Ann .... Michael Belanger
Mrs. Forrest .... Meghan Robinson
Bettina Barnes .... Theresa Marlowe
Swing/Understudy .... Laurence Overmire

Scenic Design .... B.T. Whitehill
Costume Design .... John Glaser
Lighting Design .... Vivien Leone
Production Stage Manager/
Wig Design .... Elizabeth Katherine Carr
Original Music .... Tom Kochan
Production Advisor .... T.L. Boston
Associate Producers .... Julie Halston
Mario Andriolo
Choreography .... Jeff Veazey
Directed by .... Kenneth Elliott

The play was previously presented at the Limbo Lounge in New York City, in October, 1986.

The Characters

Yo-Yo
Dee Dee
Nicky
Provoloney
Star Cat
Chicklet
Kanaka
Berdine
Marvel Ann
Mrs. Forrest
Bettina Barnes

Place

On and around a beach in Malibu.

Time

1962

PSYCHO BEACH PARTY

Scene 1

Malibu Beach, 1962. Two handsome, young beach bums named YO YO *and* NICKY, *and a sexy chick in a bikini named* DEE DEE, *are madly cavorting with a beach ball.*

YO YO (*To Dee Dee*) Baby, shake those maracas.

DEE DEE (*Squeals*) Stop teasing me, Yo Yo.

NICKY Look at that butt.

DEE DEE You guys have a one track mind.

PROVOLONEY, *a scrappy, little surfer, the joker of the group, runs on.*

PROVOLONEY Girls! Girls! Girls!

YO YO Hey there, Provoloney!

NICKY and **DEE DEE** Hi, Provoloney.

PROVOLONEY What a fantabulous day.

DEE DEE Gosh, I love the sun.

NICKY Aw shoot, we've got to get back to the malt shop. Our lunch break is almost over.

YO YO Call in sick.

PROVOLONEY Say you were run over by a hit-and-run surfer.

NICKY Nah, old Augie's a great guy. I couldn't let him down.

DEE DEE Gosh, I really love him.

STAR CAT, *the most handsome of the group, enters with a surf board.*

YO YO Hey, Star Cat, how's my man?

STAR CAT What are you clowns doing? Those waves are as high as Mount Everest.

PROVOLONEY (*Looks out*) Oh wow, look at them, man.

STAR CAT It's time to hit the water.

NICKY It's more BLT's for us. Let's hit the road, Dee Dee.

DEE DEE Sure thing. Gosh, I'm so happy. (*They exit.*)

BOYS Bye!

STAR CAT Come on guys, grab your boards, it's time to shoot the curl.

PROVOLONEY Hot diggity! (*They all run offstage.*)

CHICKLET, *a perky, fifteen-year-old girl skips on.*

CHICKLET (*To the audience*) Hi folks, welcome to Malibu Beach. I hope you brought your suntan lotion cause here it's what you call endless summer. My name's Chicklet. Sort of a kooky name and believe me, it has nothing to do with chewing gum. You see, I've always been so darn skinny, a stick, a shrimp, so when other girls turned into gorgeous chicks, I became a chicklet. Can't say I've always been thrilled with that particular nomenclature but it sure beats the heck out of my real name, Florence. I'm supposed to meet my girlfriends, Marvel Ann and Berdine here at the beach. Marvel Ann calls it a "man hunt." I don't know what's wrong with me. I like boys, but not when they get all icky and unglued over you. All that kissy kissy stuff just sticks in my craw. I don't know, maybe I need some hormone shots. I do have a deep, all-consuming passion. The mere thought fills me with tingles and ecstasy. It's for surfing. I'm absolutely flaked out about riding the waves. Of course, I don't know how to do it, not yet, but I'm scouting around for a teacher and when I do, look out world. You'll be seeing old Chicklet flying over those waves like a comet.

KANAKA, *the macho king of the surfers, enters, drinking from a coffee mug.*

CHICKLET I can't believe it. You're the great Kanaka, aren't you?

KANAKA Yes, I am the party to whom you are genuflecting.

CHICKLET Oh gosh, I'm just like your biggest fan. I was standing down front during the surfing competition—

KANAKA Hey, cool down. Pour some water on that carburetor.

CHICKLET I haven't even introduced myself, I'm Chicklet Forrest. You're like a living legend. Like Walt Disney or Helen Keller. Did you really ride the killer wave off the coast of Bali?

KANAKA In handcuffs. So how come you know so much about surfing?

CHICKLET I don't but I'm dying to learn.

KANAKA A girl surfer? That's like a bad joke.

CHICKLET Why? Couldn't you teach me? I'm a great swimmer.

KANAKA You're a tadpole. You're not meant to hit the high waves. It's like a mystical calling. Sorry, babe, sign up with the YMCA.

CHICKLET But Kanaka . . .

KANAKA Hey, little girl. I'm drinking my morning java, my grey cells are still dozing, in other words angel, buzz off.

BERDINE (*Offstage*) Chicklet! Come on!

CHICKLET Well, you haven't heard the last of me. You'll see, I'm going to be your greatest student if it kills you. Tootles. (*She exits.*)

Star Cat, Yo Yo and Provoloney run on, excited.

STAR CAT Hey Kanaka! You won't believe what's going on.

PROVOLONEY I swear Malibu Mac is going to kill the joker.

KANAKA I'm trying to drink my mother lovin java . . .

YO YO Didn't you see the cop cars down the beach?

KANAKA (*Sees them.*) Oh yeah, what's happening?

STAR CAT It's like a bad dream. Malibu Mac has been dating that high school chick, Beverly Jo.

KANAKA The homecoming queen, right?

PROVOLONEY They spent the night on the beach.

YO YO They were knocked out cold.

STAR CAT This morning they woke up, naked as they were born and some weirdo had shaved their bodies head to toe.

YO YO Not a whisker on 'em. Twin bowling balls.

KANAKA And Malibu Mac had a thing about his pompadour.

PROVOLONEY He looks like a six-foot wiener.

YO YO Talking about wieners, my stomach's saying "Feed me."

STAR CAT You're always stuffing your face.

YO YO Food is my hobby.

PROVOLONEY Yo Yo's a great chef. We've set up like a whole kitchen in our beach shack.

KANAKA Our beach shack? I never heard of two surf bums shacking up together.

PROVOLONEY You should see how Yo Yo has fixed up the place with fishnet curtains, rattan furniture, hanging plants.

KANAKA Hanging plants?

YO YO (*Innocently*) I do wonderful things with Hibithcuth. (*They all do a take.*)

PROVOLONEY My innards are screaming "chow."

YO YO Mine are screaming "give me chile dogs!"

STAR CAT See you clowns later.

PROVOLONEY (*Exiting with Yo Yo.*) Food! Food! Food! (*They exit.*)

STAR CAT Kanaka, I talked to my dad yesterday.

KANAKA Yeah?

STAR CAT I told him I wasn't going back to college. This pre-med stuff is for squares.

KANAKA But I thought you wanted to be a psychiatrist.

STAR CAT I was a kid. Now I know I want to be a surf bum. My dad hit the roof but he doesn't understand. He grew up dirt poor and made his money tooth and nail. I can't compete with that. More than anything I want his respect and I'll get that by bumming around with you.

KANAKA But you know, being a surf bum is a tall order. Only a few make the grade. It's like being a high priest, kinda. No involvements, no commitments, just following the sun. You gotta be a man.

STAR CAT I swear I won't let you down.

KANAKA You're a good guy, Star Cat. I think this is the time I show you some of my treasures. I got in my shack a necklace composed of genuine human eyeballs presented to the great Kanaka by a witch doctor in Peru.

STAR CAT Oh wow!

KANAKA Let's go. (*They exit.*)

MARVEL ANN *and* BERDINE *enter carrying beach bags. Marvel Ann is a gorgeous blonde high school vamp and Berdine is a hopeless nerd, but a nerd with spunk.*

MARVEL ANN Honestly Berdine, did you have to put that disgusting white gook all over your nose?

BERDINE Sorry, Marvel Ann, but I got this allergy that flares up whenever I go to the beach.

MARVEL ANN What are you allergic to?

BERDINE The sun. It's ghastly. My face turns beet red, my eyes close up, and I get this terrible chafing between my legs.

MARVEL ANN Charming. Help me spread out the blanket. (*They do.*)

BERDINE Marvel Ann, this blanket is really divoon.

MARVEL ANN It's coordinated with my skin tone. Chicklet, help us.

Chicklet enters.

CHICKLET I found something in the sand.

BERDINE What is it, a shell?

CHICKLET No look. (*She dangles a spider in front of Marvel Ann.*)

MARVEL ANN (*Screams in terror.*) A black widow! (*She pushes it out of Chicklet's hand.*)

CHICKLET You scared it.

MARVEL ANN Listen you two weirdos, my nerves are a frazzle. I can't believe what happened to Beverly Jo. I'm going to have nightmares all night from seeing her like that.

BERDINE I wonder what the penalty is for shaving someone's head.

CHICKLET It wasn't just her head. Couldn't you see, they also shaved her . . . (*She whispers "pussy" in Berdine's ear and they are dissolved in giggles.*)

MARVEL ANN Cut that out. I think you two have forgotten the reason we're here. This is a man hunt, capiche?

CHICKLET Why do we have to bother with them? Can't we just have a good time by ourselves?

MARVEL ANN You have a severe problem, Chicklet. You've got the sex drive of a marshmallow, you're pushing sixteen. So what if you're a straight A student, that's parent's stuff. Get with it.

CHICKLET Maybe I'm just some kind of a freak. Maybe I'll never fall in love.

BERDINE Oh you will, you will.

CHICKLET But how will I know when it hits me?

BERDINE You will, you will.

MARVEL ANN Chicklet, what are you trying to do, spoil the picture? Take off your top. You've got your swim suit on, don't you? Peel, girl, peel.

CHICKLET Darn it, it's in my bag and there's no ladies room to change in.

MARVEL ANN There's no one around. You better hurry.

BERDINE You can't take your top off here.

CHICKLET Hold the blanket up and no one will see me. (*They hold up the blanket, Chicklet takes off her smock, revealing her nude, flat chest.*) I'm hopeless. I'm built just like a boy. I wonder if I'll ever fill out.

BERDINE Hurry up, Chicklet. Marvel Ann, hold the blanket up so I can help Chicklet with her top. (*Chicklet pulls on her bathing suit top.*)

MARVEL ANN We're in luck. Look at those four gorgeous hunks of male, over there, almost enough for second helpings. Now a manuever like this takes technique. Talk to me. Don't let them think we're looking at them.

CHICKLET What should we talk about?

MARVEL ANN Anything.

BERDINE I'm reading the most exciting book. It's by Jean Paul Sartre. It's called "Nausea."

MARVEL ANN (*Posing and not paying attention.*) Oh, really.

BERDINE It's, the most clear-headed explanation of existentialism. The whole concept of free will being conscious choice against the determining . . .

MARVEL ANN (*With extreme bitchiness*) I'll see the movie.

CHICKLET Gosh, Berdine, I'm impressed. You're a real egghead.

MARVEL ANN They're looking this way. Now very slowly, let's turn our heads in their direction. (*They simultaneously turn their heads.*) Slowly. Cock your head to the side and give a little smile. (*They cock their heads and smile in unison.*) Not like that, Berdine, you look like you've got whiplash. (*Berdine straightens up.*) The blonde one is giggling. (*She giggles.*)

CHICKLET What's so funny?

MARVEL ANN Shut up. Now we go in for the kill. (*She makes a sexy growl.*)

CHICKLET What's she doing now?

BERDINE I believe she's displaying animal magnetism.

Berdine and Chicklet start growling and barking like wild dogs and apes.

MARVEL ANN What the hell are you two doing? Oh, now you've done it. They're laughing at us. How dare you. I hate you both.

CHICKLET Marvel Ann, don't lose your sense of humor.

MARVEL ANN (*Stands up.*) Oh, I'm laughing all right and so is everyone else at school, laughing at how backward you are. I ought to get the purple heart just for being seen with you. (*Turns to leave.*)

BERDINE Where are you going?

MARVEL ANN I didn't come to the beach to play. I came here to catch a man. So if you'll excuse me, I think I'll set my traps elsewhere.

CHICKLET Can we come too?

MARVEL ANN What's the point in meeting boys? You two queerbaits should get a license and marry each other. (*She exits, laughing.*)

CHICKLET What sort of nasty crack is that?

BERDINE I don't see anything wrong with having a best friend.

CHICKLET I suppose some friends get so close that they lose their individual identities.

BERDINE We're two very independent personalities.

CHICKLET She's just jealous, cause . . .

BERDINE (*Finishing her sentence.*) We've never really accepted her. How could we, she's . . .

CHICKLET dumb as-a stick. I don't think she's ever read a book . . .

BERDINE all the way to the end. Someday she'll be sorry . . .

CHICKLET that she rushed into adulthood. We're much wiser to

BERDINE/CHICKLET (*Simultaneously*) take our time.

CHICKLET I don't think virginity is such a horrible . . .

BERDINE degrading . . . .

CHICKLET awful thing. You know of course what she did with you know who in the . . .

BERDINE (*Understands perfectly.*) Uh huh. Uh huh. And did you know she . . .

CHICKLET (*Understands perfectly.*) Uh huh. But I think there's more to it. I think, well . . . you know . . .

BERDINE Really? (*Giggles.*)

CHICKLET It reminds me of that book we read, what was it?

BERDINE (*Knows the book.*) Yes, yes, yes. That's exactly the same kinda . . .

CHICKLET And look what . . . well . . .

BERDINE So true, so true. I couldn't have said it better myself.

Marvel Ann enters with Kanaka and Star Cat.

MARVEL ANN Look what I found in the sand. Two hunks of California he-man.

KANAKA I dig a mermaid whose lips are as flip as her fins.

MARVEL ANN (*Coyly*) Don't swim too fast upstream, you can still lose the race.

KANAKA I know how to glide on wave power when I have to.

STAR CAT (*To Marvel Ann*) Hey, the waves are flipping out. Come and watch me surf standing on my head.

CHICKLET (*Wildly impressed*) Can you really do that?

STAR CAT Sure. (*To Marvel Ann*) I can do lots of special tricks.

CHICKLET (*Innocently*) Really? Like what?

STAR CAT (*To Marvel Ann*) You interested?

MARVEL ANN (*Provocatively*) Very interested.

CHICKLET (*Thinks they're talking about surfing.*) So am I. Let's go right now.

MARVEL ANN I'd rather see you try those stunts on land.

CHICKLET That's not the same thing at all.

MARVEL ANN I missed your name, tall, dark and brooding.

STAR CAT They call me Star Cat.

MARVEL ANN I call you cute.

STAR CAT I'd like to call you sometime.

MARVEL ANN I'm in the phone book under my father's name, Franklin McCallister, I'm Marvel Ann.

CHICKLET You can call me too. I'm Chicklet. Here. I'll write down my number cause golly, I'd do anything to see you surf standing on your . . .

MARVEL ANN Oh pooh, the sun's playing hookey. No use sitting around here.

KANAKA Star Cat, let's help the lady.

STAR CAT You bet!

MARVEL ANN (*She holds up the blanket, the boys help her.*) Why thank you, gentlemen. Come, girls.

CHICKLET That's okay, Marvel Ann. I think I'll stay out a little longer. I'll call you when I get home, Berdine. Okle dokle?

BERDINE (*Wary*) Okle dokle.

MARVEL ANN (*Suspiciously*) Okle dokle. (*They exit.*)

KANAKA (*To Star Cat*) Good going, pal. I bet she's hot and spicy between the enchilada.

CHICKLET If Kanaka won't teach me to surf, will you? I'm a quick study. Straight A's in all my classes.

STAR CAT You think I'm impressed? Listen little girl, surfing is a man's work. Be a girl. You're more fish than dish. Me teach you how to surf? Don't make me laugh. I'd rather teach a chicken to lay an elephant's turd. Go home to mama and run, don't walk. (*He exits.*)

CHICKLET Boy, he's a grump.

KANAKA Aw, Star Cat's a raw pearl. He's just a sensitive kind of fella. Hey, look at that kite.

CHICKLET Which one?

KANAKA The red one with the flying fish.

(*Chicklet's face becomes distorted and she becomes her alter ego, Ann Bowman, a glamorous femme fatale.*)

KANAKA (*Oblivious*) When I was a kid, I was bananas over flying kites. More than anything, I'd like to be running with a kite against the wind.

CHICKLET (*Laughs*) Darling, more than anything, I'd like a cool martini, dry with a twist.

KANAKA Say what?

CHICKLET You do know what a martini is, my delicious Neanderthal.

KANAKA Chicklet?

CHICKLET (*Laughs*) I'm afraid you've got the wrong girl. Chicklet is not my name.

KANAKA Who are you?

CHICKLET My name is Ann Bowman.

KANAKA (*Laughs*) That's pretty good. You wanna be an actress?

CHICKLET I'm revealing my true nature. (*Fingers his fly.*) I'd like to see you strip down to your truest self.

KANAKA (*Pushes her hand away.*) Hey, you shouldn't do that.

CHICKLET Give me one good reason.

KANAKA You're underage.

CHICKLET My energy is as old as the Incan temples. You ever been to Peru, baby?

KANAKA Can't say I have.

CHICKLET Someday, you and I must explore the ancient temple of Aca Jo Tep. But enough about that for now, what about us?

KANAKA Hey, cool your jets, babe. If I didn't live by my personal code of honor, I might take advantage of this situation erotically, as it were.

CHICKLET Give into the feeling, Daddy-O.

KANAKA Cut the soundtrack for a minute and listen up. Let me give you the number one rule of sexual relations. No stud digs a heavy come-on from a babe. A chick can play it tough but underneath the makeup, a dude's gotta know the chick's a lady. In straight lingo, no pigs need apply.

CHICKLET (*Lies on the ground*) Forget the rules, lie here on the sand with me. Doncha love the feel of hot sand against your nude flesh?

KANAKA I don't know what you're up to but you've got the wrong hep cat.

CHICKLET Perhaps I do. I thought you were the man with the big cigar. What are you packing, a tiparillo?

KANAKA More than you can handle, kid. They ought to send you to the juvenile detention hall.

CHICKLET Aw, I'm scaring the "wittle" boy.

KANAKA Doll, when I dance, I make the moves, the chick always follows. (*He turns to leave*)

CHICKLET (*With mad ferocity*) Don't you turn your butt to me!

KANAKA (*Turns around shocked*) Chicklet?

CHICKLET I am not Chicklet, you lobotomized numbskull!!!

KANAKA C'mon stop fooling.

CHICKLET Do not test me. I will have my way. (*Laughs*) I frighten you, don't I?

KANAKA No, I ain't scared.

CHICKLET You're lying. You're yellow as a traffic light, you sniveling little prick. You're scared.

KANAKA No.

CHICKLET Look at your hands, they're shaking like jello.

KANAKA (*Hides his hands*) No, they ain't.

CHICKLET You're scared. Say it, you're scared.

KANAKA Yes!

CHICKLET Yes what?

KANAKA Yes, ma'am.

CHICKLET Ah, that's better. You're just a little slave boy, aren't you, sonny?

KANAKA I gotta get outta here.

CHICKLET You ain't going anywhere, punk. You know, I'm going to give you what you always wanted.

KANAKA You are?

CHICKLET I think we understand each other very well. I know what you fantasize about, I know what you dream about and I'm going to give it to you in spades. Now I want you to go into town and buy yourself a slave collar and a garter belt and a pair of black silk stockings. Spike heels will complete the ensemble and then my dear darling Kanaka, I'm gonna shave all that man fur off you and you'll look just like the little boy that you are.

KANAKA But what will the rest of the fellas think?

CHICKLET (*In a rage*) To hell with the rest of the fellas! I am the most important! Me! Ann Bowman! I will not be cast aside, I will not be . . . (*Becomes Chicklet again*) Of course, my Mom's an old prude, she won't think surfing is ladylike but I know I can win her over.

KANAKA (*In shock*) What?

CHICKLET My Mom. I'm gonna have to ask her permission.

KANAKA Ann?

CHICKLET My name's Chicklet, silly. So are you gonna teach me, please, please, pretty please.

KANAKA Do you remember what we were just talking about?

CHICKLET Surfing lessons.

KANAKA No after that, I mean before that.

CHICKLET Your friend Star Cat? I'm wearing down your resistance, aren't I?

KANAKA (*Very confused*) Yeah, I'll say.

CHICKLET Can we start tomorrow?

KANAKA Yeah, sure.

CHICKLET Yippee! I gotta get moving, gotta round up a board, get my Mom's okay and then tomorrow, we hit the old H_2O. Tootles. (*She exits*)

KANAKA (*Scratching his head in disbelief*) A red kite with a flying fish.

BLACKOUT

Scene 2

Chicklet's house. She enters.

CHICKLET Mom, I'm home. Gosh, the place looks spotless. Was Sadie here today?

(MRS. FORREST *enters, the spitting image of Joan Crawford.*)

MRS. FORREST Unfortunately no. Poor Sadie's brother Bubba was run over by a hit-and-run driver. You know our Sadie, always an excuse not to work, I've been on my hands and knees scrubbing all morning. And to top it off, I was experimenting cooking a veal scallopini in the pressure cooker. The darn thing exploded and I'm still finding bits of scallopini in my wiglet.

CHICKLET Well, the house looks swell.

MRS. FORREST Thank you, dear. Did you enjoy yourself at the beach? (*Puts arm around her*)

CHICKLET I guess so.

MRS. FORREST I detect a sphinx-like expression. Penny for your thoughts.

CHICKLET (*Looking for a way to tell her about surfing*) I just hate thinking of you doing all that nasty housework. You're so beautiful.

MRS. FORREST (*Laughs*) My darling daughter, I am just an old widow and a little hard work never hurt anyone.

CHICKLET You're still young. Haven't you ever thought of remarrying?

MRS. FORREST Your father was the great love of my life. I've always regretted that he died before you were born, that you never knew him. He was quite a guy. A damn good provider.

And, darling, to even think of another man would betray his memory.

CHICKLET I really love you but I don't think I'm pulling my weight around here. I've been thinking, there must be more chores for me to do, painting the inside of the trash cans, polishing the cactus plants.

MRS. FORREST Chicklet, I smell a rat.

CHICKLET I'll exterminate it.

MRS. FORREST Chicklet, what's going on up there in the old attic? (*Indicating her brain*)

CHICKLET Okay, Mom, cards on the table. I need twenty-five dollars to buy a surf board.

MRS. FORREST Out of the question.

CHICKLET Mom, it's the chance of a lifetime. The great Kanaka has promised to teach me to surf.

MRS. FORREST The great who?

CHICKLET The great Kanaka, why he's practically as famous as the President of the United States.

MRS. FORREST It's too dangerous.

CHICKLET It's as safe as playing jacks. Please let me Mom. It'll be sheer heaven or months and months of stark solitude.

MRS. FORREST I will not have my daughter cavorting with a band of derelict beach bums.

CHICKLET They're great guys. You should see them shooting the curl. It's the ultimate. A gilt-edged guarantee for a summer of sheer happiness.

MRS. FORREST Control yourself, Florence.

CHICKLET (*Fiercely*) I will not control myself. I want a mother-fucking cocksucking surfboard!!!

MRS. FORREST I can see the effect those boys are having on you. I don't like it one bit. You will not see those boys ever again. Promise me that.

CHICKLET I will not promise you.

MRS. FORREST You're cold. This is what the male sex is going to do to us. It's going to tear us apart. You don't know how lucky you are being a virgin, pure and chaste.

CHICKLET But someday I do want to marry and then I suppose I'd have to . . .

MRS. FORREST Do what? Have sexual intercourse. I know how they paint it so beautifully in the movies. A man and a woman locked in embrace, soft lighting, a pitcher of Manhattans, Rachmaninoff in the background. Well, my girl, let me tell you that is not how it is. You don't know how repugnant it is having a sweaty man's thing poking at you. (*She jabs her finger into Chicklet*) Do you like that?

CHICKLET Stop, you're hurting me.

MRS. FORREST That's nothing compared to when they poke you down there.

CHICKLET I don't believe you.

MRS. FORREST Florence!

CHICKLET I don't believe you. Sexual relations between a man and a woman in love is a beautiful and sacred thing. You're wrong, Mother, horribly wrong.

MRS. FORREST The male body is coarse and ugly.

CHICKLET Some men are beautiful.

MRS. FORREST (*In a demonic rage*) You think men are beautiful. Well, take a look at this, Missy. (*She pulls from her cleavage a jock strap*) For years I've kept this, anticipating this very moment. Do you know what this is?

CHICKLET No.

MRS. FORREST It's a peter belt. This is the pouch that holds their swollen genitalia. Isn't this beautiful? Isn't this romantic? (*She slaps Chicklet with the jock strap repeatedly.*)

CHICKLET Stop, stop.

MRS. FORREST (*Throws the jock strap at Chicklet.*) You are a very foolish girl And to think I spent long hours toiling over that veal scallopini. (*Mrs. Forrest exits. Chicklet stares at the jock strap and whimpers.*)

CHICKLET I'm sorry, Mommy, I'm sorry. (*Starts growling and making animal noises. In baby talk.*) She can't treat me this way. She's so mean and I'm too little to fight back . . . I'm so angry . . . I'm so angry . . . I'm . . . I'm (*She bursts into demonic laughter. As Ann Bowman.*) I'm alive! I'm alive! Ann Bowman lives!!!!

BLACKOUT

SCENE 3

Berdine is in her pajamas writing in her diary

BERDINE Dear Diary: Last night Chicklet showed up at my house with a real bee in her bonnet. She is determined to buy a surfboard. Her Mom said nix. Boy, parents can be grumps. Anyways, it's a good thing I won that prize money for my essay on Kierkegaard, Kant and Buber. I handed it right over. Chicklet Forrest is my best friend in the whole stratosphere. I've never told this to anyone, not even you, dear diary, but sometimes I catch her talking to herself in this weird sort of voice. I suppose some people would say she's kind of loco but you see, Chicklet is a very creative person and sometimes her imagination just sort of goes blotto but in a noodly sort of way, not a complete geek-out but just a fizzle in her research center. Sorry, that's teenage talk. Well, time to sign off, your ever faithful correspondent, Berdine.

BLACKOUT

Scene 4

The beach. Yo Yo and Provoloney enter talking

YO YO I got my menu for the luau all made up. What do you think of marinated alligator tips? You can buy 'em frozen at Ralph's. And I thought lots of finger food, but no dips, I am so tired of dips.

PROVOLONEY Yo Yo, would you stop with the food for a minute.

YO YO But, Provoloney, the luau is only three weeks away.

PROVOLONEY Do you realize how much of your life is obsessed with trivia? Finger food, dips. It really upsets me how little scope you have.

YO YO What are you talking about? I've got scope. (*Switching the subject*) What do you want to do with your hair for the luau?

PROVOLONEY (*He screams.*) See what I mean? Trivia! All this talk about recipes and hairstyles. People are gonna think you're kind of, you know, (*Makes a limp wrist*) that way.

YO YO Let 'em try. I'll bash their nuts in.

PROVOLONEY (*Trying to talk sensibly*) Yo Yo, do you ever think about the future?

YO YO Yeah, that's why I'm asking you about the alligator tips.

PROVOLONEY The far future. You're not going to be young forever. We need to plan ahead.

YO YO This was such a beautiful day. You're making me so depressed.

PROVOLONEY (*Very upbeat*) Don't be depressed, kid. Stick with me and you'll never be sorry.

Star Cat enters.

STAR CAT Hey guys, any of you seen Kanaka?

(*Kanaka and Chicklet enter.*)

KANAKA Gentlemen, the time has come for me to introduce you to the new Empress of the Seven Seas. Queen Chicklet is going to join us on the water today.

PROVOLONEY This little twirp working our waves, give me a break.

CHICKLET I'm not a twirp.

YO YO Stick to the bathtub, baby, leave the Pacific to the big boys.

STAR CAT We're too busy to be changing your diapers.

CHICKLET You think you know everything, you stuck up prune face pickle eater.

KANAKA You ready for a ride, Chickerino?

CHICKLET Kanaka, these fins are ready to hit the foam. What do you say?

KANAKA I say "Everybody, grab your surf boards and charge!" (*They all hoot and holler.*)

Lights black out and then come back on and we see Chicklet and the boys riding the high waves, laughing and screaming with joy and excitement. Blackout. When the lights come up they are carrying Chicklet on their shoulders, shouting "Hip hip hooray."

KANAKA What did I tell you, ain't she something else?

YO YO (*Making a big formal bow and kissing her hand*) I bow before the Queen Chicklet.

CHICKLET Aw, knock it off.

PROVOLONEY Welcome to the club. What do you say we make her our new mascot?

YO YO Great.

STAR CAT You know something, I am a stuck up prune face pickle eater. (*He gives Chicklet a big hug and they embrace, a bit too long. Everyone's cheers turn to ohhhhhh, and they are embarrassed.*) And I'll tell you what, I'll even teach you how to surf standing on your head.

CHICKLET (*Thrilled*) You would? Really? Just the two of us?

YO YO (*Imitating her*) Really? Just the two of us? (*All the guys giggle.*)

CHICKLET (*Embarrassed*) Well, I'd need to concentrate. I can't learn anything with you jokers around.

STAR CAT Sure, kid, just the two of us.

PROVOLONEY (*Acting silly*) Can we come, too?

YO YO Please, please, pretty please. (*Chicklet chases them around.*)

CHICKLET Oh gosh, this is the way I like it, just kids, horsing around, having picnics.

PROVOLONEY We need to give her an initiation.

STAR CAT And how.

CHICKLET Oh, no you don't.

PROVOLONEY Yo Yo, give her the Chinese tickle torture.

They grab her and Yo Yo pushes his head into her stomach tickling her with his hair, She screams. Marvel Ann enters.)

MARVEL ANN Star Cat. (*They drop Chicklet.*)

STAR CAT Hey there, Marvel Ann.

STAR CAT (*She wraps herself around him.*) What's all the brou-ha-ha?

KANAKA The Chicklet turned out to be a first class surfer.

YO YO The best.

MARVEL ANN How marvelous for you. I wish you every . . . every.

CHICKLET You should try surfing, Marvel Ann, it's great for anyone with a weight problem.

MARVEL ANN I get my exercise indoors. Star Cat, wait til you see the dress I bought to wear to the luau. It's very . . . very.

CHICKLET What, luau?

MARVEL ANN Haven't you naughty boys told Chicklet about the luau? It's just the biggest event of the whole summer.

CHICKLET You douche bags, why have you been holding out on me?

KANAKA You're just not the luau type, baby.

PROVOLONEY It's a wild night.

YO YO Practically an orgy.

CHICKLET I want to go.

MARVEL ANN Besides you'll need an escort and I've already nabbed the cutest boy in town. (*Flirts with an uncomfortable Star Cat. She strokes his hair.*)

STAR CAT Ow, you're pulling my hair.

MARVEL ANN You promised you'd go to the pier with me today. I'm in the mood for a nice big banana split. Doesn't that sound tasty?

STAR CAT Very, very. See you guys later. (*They exit.*)

CHICKLET You all think you're real clever not telling me about the luau but I'm going and I'm going to make a splash like you've never seen.

The incredibly glamourous movie star, BETTINA BARNES, *enters in a big hat and dark glasses. The boys stare at her transfixed as she unfolds her blanket and sits on the beach.*)

YO YO Zowie!

PROVOLONEY Hot dog!

KANAKA Let's check out her I. D. (*They approach her.*)

CHICKLET Hey guys, don't bother with her.

KANAKA (*To Bettina*) And then the Papa Bear said "Who's been sleeping in my sandbox?"

BETTINA (*Surprised, lowers her sunglasses*) Pardon me?

KANAKA What brings you here to grace our turf?

BETTINA (*Breathily innocent*) Am I trespassing? I had no idea.

PROVOLONEY You look real familiar. Do you know Lenny Pinkowitz?

BETTINA (*Alarmed*) Is he a shutterbug?

CHICKLET Hey guys, come on.

YO YO Can we ask you your name?

BETTINA I'm afraid I can't answer that.

CHICKLET Are you incognito?

BETTINA (*Not comprehending*) No, I'm German-Irish.

KANAKA Are there people after you?

BETTINA I have a whole motion picture studio after me and the entire press corp. Haven't you read the newspapers? I'm Bettina Barnes. (*Gasps*) I shouldn't have told you.

CHICKLET Bettina Barnes, the movie star.

BETTINA Actress.

CHICKLET You disappeared from the set of your new movie. The police think you've been kidnapped.

BETTINA I was never kidnapped. I ran away.

PROVOLONEY Why would you run away from a movie?

BETTINA You don't know what it's like being exploited by those lousy flesh peddlers and power brokers. Everyone wanting a little piece. I'm not a pepperoni.

KANAKA I saw you in that movie "Sex Kittens Go To Outer Space."

BETTINA That was a good film. The director had a vision but then I had to do the four sequels. Quel trash. I couldn't go on. They have no respect for the rights of the individual.

YO YO We'll respect you.

BETTINA (*Touched*) Would you really? Isn't that what all human beings desire, respect? That's why I'm on the lam, to get me some.

CHICKLET Where are you going to go?

BETTINA New York. I've been accepted to study with Lee Strasberg. But first I thought I'd hide out here to get some rest and relaxation. I've rented that beach house over there. I signed the lease under my real name Frieda Deefendorfer. You won't squeal on me, will you? (*The boys all promise they won't.*) You're so sweet. You can be kind of like my brothers. (*To Chicklet*) And you, you're perky. With a new hairstyle and the right makeup, you could be almost pretty.

Berdine enters.

BERDINE Chicklet! There you are. I thought I'd find you here. You were supposed to meet me at the malt shop. I was waiting there over an hour when . . . (*She sees Bettina and screams.*) Bettina Barnes! (*The boys grab her and hold her mouth closed.*)

CHICKLET She's incognito.

BERDINE Bettina Barnes. In person. You have the most beautiful eyelashes I've ever seen on any mammal.

BETTINA You're very kind.

BERDINE I loved you in "The Pizza Waitress with Three Heads." You were so real. When they trapped you on top of the Pizzeria, you made me feel what it's like to have three heads and be shot in each one of them.

BETTINA (*Intensely*) Did I really?

BERDINE Oh yes, Miss Barnes.

BETTINA (*Tenderly*) Call me Miss B. I know I could be a great actress if I found the right vehicle.

PROVOLONEY She needs wheels.

YO YO The lady needs wheels.

KANAKA We'll get you a car.

BERDINE No, she means she needs a great role that will reveal the many facets of her kaleidoscopic persona.

BETTINA (*Confused*) What did she say?

BERDINE Sometimes even the great don't understand their own power. You are more than a mere sex kitten. You are the feminine embodiment of the nietzschian superman. Ever striving, striking a blow for the truth in the eternal battle of the sexes. Onward, Bettina! "And whatever will break on our truths, let it break! Many a house hath yet to be built." Thus spake Zarathustra.

BETTINA That's what I've been telling my agents for months. You're smart. What's your name?

BERDINE Berdine.

BETTINA I desperately need a secretary slash companion slash masseuse. How would you like a job for the summer?

BERDINE I don't know, Miss B. I've got a big reading list to get through. And I'm still not finished with "The Idiot."

BETTINA (*With great sympathy*) You've got man trouble?

PROVOLONEY Hey guys, let's invite Miss Barnes to the luau.

BERDINE What luau?

KANAKA The first full moon of the summer, we have a luau slash barbecue. It's a night no one ever forgets.

BERDINE (*Sarcastically*) Gee, thanks Chicklet for inviting me.

CHICKLET I just heard about it.

BERDINE Like hey I really believe that.

CHICKLET It's the truth.

BERDINE The truth is that we're not connecting at all anymore.

CHICKLET What are you talking about?

BERDINE Let me spell it out for you then. In the past few weeks, you never return my phone calls, you've cancelled out of the last five times we're supposed to get together and today you stood me up at Augie's malt shop. I don't think you want to be best friends anymore.

CHICKLET I'm sorry, I just . . .

BERDINE (*Holding back tears*) Everyone said we were too close. I never thought this could happen. Not to us.

BETTINA Please don't argue on my account.

CHICKLET Don't cry. Look, let's talk about this in private. How about meeting me at Augie's tomorrow.

BERDINE So you can stand me up again? No, thank you. Chicklet, my closing remarks to you are these. I hope you enjoy all your new hipster friends cause you just lost your best and oldest one. Miss Barnes, I've reconsidered and I'd love to be your secretary. When do I start?

BETTINA Pronto. We're going to have a great time. (*Takes her arm*) I'm going to let you in on all my innermost secrets. Let's go back to my bungalow and have lunch. You do know how to make Crab Louis, don't you?

BERDINE I don't think so.

BETTINA No sweat. We'll have peanut butter and jelly . . . (*As an afterthought*) on toast points.

PROVOLONEY Think about the luau.

KANAKA Think about me.

BETTINA (*Seductively*) How could I forget you.

YO YO (*Extends his hand to Bettina to shake hands.*) It's been great meeting you.

BETTINA (*She turns to Yo Yo and takes his hand.*) My, what great big hands you have.

YO YO (*Leering*) You know what they say about big hands and big feet.

BETTINA (*Studying his hand intently*) Yes, most interesting.

CHICKLET Are you a palmist or something?

BETTINA No, nothing like that. I just have these incredible instincts about people. I seem to know how they tick.

YO YO So what do you see?

BETTINA I bet you're very good with hair.

YO YO You mean running my fingers through it.

BETTINA No, I mean setting it.

YO YO (*Upset at the suggestion he's a fag.*) Hey, wait just a minute . . .

BETTINA (*Very soothing and gentle*) That's nothing to be ashamed of. It's a special gift. (*The other guys snicker.*) I've got a slew of wigs with me. Let's go to my bungalow, lock the door and play beauty salon.

PROVOLONEY (*Acting sexy*) Can I come too? I'd love to lock the door and play with you.

BETTINA Hey, Berdine, as a great philosopher once said "the more the merrier." Let's go!

YO YO Yeah, go, go, go. (*Bettina exits followed by Yo Yo, Provoloney and Berdine. Kanaka pulls Chicklet back.*)

KANAKA Hey, Chicklet.

CHICKLET Don't you want to go to Bettina's?

KANAKA Nah, it's kids stuff to be impressed with her. (*Checks to see if they are alone.*)

CHICKLET Who are you looking for?

KANAKA I want to make sure we're alone. Uh, it's Yo Yo's birthday coming up and . . .

CHICKLET I thought he said it was . . .

KANAKA No, it's real soon and I thought you could help me make him a present.

CHICKLET Like what?

KANAKA A kite. He's flipped over kites. What do you think of that?

CHICKLET A kite. That's okay.

KANAKA Kites. He becomes like a different person when he's flying a kite.

CHICKLET I never made one before but . . .

KANAKA (*To himself*) What were we talking about? Do you see that fish jumping out of the water?

CHICKLET No, where?

KANAKA I'm crazy for fish, aren't you?

CHICKLET (*Shrugs*) Feh. Kanaka, are you all right?

KANAKA (*Giving up*) No, I must be out of my mind. Forget it. Geez, I'm embarrassed. Is my face red? (*When Chicklet hears red she laughs wildly and turns into Ann Bowman.*)

KANAKA (*Elated*) It was a red kite!

CHICKLET (*As Ann Bowman*) It most certainly was, darling. As red as your ass when I finish spanking you.

KANAKA Oh yes, Mistress Ann. I've been a bad boy. I need a spanking.

CHICKLET I've got you under my spell. You would do anything I asked. (*She turns into Tylene, a black checkout girl.*) But if she asked me to work overtime at that Safeway, she be out of her mind.

KANAKA Ann?

CHICKLET Who you be calling Ann, my name is Tylene. Tylene Carmichael Carmel.

KANAKA What?

CHICKLET I be working at the checkout, it goin' on four-thirty and I'm fixin' to leave. My boyfriend, he's taking me to see Chubby Checker.

KANAKA Ann, come back, Ann, are you there?

CHICKLET Would you let me finish? What I am saying is my supervisor, Miss Feeley, she asks me to work overtime. She thinks she so cool, she . . .

KANAKA (*Shakes her*) Stop it. Bring Ann back!

CHICKLET (*Indicates a switchblade's in her pocket*) Back off, I cut you. I cut you. I got me a blade. I cut you.

KANAKA (*Terrfied*) That's cool. That's cool.

CHICKLET No way no white son of a bitch be grabbin at me. No way, no way . . . (*Returns as Ann*) No way you can escape my domination. The world has tried to suppress me, to deny my very existence but I have risen like a phoenix to claim my birthright.

KANAKA What's that?

CHICKLET World domination. Ann Bowman, Dominatrix Empress of the planet Earth. Has a catchy ring, don't you think?

KANAKA Yes, Mistress Ann.

CHICKLET I wonder if your little friends might make excellent slaves. We must catch them in butterfly nets and put them in cages. Once their spirit is broken, they shall learn to serve their Mistress Ann.

KANAKA Cages. But won't they suspect you're up to no good?

CHICKLET I am not only a first class general. I am also a brilliant actress. I will pose as dear little Chicklet and infiltrate the teen set.

KANAKA Look, I think I've gotten in over my head. I can't do something like this.

CHICKLET (*Grabs him*) You deny me! No one denies me, darling. You need what only I can offer. Face it, you're weak, you're a pushover for me. You sing to the coppers and I'll finger you as the fall guy. You made me lose my temper. It's time for fun and games. Shall we proceed to your place? Kanaka, move it! (*She throws her head back and laughs. They exit.*)

BLACKOUT

SCENE 5

The Beach. Provoloney and Yo Yo enter.

YO YO I don't know, Provoloney, it sounds too easy.

PROVOLONEY I tell you, the ideas that make millions are deceptively simple. Bettina Barnes is on the lookout for a movie that will win her an Oscar. We've got to find it for her.

YO YO But that means writing and I'm not so good with sentences.

PROVOLONEY In Hollywood, only flunkies do any writing. The smart guys write treatments. The studio pays big money just for ideas. We come up with a great notion for a flick and we can rake in the moola without putting in a comma.

YO YO You have any ideas?

PROVOLONEY My brain's bursting with them. Westerns, sci-fi, musicals.

YO YO Well, I think . . .

PROVOLONEY Quiet on the set. I need inspiration. I need a concept.

YO YO I think Bettina should play the richest woman in the world.

PROVOLONEY (*His eyes closed*) Yeah, my mind's working now. Go on.

YO YO Her old man wants her to marry this prince but he's kind of a drip so she ankles out of Phily and heads westward to Malibu.

PROVOLONEY It's all coming to me. I'm cookin'. Go on.

YO YO She's got so much cash that she buys the whole beach. There's this real hot surf bum who lives there and he don't like the idea of being evicted. They decide to smoke the peace pipe and the stud offers to teach her to scuba dive.

PROVOLONEY This is great. I can see the whole thing. A billboard fifty feet high. Bettina Barnes in a wet suit.

YO YO I see this real big scene when they first dive underwater. (*Yo Yo mimes going underwater.*)

PROVOLONEY (*He dives too.*) They swim past picturesque coral reefs and dolphins.

YO YO And they bump into each other. (*They mime all the next activity.*)

PROVOLONEY And they get their feet caught in some seaweed . . . and their bodies are locked into each other.

YO YO They can't get out?

PROVOLONEY (*Transfixed*) Uh uh. Their eyes meet. Every night he's dreamt of her long flowing hair, her ivory skin, her biceps.

YO YO She feels powerless to resist his raw brute strength. Is this where they kiss for the first time?

PROVOLONEY They've always wanted to but they were too scared.

YO YO I guess underwater it doesn't matter much.

PROVOLONEY I guess not.

They slowly kiss. Cannons go off. Bells ring. The 1812 Overture is played. They break apart.

PROVOLONEY (*Scared*) Uh, Yo Yo, I better write this down before I forget it.

YO YO (*Thrilled*) I won't forget it.

PROVOLONEY (*Embarrassed and remorseful*) I met this lady who works in the library. She said she'd teach me how to use her typewriter.

YO YO That's good.

PROVOLONEY Yeah. Maybe afterwards, I'll . . . I'll ball her. (*Provoloney exits.*)

BLACKOUT

Scene 6

The beach beyond Bettina's house. Berdine is writing in her diary.

BERDINE Dear Diary. Gear up for another helping of Berdine's flaming self pity. I miss Chicklet so much. Ever since she got that darn surf board, nothing's been the same. I wish I'd never given her that money. A girl's best friend is something very special. And Chicklet's more than just my best friend. It's like we're one person. I know that sounds kooky but it's true. Oh, life is but a meaningless charade, death the ultimate absurdity. I am living proof of Sartre's existential concept of nausea. Gosh, I wish I had a Tums. Of course, I've been very busy working for Miss Barnes. She's a nice lady but very complicated.

Bettina enters stretching.

BERDINE Good morning, Miss B!

BETTINA What a splendiforous morning. I can't tell you how grand it feels to be away from that salacious Hollywood rat race. I was so tense. You can't imagine the hubbub in my lower lumbar region.

BERDINE Well, this week has done wonders for you. You look like a completely different person.

BETTINA (*Suspicious and paranoid*) Who? What's her measurements?

BERDINE No, what I meant was . . . oh . . . (*Sees telegram in her hand*) Oh! Miss Barnes, that telegram arrived that you were waiting for.

BETTINA (*Excited*) Oh wow, I'm scared to open it. It's from the studio. I've asked them to release me from my contract. (*Opens it*) I'm too scared to read it. It's awful being this vulnerable. (*To Berdine*) You read it to me.

BERDINE (*Reading*) Dear Bettina, up yours, stop, with turpentine, stop. New picture "Sex Kittens Go Bossa Nova" starts lensing September first. Be there or expect legal action. Stop. Love Sid Rosen. (*Stops reading*) Oh Bettina, I'm so sorry. You poor little thing.

BETTINA (*Tough as nails and in a low rough voice*) That cheap son of a bitch can't do this to me. He slaps me with a subpoena and I'll have his balls on a plate.

BERDINE (*Shocked*) Bettina.

BETTINA (*Pacing furious*) After all the money I made for those bastards. They can't do this to me. I'm Bettina Barnes. I'm no flash in the pan that'll take any piece of crap. I'm playing hard ball, baby.

BERDINE Have you read the script? Maybe it's not bad.

BETTINA Not bad! Lassie could fart out a better script.

Yo Yo and Provoloney enter. Provoloney is tricked up in his notion of a hollywood movie mogul.

PROVOLONEY Hey there; Miss Barnes, I hear you got some work you'd like us to do.

BETTINA (*Soft and vulnerable*) Oh, yeah, something. I needed something done. I'm so forgetful. (*Remembers*) Oh, yes. Last night I was sleepwalking and I suddenly woke up and discovered this adorable little garden in my back yard. During the last storm, all the little trees and shrubbery must have broken and it's a dreadful mess. Could you clear it up for me? And then we can have swell parties. I make delicious jalapeno pancakes.

YO YO Sure thing. We'll clean it up.

PROVOLONEY (*Nervously*) Excuse me Miss Barnes, do you think I could talk to you for a moment?

BETTINA But of course.

PROVOLONEY (*With an air of bravado*) I never told you this before but this surf bum business is just a facade, I'm really a screenwriter.

BERDINE You're what?

YO YO He's a screenwriter.

PROVOLONEY Written tons of stuff, TV, radio. I've got a development deal going for me at Columbia. Meeting you yesterday gave me the inspiration for a new picture. A big picture, cinemascope, 3-D, smell-o-vision.

BETTINA (*Touched*) Really, I inspired you?

PROVOLONEY You certainly did. It's just a treatment, really, an idea.

YO YO But it's a great one.

BETTINA I love a man with a big idea.

PROVOLONEY Columbia's been putting the screws on me to make it with Kim.

BETTINA (*Very impressed*) You know Kim Novak?

PROVOLONEY Great gal but dead eyes, blank, an empty screen. This idea . . .

BETTINA Oh, tell me all about it.

PROVOLONEY The setting: Malibu Beach. I see you as the daughter of a shipping tycoon. You . . .

BERDINE . . . leave finishing school and meet a handsome surf bum who teaches you how to scuba dive. "The Girl From Rock n' Roll Beach," Starring Mamie Van Doren, Allied Artists, 1960, Albert Zugsmith, Producer.

PROVOLONEY Yeah, well, it's a lot like that, only better. You can have the whole megillah for two thousand dollars.

BETTINA Two thousand dollars. It sounds most intriguing but I think for my first independent feature, I should play a typical girl of today, someone who the audience can identify with and yet a girl with a personal problem, like psoriasis. However, maybe we can develop this further.

PROVOLONEY Bettina baby, I don't want to pressure you but . . .

BETTINA (*Looks offstage*) Oh, look, there's your little friend, Chicklet. I don't know, there's something kind of funny about her.

Chicklet enters with a wild red feather boa, and smoking out of a long cigarette holder.

CHICKLET (*In Ann Bowman's voice*) Berdine darling! It's been eons since we last met.

BERDINE (*Shocked*) Chicklet?

CHICKLET Miss Barnes, a delight as always. (*To the boys*) Hello, boys. (*They all say "Hi" in a dazed manner.*) I do hope these boys have been showing you a good time. They taught me how to surf and now I'm positively addicted to shooting the curl, as they say.

BETTINA They're helping me fix up my backyard.

CHICKLET How utterly fab. Boys, I have a little job for you.

YO YO Chicklet, are you feeling all right?

CHICKLET Just swellsville. I'd like to have a cage built.

PROVOLONEY A bird cage?

CHICKLET No, something suitable for a bigger animal, or animals.

BERDINE Chicklet, what are you talking about?

CHICKLET (*Becomes herself*) Berdine. Where am I? (*Sees the boa and cigarette holder*) What's all this?

BERDINE You tell me.

CHICKLET (*At a loss*) Ohhh, I found it in the garbage outside the Club Transvestite. (*She laughs hysterically but no one else does.*) Eek.

PROVOLONEY You wanted us to build you a cage.

CHICKLET A cage? Don't be a doofus . . . Anyways, now that I am here . . . Berdine, I feel awful for the way I've been treating you. I don't know what could possess me being so rude like that. You should just belt me. Go on and belt me.

BERDINE I couldn't.

CHICKLET Really. You're like my . . . How do I . . .

BERDINE I know. You are too.

CHICKLET But more than that. We've always . . .

BERDINE That's true. But still sometimes . . .

CHICKLET Oh, but we . . .

BERDINE Yeah, but I wouldn't want . . .

CHICKLET You don't really want . . .

BERDINE I just don't . . .

CHICKLET Trust me. C'mon. Please Berdine, please go on being my best friend for a zillion more years. What do you say?

BERDINE For a zillion trillion more years. To infinity. (*They hug.*)

CHICKLET Will you be my escort to the luau?

BERDINE You don't think I'm too much of a nerd-brain?

CHICKLET Of course not.

PROVOLONEY What are you two going to do for the talent show?

CHICKLET What talent show?

YO YO That's part of the tradition. Everyone's gotta getup and do an act. I'm doing my Jane Russell imitation. (*Pulls his shirt out like bosoms*) Boom titty boom.

BERDINE I know. Remember that act we did for the Kiwanis Club Variety Night? The costume is in my attic.

CHICKLET You got yourself a partner. (*They shake*)

BETTINA I'm glad you patched things up. I'm so in awe of friendship. I mean, never having any. We better get started on the garden before it gets dark. Come on, kids. (*All the kids including Chicklet and Berdine exit laughing and singing.*)

Star Cat and Marvel Ann stroll on

MARVEL ANN Star Cat, you mean little devil, I was up all night thinking about you.

STAR CAT (*Excited*) You were?

MARVEL ANN Uh huh. Couldn't sleep a wink. You wanna know what I was thinking?

STAR CAT Empty that beautiful head of yours.

MARVEL ANN I was thinking that you and I are going to be united as one forever.

STAR CAT (*Nervously*) Gee, Marvel Ann, are you sure I'm good enough for you? I wouldn't want you to settle.

MARVEL ANN Settle? You're the dreamboat of all time, generous, always thinking of others, sensitive.

STAR CAT Aw, I'm just a good for nothing surf bum.

MARVEL ANN That's not true. You're just riddled with greatness. I look in your eyes and honestly, I see dollar signs.

STAR CAT You don't understand. I'm rejecting those false values. I refuse to worship the golden calf.

MARVEL ANN (*Petulant but still pleasant*) You don't know what you want. I think it's a horrid shame that you're throwing away a great future as a psychiatrist. All your wonderful compassion going to waste. (*Star Cat tries to interject*) Oh, I know what you're going to say, "I just want a little shack by the water." Well, you can't expect me to live like that. Imagine me serving my friends Steak Diane Flambé in a lean-to. (*Star Cat tries to interject*) Don't say a word, I know what you're thinking, "Marvel Ann is such a lovely person, in time she'd grow used to such a life." (*With growing emotion and intensity*) Well, I'd be humiliated. Oh, I can read you like the funny papers. (*With growing fury*) You think I'm so head over heels in love with you, I'll accept whatever crumbs you have to offer. Well, no siree Bob, I am hardly a desperate female. Ohhh, look at that awful expression in your eyes. I bet you think you don't even have to marry me, that I'd shack up with you like a common whore. Now you've really done it. I am livid. How could you think of such filth! You are a selfish, egocentric creep and my advice to you is to straighten up, buckle down and apply yourself like any other decent, normal Presbyterian!! (*She stalks off in a fury*)

Chicklet enters.

STAR CAT (*Angrily*) Hey, what are you doing here?

CHICKLET I didn't know you owned this beach. I don't see your initials carved into the ocean.

STAR CAT Sorry. I didn't mean to bark at you.

CHICKLET (*Sympathetically*) Girl trouble?

STAR CAT Yeah, that dame wants to put a ball and chain around my neck.

CHICKLET Well, don't you dare let her. I think it's swell the way you guys live.

STAR CAT You do?

CHICKLET Sure. Flying about as free as a gull, never having a care in the world.

STAR CAT You're on my beam. Marvel Ann doesn't understand me at all. She thinks she can see through me like wax paper but she's wrong. I'm an extremely complex person with deep rooted neuroses and anxieties. You wouldn't understand that, you're just a kid.

CHICKLET (*Offended*) I am not just a kid. I'm capable of intensely passionate adult feelings. If you didn't have so much sea foam in your eyes, you'd notice I'm a budding young woman.

STAR CAT (*Amused*) Honey, your buds have a long way to bloom.

CHICKLET Evidently some people don't share that opinion.

STAR CAT Like who?

CHICKLET Oh, some people.

STAR CAT Like nobody.

CHICKLET Like Kanaka. He thinks I'm, how did he put it? I'm a luscious voluptuary.

STAR CAT Liar. I know Kanaka. He could have any dame in Malibu.

CHICKLET Well, he wants me.

STAR CAT How do you know?

CHICKLET It's one of those mystical things a woman feels instinctively in her soul.

STAR CAT Get over it.

CHICKLET (*Defensively*) He taught me how to surf, didn't he? And he tries to see me every day and he always makes sure we're completely alone. As a matter of fact, I'm headed over to Kanaka's shack right now, for an extremely intimate tête-a-tête.

STAR CAT I don't believe it.

CHICKLET *Chacon á son gout.* That means, each to his own, you dope. He thinks I'm special.

STAR CAT I think you're trying to make me jealous. What a screwy kid you are. I bet you've got a great big fat crush on me.

CHICKLET (*Blushing*) If we were at war with the Soviet Union, I wouldn't even let you into my bomb shelter.

STAR CAT Hey c'mon, let's call it a truce. I like you, kid. I do. And I think you're very special.

CHICKLET Please don't patronize me.

STAR CAT (*Turns her around and holds her chin*) You are special.

CHICKLET (*Vulnerable*) I am?

STAR CAT And cute.

CHICKLET I am?

STAR CAT You need somebody to protect you.

CHICKLET Protect me from what?

STAR CAT (*Friendly*) Oh, from big bad wolves. You could be a tasty morsel, to some wolf.

CHICKLET What about to you?

STAR CAT I suppose I could be dangerously tempted.

CHICKLET Oh, Star Cat.

Star Cat opens his mouth to sing. We hear an obviously dubbed recording of a teen idol singing the "Chicklet Theme Song." Suddenly, the record gets stuck, and we hear the needle scratch across the record. There is an uncomfortable silence.

STAR CAT I guess I'll have to tell you how I feel. You're a one of a kind girl, Chicklet, like no one I've ever met.

CHICKLET What about Marvel Ann? Is she one of a kind too?

STAR CAT (*Smiles, embarrassed*) Well . . .

CHICKLET Star Cat, what do boys do when they're alone with a girl?

STAR CAT You can't ask me such a question.

CHICKLET Why not? I want to know.

STAR CAT They neck. I don't know.

CHICKLET What do you do with Marvel Ann?

STAR CAT This is embarrassing, Chicklet.

CHICKLET Tell me.

Romantic music sneaks in through the end of the scene.

STAR CAT She nestles real close to me.

CHICKLET (*Cuddles next to him*) Kind of like this?

STAR CAT (*Horny and nervous*) Yeah, sort of like that. I hold her in my arms. And she holds me back.

CHICKLET Like this? And then what do you do?

STAR CAT I kiss the back of her neck. I can't do this with you.

CHICKLET Pretend I'm Marvel Ann. I need to know this sort of thing. For my own protection.

STAR CAT I stroke her arm and she kisses my chest. (*Chicklet kisses his chest*) And we can feel our hearts beating as one. We find ourselves swaying to the same personal rhythm.

CHICKLET You take your clothes off, right?

STAR CAT (*Lost in the moment*) Uh huh.

CHICKLET You got your clothes off. Then what?

STAR CAT I caress her smooth satiny flesh. It glistens in the moonlight. She gently touches my muscles with her fingertips.

Our bodies seem to float to the ground. We're entwined. And then I slowly slide my penis into her vagina. Simultaneously, she licks her index finger and inserts it up my rectum as I pump my penis . . .

During this last graphic part, Chicklet is horrified and at the end of his speech, she screams as if in a horror movie and runs away.

STAR CAT (*Shouting after her*) Chicklet, come back!

BLACKOUT

SCENE 7

Kanaka's shack. Star Cat enters.

STAR CAT Kanaka, where are you? You home?

Kanaka enters

KANAKA Hey pal, what are you doing in my shack without an invite? I don't dig surprise visits.

STAR CAT I'm looking for Chicklet.

KANAKA She's not here, not yet.

STAR CAT But she will be.

KANAKA Yeah, and what's it to you? She's not your chick.

STAR CAT And she shouldn't be yours either. She's only a kid.

KANAKA That's all you know.

STAR CAT If you've laid a finger on her . . .

KANAKA Hey, cool out. You don't know the score. There is more to that Chicklet than meets the old eyeball. There's like two Chicklets in one, man.

STAR CAT What are you talking about?

KANAKA It's wild. She's like twins in one bod. One's an angel and the other's a she devil. She calls herself Ann Bowman and she's like a demon. And the weird thing is, I can turn her off and on like a flashlight.

STAR CAT You're talking crazy.

KANAKA (*Desperate*) Can I trust you, buddy? Will you swear by the code of the King of the Sea you won't tell anyone any of this?

STAR CAT Yeah, I swear.

KANAKA I got it heavy for Ann Bowman. She's like a drug running through my veins and I can't shake her. I'm even gonna let her shave me, man.

STAR CAT You're not making any sense.

KANAKA Nothing makes sense. But I need her. I need Mistress Ann.

STAR CAT Get a hold of yourself.

KANAKA She's power mad. She's plotting to take over the world. First Malibu and then Sacramento. She wants to set up concentration camps for her enemies and public executions and her own NBC variety series.

Chicklet enters unseen by them

STAR CAT If this is true, you've got to stop this!

KANAKA I can't give her up. I'd kill for Ann Bowman.

CHICKLET Who's Ann Bowman?

STAR CAT Stay out of this.

KANAKA Star Cat, I want you to meet a friend of mine. Hey, Chicklet, you remember that kite we saw, that . . .

STAR CAT You son of a . . . (*Star Cat tries to punch out Kanaka. They fight. Chicklet tries to get between them. Suddenly they all start to move in slow motion and we see Chicklet get in the way of Star Cat's punch and slowly drift to the floor.*) Chicklet, are you all right?

KANAKA Now you've done it, man. (*They both hold her as she comes to*)

CHICKLET What happened? Where am I?

KANAKA In my beach shack.

There's wild knocking at the door

KANAKA The door's open.

Mrs. Forrest enters in a furious state

MRS. FORREST Well, this is a pretty sight, I must say.

KANAKA Who the hell are you?

CHICKLET Mom, what are you doing here?

MRS. FORREST Young lady, you are in big trouble.

STAR CAT Mrs. Forrest, you don't understand.

MRS. FORREST Indeed I do understand. I also know the penalty for seducing a minor. You and your buddy will be sitting in stir for quite a while.

CHICKLET Mother, would you stop. Kanaka and Star Cat are my friends. There was nothing dirty involved.

MRS. FORREST How dare you speak to me in that manner. I see now clearly the effect of a permissive childhood. All the gentle caring, the indulgences, the little treats. How wrong I was. Life will be quite different from now on. I am going to mete out a severe punishment for you, young lady, most severe indeed.

CHICKLET Mother.

MRS. FORREST Get in the car. (*Chicklet exits. To the boys.*) You two scum bags had better get yourselves a good mouthpiece, cause I'm gonna tear your peckers off in that courtroom. Good evening, gentlemen.

BLACKOUT

SCENE 8

Berdine is in her bedroom writing in her diary.

BERDINE Dear Diary: This entry is strictly confidential. Chicklet's Mom is on the warpath. She locked the Chicklet in her room and has refused her all visitors, yours truly included. Panicsville, here I come. The luau is tomorrow night! Chicklet and I simply have to be there. We've been rehearsing our Siamese twin act all week. It's gonna be the greatest thing ever. I swear, grownups think they can run the whole world. Like Nathan Hale or Lafayette Escadrille, there is only one person who refuses to bow down before tyranny, I Berdine! I'm marching over to Chicklet's right now and get her out of there. I defy you stars, nothing and I mean nothing is going to stop us from going to the luau.

BLACKOUT

Chicklet's bedroom. Chicklet is bound and gagged. A T.V. tray with dinner is placed before her. Mrs. Forrest enters with creepy serenity.

MRS. FORREST What a dinner. I'm so stuffed I can hardly move. I certainly enjoyed my T-bone steak, so bloody rare and juicy. (*Thoughtfully*) I may have overcooked the lima beans. Vegetables are delicate creatures. (*With vulnerable charm*) Still, I have to admit, it was delicious. (*Still lovely*) This meal could have been yours, Chicklet, if you hadn't chosen to disobey me. Do you finally see what I mean about making the right choices in life? It's a rough world, darling, with a lot of crummy people out there. You can't be impressed with them. (*With force*) Believe me, they stink! (*Back to her charming manner*) I'm afraid I still see defiance in your eyes. You have so much to learn. (*She touches the gag restraint. Jokes.*) I bet you think I've taken this gag too far.

(*Laughs at her joke*) That's funny. (*She gives the gag a tighter tug*) I think we'll keep this on a wee bit longer. (*She exits*)

(*Berdine enters swinging in through the window on a rope made of bedsheets*)

BERDINE Chicklet! What has she done to you? (*She tries to untie her*) You poor helpless thing. How did she do this? These must be army knots. Don't be mad but I think our top priority should be your arms. I hope this experience won't make you bitter and pessimistic. Just hold on. I'm not saying you should be a grinning idiot but as Schopenhauer says "we should strive for a tragic optimism." (*Chicklet grunts*) It's not easy, the greater the intelligence, the greater the capacity for suffering. (*Chicklet grunts*)

Mrs. Forrest enters unbeknownst to Berdine whose back is to her. Chicklet sees Mrs. Forrest and grunts trying to warn Berdine.)

BERDINE I can't get it. We'll have to get you out of here the way you are. Give a little hop. (*Berdine turns around and sees Mrs. Forrest*)

MRS. FORREST (*Exuding charm*) Hello Berdine. How kind of you to visit us. I've made a terrific bunt cake. Care for a slice?

BERDINE (*Totally freaked*) That's okay. My Mom made butterscotch pudding for dessert. I've really got to get along.

MRS. FORREST Such a pity. I was hoping you'd watch "Bonanza" with us. Are you planning to take Chicklet with you?

BERDINE Uh yes, actually. We've been rehearsing . . . I mean we've been working on a science project together. Mendel's theory of propagation and all that stuff.

MRS. FORREST I'm afraid Mendel will have to propagate without the help of my Chicklet. She's been a naughty girl and naughtiness must be punished. Chicklet lied to me and more importantly she lied to herself. Berdine, you must be brutally honest with yourself, cruelly honest. Rip away the cobwebs of delusion. Dig and find the ugliness at the base of your soul, expose it to the light, examine it, let it wither, then kill it!!! Girl, know thyself! (*Trying to control her emotions*) It's the only way.

BERDINE (*Caught up in the debate and forgetting Chicklet*) Mrs. Forrest, I fervently disagree. (*Chicklet grunts desperately*) One must seek self knowledge but illusion is necessary to preserve a sense of innocence.

MRS. FORREST (*Pulls Chicklet to her*) None are innocent, all are guilty.

BERDINE (*Realizes Mrs. Forrest isn't on her wave-length*) Mrs. Forrest, you're a fascinating conversationalist but I've really got to get Chicklet out of here.

MRS. FORREST (*Forcefully*) Chicklet is grounded!

BERDINE Get out of my way, Mrs. Forrest. I am rescuing Chicklet. You are not responsible for your actions.

MRS. FORREST You take one more step and you'll be a nerd with no teeth.

BERDINE To save Chicklet, I would gladly wear a complete bridge. (*Berdine moves and Mrs. Forrest grabs her. They wrestle to the ground and fight it out. Finally Berdine gets the upper hand and sits on Mrs. Forrest's chest, pinning her down.*) Chicklet, run for it!

MRS. FORREST (*Gasping*) Get off me! You big cow. (*Chicklet with her feet bound slowly hops offstage while Berdine talks to Mrs. Forrest*)

BERDINE (*Ties Mrs. Forrest up with bedsheets*) I'm really sorry, Mrs. Forrest, for being so disrespectful. This is highly uncharacteristic behavior for me but you know, lately I've been cramming myself with Sartrean existentialism so maybe I'm unduly influenced by his commitment to extreme action. Gosh, this is deep.

BLACKOUT

Scene 9

The luau. Lights up and Provoloney, Yo Yo, Kanaka, Bettina, Nicky and Dee Dee are all having a wild time. Star Cat enters.

STAR CAT Marvel Ann, Marvel Ann! Has anybody seen Marvel Ann?

EVERYONE No!

NICKY Hey cats, let's Limbo!

They do a big limbo number and hoot it up. At the height of the festivities Marvel Ann enters, her hair half shaved off. Bettina is the first to see her and screams.

MARVEL ANN (*Hysterical*) My hair! My hair! I'm gonna kill the bastard who did this.

STAR CAT Marvel Ann, what happened?

MARVEL ANN I was lying on the beach with my eyes closed. Someone knocked me out, I woke up and the bastard was shaving my head. They'd already shaved my beaver.

PROVOLONEY Couldn't you see who it was?

MARVEL ANN No, they had glued stripper's pasties over my eyes. I'm so humiliated.

KANAKA (*In terror to Star Cat*) Ann Bowman strikes again.

BETTINA Honey, in a few months you'll have a cute pixie.

Marvel Ann groans. Provoloney jumps up trying to get everyone's attention.

PROVOLONEY Quiet, everybody. QUIET! (*Everyone settles down to watch the show*) Good evening and welcome to Provoloney's Pacific Follies. How is everybody out there? Ready for a great show? Let me hear you.

NICKY Boo! Get on with the show. (*Everyone joins in booing*)

PROVOLONEY I love these audiences, the greatest in the world. I tell you, coming over here tonight I couldn't help but be reminded of the story of the Stewardess in from Cleveland. She arrives at . . .

NICKY We heard that already. Bring on the girls. (*Everyone joins in*)

PROVOLONEY Rough house. Okay, you want entertainment, I'll give you entertainment with a capital E. There's nothing I like better than discovering young talent. And I . . .

NICKY Where did they discover you? Under a rock? Get on with it.

PROVOLONEY (*Getting mad*) What I'm doing is laying the foundation for the evening at . . .

NICKY You're laying an egg. (*Everyone laughs*).

PROVOLONEY I've gotten big laughs from tougher crowds than you.

NICKY Before or after you dropped your pants? (*Everyone laughs*)

PROVOLONEY (*Furious*) That does it! I don't have to take this. Do your own stinkin' show. (*Star Cat jumps up and soothes Provoloney's ego*)

STAR CAT Aw, c'mon, he's just joshing you. You're doing great. Go on. Guys, give him some support. (*They applaud*)

PROVOLONEY Well, if you insist. Without further ado (*He gives Nicky a dirty look*) please give a warm hand to a sister act that ends all sister acts. Straight from exotic Siam, the spectacular, the inseparable, Hester and Esther. Take it away girls.

Chicklet and Berdine enter in a wild red siamese twin costume joined at the hip

CHICKLET My name is Esther.

BERDINE My name is Hester.

BERDINE/CHICKLET (*In unison*)

LIFE AIN'T ALWAYS A PIP
WHEN YOU'RE JOINED AT THE HIP.

IF JUST A SMALL BUMP
DOES STRANGE THINGS TO YOUR RUMP,

AND A HOT STRIPPER'S GRIND
REALLY ACHES YOUR BEHIND,

BUT ENUF OF THIS KVETCHING,
WE STILL LOOK MOST FETCHING,

SO VO DE OH DO,
LETS GET ON WITH THE SHOW.

Chicklet and Berdine begin singing a song such as "The Lady in Red." In the middle of the song, Chicklet begins talking to herself. Berdine continues to sing.

CHICKLET Red . . . red . . . red dress. (*mutters*) Take that off. You look like a whore. Take that dress off. (*Cries like a baby*) I'm angry. I'm angry. I don't like this. I can't move. Get me out. (*Berdine continues to sing nervously—Chicklet makes animal sounds*)

BERDINE Chicklet, please. "The Lady in Red," the fellas are crazy about the . . .

CHICKLET (*Muttering*) Crazy, crazy, the fellas are crazy . . . about ME! Me, Ann Bowman, live, onstage! (*Laughs raucously*) At last, in the spotlight.

BERDINE (*Nervously improvising*) Now Chicklet's going to do some impersonations for you. Who are you doing, Chicklet?

CHICKLET (*As Ann*) Get your hands off me, you blithering bull dyke.

BETTINA What's going on?

CHICKLET (*As Ann*) Silence! Now that I have your attention, I'd like to sing my song, my SOLO! (*Crooning*) More than the greatest love the world has known . . . (*A little girl*) Stop, I don't like your singing, you scare me. (*As Ann*) Shut up you little bitch! (*As Tylene*) Don't you be talking to that chile like that. (*As Ann*) Do not underestimate my fury, Tylene. (*As Tylene*) I ain't scared of you, mother. (*As Dr. Rose Mayer*) Excuse me, if I may interject. This is Dr. Rose Mayer speaking. If you have a personal grievance, by all means you are entitled to a fair hearing but let us not air out our dirty laundry in public. (*As Ann*) Butt out, you blabbering battleax. (*As Dr. Rose Mayer*) Once more I must interject. Ann, the question I ask of you is why? Why cause all this tsouris, this unhappiness. (*As Ann*) Enough! You insolent fools! I am taking over Chicklet's mind once and for all. Chicklet is officially dead!

BERDINE Stop it, stop it!

CHICKLET (*As Ann*) I warned you not to touch me. (*She starts to strangle Berdine. Star Cat and Kanaka try to separate them. Chicklet pulls out a straight razor and the chase in on. Chicklet is on the rampage chasing all the kids, dragging Berdine behind her.*) It's a shave and a haircut for all of you. How about white sidewalls, honey. (*She moves toward Bettina*) I'll get you anyway, Peewee.

BETTINA (*Holding her ponytail*) It's a fake! It's a switch! Help! Help! (*Star Cat and Kanaka subdue Chicklet. They pin her arms back and grab the razor. Berdine is in hysterics.*)

STAR CAT Let's get them out of that costume. (*They break away the siamese twin costume, freeing them. Bettina comforts Berdine*)

Mrs. Forrest enters

MRS. FORREST I thought I'd find her here. I'm going to have all of you arrested for kidnapping.

STAR CAT Mrs. Forrest, your daughter is mentally ill.

MRS. FORREST My little girl is as normal as I am.

CHICKLET (*In the voice of Tylene*) I gotta go back to work at the Safeway.

MRS. FORREST (*Near hysteria, grasping at straws*) She wants to be an actress. She's putting on a character. (*Breaks down*) She's not sick!

CHICKLET (*As Ann*) You're so right, Mrs. Forrest, I am hardly the lunatic they are painting me to be. I am totally in control.

STAR CAT You are merely a delusion of Chicklet Forrest that enables her to express anger and rage.

CHICKLET (*As Ann*) Fancy phrases. And a big basket. I'd like to strap you on sometime.

STAR CAT That is highly unlikely since you are about to be obliterated.

CHICKLET (*As Ann*) Party pooper.

STAR CAT You don't frighten me. I'm flesh and blood. You're a psychological manifestation. I can conquer you.

CHICKLET (*As Ann*) There's no man alive strong enough to conquer me . . . maybe Bob Hope.

STAR CAT I'm going to place you under hypnosis and through the technique of past regression get to the root of the trauma that fragmented Chicklet's personality.

MRS. FORREST I can't allow this. He doesn't know what he's doing.

PROVOLONEY He's had three semesters of psychiatric training.

STAR CAT Look into my eyes. I'm taking you back in time.

MRS. FORREST Someone stop this madness!

CHICKLET (*As Ann*) Oh shut your hole. Go on darling Doctor Star Cat.

STAR CAT I want to speak to Chicklet. Chicklet, are you there?

CHICKLET It's hard, I feel so far away, I can't . . . (*She begins to sound like a radio with static*)

MRS. FORREST She's babbling. (*She exits*)

STAR CAT It's a bad connection. Chicklet, I know you are there. We are here to help you. Trust me. Are you there? (*Chicklet is sounding like a radio quickly switching stations*)

KANAKA (*Sincerely*) Maybe you should try her on FM.

STAR CAT Talk to us Chicklet, talk to us.

CHICKLET (*Static noises clearing as Dr. Rose*) . . . lieve you will have greater success conversing with one of us.

STAR CAT Who am I talking to?

CHICKLET (*As Dr. Rose*) Dr. Rose Mayer, you're on the air.

STAR CAT Who exactly are you?

CHICKLET (*As Dr. Rose*) A radio personality, and a syndicated columnist.

PROVOLONEY This is weird, man, too weird.

CHICKLET (*As Dr. Rose*) I serve a very important function in Chicklet's life. Any situation that gets a little mishugga, that requires tact or diplomacy, I come in. In toto, I'm a people person.

STAR CAT And who is Tylene?

CHICKLET (*As Tylene*) I am her ambitious self. Come September first, I am attending night school where I can study keypunch and office management skills.

Suddenly Chicklet turns into Steve, an all American boy.

CHICKLET (*As Steve*) Whoa, can I just say something for a minute?

STAR CAT I believe we're meeting someone new. What's your name?

CHICKLET (*As Steve*) Steve.

STAR CAT Are you also a radio personality?

CHICKLET (*As Steve*) No. I'm a male model.

STAR CAT Describe yourself.

CHICKLET (*As Steve*) I'm a forty regular. (*Fidgety*) I'm very important to Chicklet. I'm her athletic self. I enjoy all sports, ice hockey, kayaking, golf, competition bowling. Of course I do try to be a well-rounded person. I love old romantic movies, snuggling up by a fire. I guess what I look most for in a girl are great legs and a sense of herself. (*He winks at Bettina, who gasps*)

STAR CAT Are there any more of you?

CHICKLET (*As Steve*) Gosh, let's see, there's a veterinarian, a couple singers, a reformed rabbi, a lighting designer, the accounting firm of Edelman and Edelman, a podiatrist . . . (*As Chicklet*) Help me.

STAR CAT Chicklet, is that you?

CHICKLET (*As a little girl*) Uh huh. (*She sings*) "IT'S RAINING, IT'S POURING . . ."

STAR CAT How old are you?

CHICKLET Eight. Seven and a half.

STAR CAT Where are you?

CHICKLET In a room, Mama calls it the hotel. There's a playground across the street. My brother Frankie and me like to go on the swings.

BERDINE She doesn't have a brother.

CHICKLET I do too have a brother. He's seven and a half.

YO YO Twins.

CHICKLET Mama says we can't go on the swings alone. She says it's too dangerous. Mama's going to take us to the movies today. She says she's gonna . . .

Mrs. Forrest appears in a strange light, she is in the past, dressed in a red dress like a sexy young whore in the 1940's

MRS. FORREST (*Gently*) Baby, I'm so sorry. We're gonna have to go to the movies another day. Mama's gotta work. Fellas, come on in. These are my twins, ain't they cute?

CHICKLET But you promised you'd take us to the movies.

MRS. FORREST Well, I'm sorry. What do you want from my life? You wanna eat, don'tcha? Anyways, we gotta do our bit for the boys who go overseas. These guys are in the Navy and your Mama is making sure they are very well entertained. (*She giggles. To the children*) Now darlings, go outside and play. I'll meet you in the playground in an hour.

CHICKLET You're not fair.

MRS. FORREST Florence, I don't want anymore lip. Take Frankie and go outside and play. And don't you go near those swings. (*She turns to the sailors*) Sorry guys, being a Mom ain't easy. Now what was your name again, good looking? Please to meetcha, Johnny. Just call me Ann. Ann Bowman. (*She exits*)

CHICKLET (*In her normal voice*) I was so angry. I wanted to hurt her. I took Frankie's hand and we crossed the street to the playground. There were these awful slum children playing, pounding strange primitive instruments. A sharp breeze caused the wild flowers to have the wizened faces of starving circus clowns. The sky seemed so threatening, as if the clouds were created of demented angels warning me to flee. But I couldn't. I can't. Don't make me go on. Please.

STAR CAT You must. What happened next?

CHICKLET I look down and there's a pale green snake slithering along the crack of the pavement, a cooly seductive creature on its way to a lizard ball. This veridian temptress stops to deliver me a message. A perverse billet-doux that I must disobey my mother. No, no, I can't do that. I love my mother. She's kind and beautiful. The snakes multiply, in a moment, there are reptiles covering the jungle gym making those steel bars as green as grass and terrifyingly alive. And all of them whispering "Go on, go on, go on the swings. Your mother doesn't love you. She loathes the very sight of you." I looked at my little brother, wearing his red overalls with the little fishes. I said, "Frankie, let's go on the swings. It'll be fun. I don't care what Mama said." He got on the swing and I pushed him. Harder and harder I pushed him until he was soaring into the clouds and that's when I dared him. I dared him, "I bet you can't stay on with no hands." He took me up on the bet and let go, and my wonderful little twin brother, this adorable little boy who loved and trusted me, he flew off the swing and into the outstretched arms of those ghastly angels and I never saw him again until we found his crushed, little body in the dumpster next door!

She dissolves into tears, Star Cat holds her. Mrs. Forrest appears again as she is today.

MRS. FORREST (*Devastated*) It's all true. All of it true. I was so ashamed. I blamed myself for the death of my boy. But I always loved my little girl. (*To Chicklet*) You must believe that. I did love you. I do. And when Chicklet lost her memory of that day, I took it as a blessing from God. I vowed to create a new life for us. I changed my name, moved to a new city. I suppose I tried too hard, went too far and now . . . now I see I'm doomed to failure.

CHICKLET Mother, hold me. (*They embrace*)

BERDINE (*Sobbing*) I was supposed to be her best friend but I never knew.

KANAKA How do you feel, Chicklet?

CHICKLET As if a thousand doors have been opened.

PROVOLONEY But what does this all mean?

STAR CAT It's really very simple. Chicklet did her best to suppress this traumatic childhood episode by denying herself all normal human emotion, so she created various alter egos to express emotion for her. She associated the sex drive with her mother, so she in effect became her childhood vision of her mother, Ann Bowman, whenever placed in a potentially erotic situation.

KANAKA Is this condition contagious?

STAR CAT Indeed not. Over eighteen percent of all Americans suffer from some form of multiple personality disorder. It is not communicable and in most cases, treatable with medical care.

BETTINA (*Energetically*) This is the most exciting story I've ever heard. This is the project that's going to win me an Oscar.

PROVOLONEY Huh?

BETTINA A surfer girl with a split personality. A prestige picture if I ever saw one. (*To Chicklet*) Honey, I want to option this property, and believe me I'll pay top dollar. I can't promise casting approval but you can trust my integrity.

MRS. FORREST I don't know. This is an invasion of . . .

CHICKLET Mother, this is important. I want the public to know what it's like to suffer from a multiple personality disorder. And Berdine, will she be in the picture? She's very important, you know.

BETTINA Oh, sure, sure, a character part.

STAR CAT But Bettina, do you really think you're ready to interpret such a complex role?

BETTINA (*With artistic intensity*) I don't think, I feel. I know this girl. I feel her torment. I am Chicklet! (*Suddenly switching to her practical show business nature*) Yo Yo and Provoloney, I'm taking you to New York with me as technical consultants on the Malibu scene.

YO YO Wow, New York!

PROVOLONEY The Philharmonic!

YO YO The New York City Ballet!

PROVOLONEY Balanchine!

YO YO The Frick! Provoloney, should we tell them about us?

PROVOLONEY Yeah, since this is the time for truth telling. Yo Yo and I are lovers. (*Everyone gasps*)

YO YO Yes, and we're proud of it. I've read all about the persecution of homosexuals, how in big cities, bars are raided and innocent people arrested, their lives ruined. But someday, someday we're going to fight back and the laws will be changed, and our brothers and sisters will march down the main streets of America shouting that we are proud to be who we are!

PROVOLONEY Oh, Yo Yo, I really love you. (*They embrace. The crowd sighs in sympathy.*)

BETTINA Come on everybody, let's move this party to my place. I've got the best record collection in town. (*They all hoot and holler and exit except for Berdine*)

BERDINE (*Alone onstage, holding the siamese twin costume*) Life sure is wacky. Here Chicklet and I were best friends and I never really knew her. If I don't know *her,* can I ever truly know anyone? Star Cat thinks science can tell us everything, and Bettina says if she feels things, they're true. Oh, sweet, lonely Schopenhauer and crazy ole Nietzsche and dear, committed Jean-Paul, all of you searching and never settling for an easy answer to life's eternal puzzlement. I hereby vow to carry on your never-ending quest. I know now that my true calling is to be a novelist and devote my life to exploring the fathomless possibilities of the human comedy. Hey, wait for Berdine! (*She runs off*)

BLACKOUT

Scene 10

The beach at twilight. Star Cat is walking along the beach, wearing a tie and jacket. Kanaka enters carrying a suitcase.

KANAKA Hey, my man. It's time to shove off. You gonna say farewell to your old chum, Kanaka?

STAR CAT You off to Tahiti?

KANAKA (*Embarrassed*) No, uh not Tahiti, exactly.

STAR CAT The Ivory Coast?

KANAKA New York.

STAR CAT New York. What kind of place is that for the King of the Surfers?

KANAKA Bettina. She wants me with her. She needs me.

STAR CAT I had no idea. You and Bettina.

KANAKA Yeah well, you know Bettina and her incredible instincts about people. She says our personalities sort of fit together like a crazy jigsaw puzzle. But I told her, I'm the kind of guy that needs my freedom. I don't put up with no bunk, no star tantrums.

From offstage, we hear Bettina shouting like a fishwife

BETTINA Kanaka! Don't keep me waiting! We've got a nine o'clock plane to catch and I'm not missing it on account of some slow as molasses beach bum. Move it!

KANAKA (*Subserviant*) Yes, Bettina. (*To Star Cat*) Ciaou, kid. (*He exits*)

STAR CAT (*To himself*) The great Kanaka. What a mystery.

(*Chicklet appears in a beautiful gown, somehow grown up and lovely*)

CHICKLET Good evening, Star Cat

STAR CAT (*In shock*) Chicklet?

CHICKLET It's a beautiful night. The King of the Sea must be having cocktails.

STAR CAT Chicklet, you've become a young woman.

CHICKLET Have I? Star Cat, I . . .

STAR CAT I'm not Star Cat anymore. Call me Herbert. Herbert Mullin. Everything seems so different now. I'm leaving the beach.

CHICKLET Where are you going?

STAR CAT Back to college. I think I could make a good psychiatrist.

CHICKLET Do you really want to, with all your heart?

STAR CAT I do. I want to make sure a monster like Ann Bowman never appears again.

CHICKLET I'll miss you, Star Cat . . . I mean, Herb.

STAR CAT I was wondering . . . would you wear my pin?

CHICKLET (*Thrilled*) Your pin. Does this mean we're exclusive?

STAR CAT Well, I'll be all the way in Boston. You can't expect a guy to . . .

CHICKLET (*Mad*) Well, forget it, you creep. I'll be darned if I'll keep the home fires burning while you're pawing some Beacon Hill, blue blooded beasel.

STAR CAT That sounds like Ann Bowman.

CHICKLET I hope so.

STAR CAT You're quite a girl. The only girl for me. So will you wear my pin?

CHICKLET Will I ever! It's the ultimate. It positively surpasses every living emotion I've ever had! (*She whirls around and takes his arm and they walk down the surf to their new happiness*)

BLACKOUT

THE LADY IN QUESTION

Charles Busch in *The Lady in Question*. Photo Credit: T. L. Boston.

The Cast

The Lady in Question was originally produced by the WPA Theatre (Kyle Renick, Artistic Director) and subsequently moved to the Orpheum Theatre under the auspices of Kyle Renick and Kenneth Elliott, under the direction of Kenneth Elliott, with set design by B. T. Whitehill, costume design by Robert Locke and Jennifer Arnold, wig design by Elizabeth Katherine Carr, and lighting design by Vivien Leone, and with the following cast, in order of appearance:

Voice of the Announcer .... James Cahill
Professor Mitteihoffer .... Mark Hamilton
Heidi Mittelhoffer .... Theresa Marlowe
Karel Freiser .... Robert Carey
Professor Erik Maxwell .... Arnie Kolodner
Hugo Hoffmann .... Andy Halliday
Baron Wilhelm Von Elsner .... Kenneth Elliott
Gertrude Garnet .... Charles Busch
Kitty, The Countess of de Borgia .... Julie Halston
Augusta Von Elsner .... Meghan Robinson
Dr. Maximilian .... Mark Hamilton
Lotte Von Elsner .... Andy Halliday
Raina Aldric .... Meghan Robinson

The Characters

Voice of the Announcer
Professor Mittelhoffer
Heidi Mittelhoffer
Karel Freiser
Professor Erik Maxwell
Hugo Hoffman
Baron Wilhelm Von Elsner
Gertrude Garnet
Kitty, the Countess de Borgia
Augusta Von Elsner
Dr. Maximilian
Lotte Von Elsner
Raina Aldric

Time: 1940

Place

The Bavarian Alps, outside the train station at Ludwigshafen, and the Schloss of the Baron Von Elsner.

THE LADY IN QUESTION

PROLOGUE

A large four-paneled screen covers the width of the stage. It is a giant sized travel folder with the title "Tour Carefree Bavaria." The mood is dark, grey, ominous. Lush movie Soundtrack Music is heard full of drama and triumph. The Music quiets down to a feeling of suspense. A VOICE OVER *of a sonorous, old time announcer is heard.*

VOICE OVER The year is 1940. Adolph Hitler's armies make his dream of European annexation a reality. Norway, the Netherlands, Belgium and France all fall before the monstrous power of the German fighting machine. Fear of fifth columnists makes idle chatter a thing of the past, as people across the continent live in terror.

During the voice over, KAREL, *a handsome, young Nazi stormtrooper goosesteps across the stage and exits.*

VOICE OVER Nowhere is this more evident than in Hitler's own Bavaria. Free speech and free travel are but a distant memory, and those attempting to escape look with sad eyes to their local train terminal as a desperate symbol of hopes and dreams passing by.

The sounds of a train pulling into the station are heard as the lights come up on Act I, Scene 1.

ACT ONE

SCENE 1

The train station at Ludwigshafen. Afternoon. PROFESSOR MITTELHOFFER, *a kindly, mildly eccentric old man awaits the train from Paris. With him is his daughter* HEIDI. *She is in her early twenties, very pretty, courageous and something of an emotional spitfire. Her fierce temper belies her fragile, Dresden doll appearance.*

PROFESSOR Heidi, I hope we have not missed his train. You should have woken me earlier from my snooze.

HEIDI Papa, don't be silly. We're early. Professor Maxwell is arriving on the 11:58. And besides, you needed your rest. You've been slaving over your new translations for weeks.

PROFESSOR "The Complete Letters of Thomas Jefferson." How Germany needs his wise words today.

HEIDI How Germany needs her great men today. True greatness and not this (*With gutteral fierceness.*) revolting imitation of . . .

PROFESSOR Shhhh, Heidi! You mast control your passionate nature. You inherited that from your mother, may she rest in peace.

HEIDI Do you miss her terribly?

PROFESSOR Very much so. (*He sneezes.*)

HEIDI Oh Papa, why are you not wearing your muffler? How many times have I told you?

PROFESSOR I must have left it where I left my spectacles.

HEIDI (*Takes his glasses out of her pocket.*) Here are your spectacles. I was wondering when you'd miss them.

PROFESSOR My little mischief-maker.

HEIDI What am I to do with you? Sometimes I feel like I am your wife. I like that feeling, Papa. I love you more than anything in the world. I'd kill for you.

PROFESSOR That is not good, liebchen. A young girl must have her own life. I do not want you to develop an Elektra complex.

HEIDI Papa, I promise you I won't.

Karel, a handsome young stormtrooper, enters.

HEIDI Look, Papa, there's Karel.

PROFESSOR Heidi, don't . . .

HEIDI Hello, Karel!

KAREL (*Comes over.*) Heidi, Professor Mittelhoffer, Heil Hitler.

PROFESSOR Good morning, Karel.

KAREL It is customary in the new order to reply "Heil Hitler."

PROFESSOR You must forgive me, my lumbago.

HEIDI (*Flirtatiously.*) Karel, it's been so long since we've . . .

KAREL (*Ignoring her.*) Professor, what brings you to the terminal so early?

PROFESSOR I am meeting a colleague.

KAREL A foreign colleague?

PROFESSOR As a matter of fact, yes.

KAREL From what country?

PROFESSOR I am not aware of his citizenship.

KAREL (*With mounting intensity.*) Why does he keep this a secret?

PROFESSOR I imagine it is his choice.

KAREL He has no choice. Why is he in Germany?

PROFESSOR To gaze at our lovely alpine scenery?

KAREL Do not treat me like a fool! I am no longer your pupil. No more can you make me sit in the corner with a dunce-cap. I would not want to report your activities to my superiors.

HEIDI Karel, you must not speak to my father that way.

KAREL Your father is a renowned intellectual, a loathsome species, and therefore under suspicion. It is my duty to leave nothing unnoticed.

HEIDI (*Flirting.*) Then you've been shirking your duties.

KAREL I have not.

HEIDI You haven't noticed my pretty new frock.

KAREL It is most becoming.

PROFESSOR Excuse us. We must see if the train is late.

HEIDI Oh, Papa, why don't you check?

PROFESSOR Heidi, my . . .

HEIDI Go, go, go.

PROFESSOR Heidi!

HEIDI Go.

The Professor exits.

KAREL Your father, he does not like me.

HEIDI No one likes little boys with bad manners.

KAREL I obey the code of the new order.

HEIDI Karel, I've missed you.

KAREL You can see me whenever you choose.

HEIDI I miss the boy I once loved so dearly. I'm afraid he no longer exists.

KAREL Heidi, don't.

HEIDI I miss the boy I tutored every day. Your face was so cute when you'd strain for the simplest answers. For ten points: Name three tragedies by William Shakespeare.

KAREL Shakespeare is dead. There is only Schiller and Goethe.

HEIDI (*Grabs his head.*) Look at me! How do I crack open that big, good-looking, dumb head of yours? How do I let in some truth?

KAREL (*Reciting.*) Adolf Hitler is our savior. The Third Reich will last a thousand years.

HEIDI (*With wildly fierce emotion.*) Shut up and look at me! How do I make you feel, feel something! Anything! For chrissake, be a human being!

KAREL (*Breaking into passion.*) I am a human being, Heidi, and I do love you, and I'm scared for you. Do not fall back with the malcontents. They will all perish. There is still a place for you in the Hitler Rhinemaiden brigade.

HEIDI I wouldn't play canasta with those goose-stepping lezzies.

KAREL (*Hardened.*) I see we are both not the young people we once were.

Professor Mittelhoffer enters with PROFESSOR ERIK MAXWELL, *a handsome American. He carries a suitcase.*

PROFESSOR Heidi, our guest has arrived. We must go.

KAREL Do not hurry, Professor. I should like to officially greet your esteemed colleague.

PROFESSOR Professor Maxwell, this is my daughter, Heidi, and my former student, Karel Freiser.

ERIK I'm flattered that I merit an official greeting. (*Puts down suitcase, Stage Left.*)

HEIDI Your train was exactly on time.

ERIK Yes, it arrived with frightening German efficiency.

KAREL You will become accustomed to our well-organized society.

ERIK It is a lovely country, the land of beer, Wagner and terror.

PROFESSOR (*Nervously.*) He means terriers, schnauzers, dogs.

KAREL My English is not fluent. Of course, English is a gutter language, ultimately to be extinguished.

ERIK (*Matter of factly.*) While it's still spoken, up yours, asshole.

KAREL I do not comprehend. Was heisst "asshole?"

ERIK It means your Führer.

PROFESSOR Take my word, Karel, in America, it is used most selectively. Come, you must be hungry.

KAREL One moment. What is your business here in Germany?

ERIK It is my business and none of yours, bub.

KAREL Perhaps it should be the business of the prefect of police. Enjoy your visit, Professor, and let us hope it will be brief. Heil Hitler. (*He looks at Heidi and exits.*)

ERIK A graduate of Hitler's charm school.

HEIDI It is foolish to bait him, Professor Maxwell.

ERIK Forgive me. It was foolish, foolish and selfish. My big mouth will only reflect on you. I'm very sorry.

HEIDI Your bitterness is understandable.

ERIK I'm beside myself with worry. Since I received your letter, I haven't slept a wink. How is she? Have you spoken to her? Has there been any word?

PROFESSOR Yes, there has been word. Can you take it?

ERIK I can take it.

PROFESSOR Your mother is to be executed on Friday.

Erik starts to swoon, they catch him.

PROFESSOR Buck up, my friend.

ERIK (*With rapid-fire delivery.*) The monsters! I could kill every one of them with my bare hands. Why should they want her dead? She's an actress. She knows nothing about politics. Dead! That word has nothing to do with my mother. My mother is life, life itself! Why? Why?

PROFESSOR I have known your mother a great many years. She is a brilliant actress, but "careful" is not a word in her vocabulary. She befriended a young, radical playwright, the hope of the German theatre. (*Embarrassed.*) It was rumored they became lovers.

ERIK (*With a deadpan no-nonsense air.*) Professor, let me tell you right now, my parents divorced when I was little. My father was awarded custody and my mother returned to Europe where she has lived her own life. I do not judge her. Please go on with your story.

PROFESSOR Using her legendary name, they mounted a production of the young man's most fiercely anti-Nazi play. On the opening night, the S.S. raided the theatre, killed the playwright and arrested your mother on the grounds of treason. She is in a prison a few miles away.

ERIK This is a nightmare!

PROFESSOR You will wake up, my friend, and soon. We have devised a plan of escape.

ERIK Escape? Is it possible?

HEIDI Yes, but exceedingly dangerous.

PROFESSOR The plan involves the formidable figure of the Baron Von Elsner.

ERIK Who is this man?

HEIDI A decadent nobleman who has risen high in the Nazi regime. There are terrible tales of his numerous depravities.

ERIK (*With genuine highminded interest.*) Spare me nothing.

PROFESSOR Later, but for our plan to succeed, we need a confederate planted in the Baron's ancestral home. You can see it looming darkly in the mountains.

ERIK What does the Baron's house have to do with my mother? None of this makes sense.

HEIDI (*Urgently.*) You must do exactly as my father says.

ERIK Of course, I trust you both completely. How do I find an ally in the Baron's home?

HUGO *enters, Hugo is an intense highstrung fellow in his thirties. A touch of Peter Lorre.*

PROFESSOR That I do not know, but the escape must take place tomorrow night.

HEIDI Papa, there is Hugo Hoffmann.

PROFESSOR Hoffman is a noted painter. He has used his gift to forge letters of transit. If we are lucky enough to get your mother out of prison, we will need them to cross the border. He has made four of them. Be careful what you say. There are ears everywhere.

HUGO Professor, how good to see you. (*Under his breath.*) I'm afraid the Baron Von Elsner may be on to my activities. (*Looking at Erik.*) Is this the one?

HEIDI Yes, our friend has many contacts in the theatre and would like to see your sketches.

ERIK Yes, I'm sure they will travel well in America.

HUGO Compliment my tie. I will give it to you. Protest, then accept it. The letters of transit are inside the fabric.

ERIK I do so admire your necktie.

HUGO Then you must take it as a souvenir of our great country.

ERIK You are far too generous.

HUGO No, I insist. (*Takes off his tie and gives it to Erik.*)

HEIDI The Baron.

BARON VON ELSNER *enters. The Baron is a dignified, imposing man in his forties, a cold-blooded killer but with a silky charm.*

BARON Could that be the very talented Hugo Hoffmann?

HUGO (*Terrified.*) Baron, this is an honor.

BARON I must commend you on the restoration of my frescoes. Most skillful.

The rest of this scene is underscored by tense, suspenseful Music.

HUGO Thank you, Baron Von Elsner.

BARON However, your latest creative endeavor disturbs me.

HUGO The mural at City Hall? It is most reverential.

BARON You are very clever. It took careful observation, but then I discovered it.

HUGO I don't know what you mean.

BARON The magnificent detail surrounding the figure of the Führer is actually a code. A call to arms to your ridiculous resistance movement.

HUGO That is not true. Perhaps someone has tampered with my painting.

BARON That could be possible. Come with me to the prefect's office so we can clear up this misconception.

HUGO By all means. Some traitor has defaced my work. Herr Baron, if I could stop and use the facilities, I'd be most grateful.

BARON Of course, Hugo, of course.

Hugo starts to make a run for it. Karel enters to block his way. Hugo turns to the Professor.

HUGO Help me, help me, please.

PROFESSOR What can I do?

Hugo jumps off the front of the stage and makes a run for it.

BARON Halt! Halt in the name of the Führer!

Baron shoots Hugo in the back. Hugo falls down, dead beyond the view of the audience. Heidi screams. The Baron and Karel exit. Erik, the Professor and Heidi are horror-struck and hurry away. Erik leaves his suitcase Stage Left. The lights dim.

VOICE OVER Yes, human life Is cheap in the fatherland. The time has come for all men to come to the aid of humanity, to cast off self interest and band together. But, as always, there are SOME PEOPLE who ignore the cataclysm around them. SOME PEOPLE who live only for their hedonistic pleasure. SOME PEOPLE WHO DON'T GIVE A GOOD GODDAM FOR ANYONE BUT THEIR OWN STINKIN' SELVES!

The glamorous, internationally acclaimed American concert pianist, GERTRUDE GARNET* *enters, having just arrived on the Paris train. She's elegantly dressed in a traveling suit and furs. She speaks in a grand, very affected manner that disguises her honky tonk background. At this moment, she's in a terrible snit.*

---

*Pronounced GAR-NAY.

GERTRUDE Where is she? Where is my maid? Suzette! Suzette! If that dreadful girl thinks she can leave me high and dry without my cosmetic bag, she's got another think coming. (*Looks around.*) Conductor! Conductor! Where is everyone? Kitty! Kitty!

KITTY, THE COUNTESS DE BORGIA, *enters. Kitty is Gertrude's long-time buddy from her vaudeville days. Kitty is an attractive blonde, wisecracking, tough as nails but with a heart of gold. Now married to a nobleman, Kitty, too, can affect a high tone when it's required.*

KITTY Hold your horses, Gertie. These gams are still moving on Palm Beach time.

GERTRUDE This is absolutely appalling. How could Suzette do this to me? Quitting without even giving notice.

KITTY You shouldn't have slapped her across the face with that paillard of veal.

GERTRUDE I was making a point.

KITTY You sure made it. The dame jumped off a moving train.

GERTRUDE I never dreamed she'd be so vindictive. Fleeing with my cosmetic bag. The lashes alone are worth over a thousand dollars. Why are there so many soldiers about with their great scowling faces?

KITTY Honey, I say we get back on that train and skip this part of the tour.

GERTRUDE (*Aghast.*) Skip this part of the tour? Kitty my recitals in Munich, Frankfurt, and Ludwigshafen were scheduled four years ago and are completely sold out.

KITTY Give 'em back their money and let's beat it. This whole country gives me the creeps.

GERTRUDE Kitty, I am an artist, the leading concert pianist on the international stage and when Gertrude Garnet says she'll appear, she appears, hands oiled and ready. Where is the car from the hotel?

KITTY (*Laughs.*) You know, Gertie, this reminds me of our old vaudeville days when we were left stranded in Altoona.

GERTRUDE Kitty, this is hardly the time.

KITTY We were booked on the same bill as that slimy escape artist.

GERTRUDE He was a mentalist. Is that the car?

KITTY Whatever, he escaped with the cashbox.

GERTRUDE (*Becomes her tough former self.*) And because you gave him the romantic fisheye, the manager thought we was in cahoots.

KITTY I never gave him the fisheye.

GERTRUDE Ah, you were dropping them eyelids like they were a fire-curtain. And that stingy manager, he was as tight as Kelsey's nuts. (*Regains her soignee tone.*) Kitty, I am not in the mood for strolling down memory lane.

KITTY Well, you should. You've become just too hoity-toity since you took up that egghead music.

GERTRUDE That egghead music has paid off in spades.

KITTY I still say you were a lot happier when we were in vaudeville and I played fiddle to your honky-tonk p*i*ana.

GERTRUDE Now you're a wealthy countess. I hardly see you renewing your union cards.

KITTY Sister, after having the Count de Borgia rubbing his old sausage on me, gimme a split week in Pittsburgh.

GERTRUDE Stop that. We've risen to the top of high society and do you know how we made it?

KITTY Behind a lot of wives' backs.

GERTRUDE No, because it was our destiny. I've been seeing the most marvelous mystic, so wise, and terribly profound.

KITTY Not another one. That last holy man gave me one helluva goose.

GERTRUDE Not the swami. He's laid out for me the entire blueprint of life. He calls it his New World Philosophy. Every thing that happens to us happens because we make it happen. There was no luck involved in my career. (*With a rather frightening hard edge.*) I made my luck.

KITTY So you mean somehow we wanted to be stranded in this train station?

GERTRUDE Indeed. Perhaps instinctively we know that some great adventure lies in store for us. You see, darling, the rhythms and patterns of millions of years of civilization have brought you and me to this very moment. Now it remains for us to choose how we're going to handle this occasion. We *can* change the pattern.

KITTY (*Not impressed.*) Change the tune, girl, the record's got a scratch on it.

GERTRUDE Stop that, Kitty, this is important.

KITTY I just have trouble believing that if our train had crashed, it would have been because I chose it.

Erik enters and as he passes the ladies on his way to get his suitcase, he can't help hearing what they are saying.

GERTRUDE Entirely possible. Sometimes I think all these people who say they're being persecuted, perhaps they chose it too. Unconsciously, of course. It does make it rather hard to sympathize, though, doesn't it?

ERIK That is the stupidest hog wash I've ever heard.

GERTRUDE (*Haughtily.*) I beg your pardon!!??

ERIK That half-baked philosophy is extremely dangerous.

GERTRUDE (*Aside to Kitty.*) Kitty, he's a nut, move over. (*Pulls Kitty over a bit Stage Right.*)

ERIK Open your eyes, lady. Innocent people are disappearing around you. The Nazis are planning to tattoo people to separate them from the rest of us. There are stories of hideous camps built to isolate those out of political favor.

GERTRUDE (*Blithely.*) Such an alarmist. Besides, we all have many reincarnations. This one may be dreary, chances are the next one will be all champagne and caviar.

ERIK One day, you're going to be shaken out of this foolishness and I'll feel very sorry for you.

GERTRUDE Sing no sad songs for me, darling. Come, Kitty.

ERIK You're famous, aren't you?

GERTRUDE Extremely famous and extremely bored.

ERIK You're Gertrude Garnet, the pianist. (*Pronounces her name like the birth stone.*)

GERTRUDE Gertrude Garnet. (*Garnay.*)

KITTY You're an American. Are you here for work or amusement?

GERTRUDE Kitty.

ERIK I have important work in Germany.

KITTY I hope it won't take up all of your time.

GERTRUDE (*To herself.*) I can't believe I'm waiting out here without a car.

ERIK Where are you staying?

GERTRUDE	KITTY	ERIK
We're staying with friends.	The Hotel . . .	I don't mean to pry.
Kitty, don't . . .	The Hotel Mitzi.	I thought perhaps we . . .

ERIK The Hotel Mitzi. I read about that in the newspaper. Yes, it was confiscated last week. When the concierge protested, he and the entire staff were executed.

KITTY How dreadful.

GERTRUDE Dreadful indeed. It's Octoberfest and we'll never find another reservation.

The Baron enters.

KITTY What are we going to do?

Gertrude approaches the Baron and asks him, in German, where she can find a hotel.

GERTRUDE *Mein Herr, mein Herr, entshuldigen Sie bitte, mein Herr. Meine Freudin und ich suchen Unterkunft.*

BARON I speak English, Gertrude.

GERTRUDE (*Pleased.*) Oh.

BARON I would recognize you anywhere. I am the Baron Von Elsner. (*Attempts to take her hand, she withdraws it.*)

GERTRUDE (*Laughing.*) I'm afraid I never let anyone touch my hands. They're insured by Lloyds of London.

BARON (*With great charm.*) I can well understand. I have many of your recordings in my home. Your boxed set of Schubert is a particular favorite.

GERTRUDE The German composers are so good for the fingers. Have you heard my Beethoven "Appassionata?"

BARON It haunts me. I'm particularly fond of your Schumann "Fantasy Stucke."

GERTRUDE Oh, and this is my traveling companion, the Countess de Borgia.

BARON (*Takes her hand.*) And are your hands insured?

KITTY (*Coldly.*) Just personal liability.

BARON (*With veiled irony. To Gertrude.*) Your friend is very amusing. (*To Kitty.*) You must visit our local circus. Unfortunately, our leading clown was mauled to death by an angry lion. I have not been introduced to your other friend.

GERTRUDE We just met him.

ERIK Professor Erik Maxwell.

BARON And your field of expertise?

ERIK Nutrition. I'm making a study of German dietary habits.

BARON Yes?

ERIK I believe there is a connection between the heartiness of German beer and bread and your legendary ambition.

BARON We do eat well, but you must not forget, we are the master race. Now, my dear Madame Garnet, you were asking me something.

GERTRUDE The Countess and I are in terrible straits. We had reservations at the Hotel Mitzi, and now I heard it's closed. Could you recommend some first-class hostelry?

BARON The Mitzi was a dreadful place. May I offer you the use of my Schloss?

KITTY Come again.

GERTRUDE His Schloss, dear, his villa. We couldn't possibly accept.

BARON It is quite lovely, right on the lake at Shauffehausen.

KITTY I've never been inside a real German slush.

GERTRUDE Schloss, dear. Perhaps we could spend the night, until we find further accommodations.

BARON Delighted. Professor Maxwell, you must join us for dinner. I find your theories most intriguing.

ERIK I will be there. Goodbye, ladies.

KITTY Then we'll see you later at the Baron's schnapps.

GERTRUDE Schloss, dear.

KITTY Right.

ERIK Till then. (*He exits.*)

BARON Shall we go? I'll have my manservant collect your luggage.

GERTRUDE Just those thirty-seven pieces. This is such a lovely surprise. Baron, I can't wait to see your magnificent shlong. I mean, schloss! (*Mortified by her blunder.*)

They all exit.

BLACKOUT

Wagner's "Liebestod" is heard in Liszt's piano transcription. As the action moves into the next scene that evening, the music becomes Gertrude's playing in the adjoining salon.)

ACT ONE

Scene 2

The Schloss of the Baron Von Elsner. That evening. The ski lodge has been the Von Elsner's vacation home for generations and reflects their malevolence in its cold, grey austerity. A grotesque boar's head is their notion of whimsical decor. There is a front door USC and a fireplace DSL. Above the fireplace is a portrait of Hitler. A large sofa Center Stage is the only furniture. A staircase starts USR and goes to a landing above the front door. There are two doors on this landing. Downstairs SR there are two doors. One to the kitchen (large swinging door) and DS of that door is the door to the concert room. On SL above the fireplace an archway leads to the library. We hear Gertrude playing the piano in the concert salon. Karel enters the front door with the very elegant BARONESS AUGUSTA VON ELSNER. *White haired and magnificent, she is the Baron's mother. Her aristocratic charm masks an evil, cold spirit.*

AUGUSTA Ah, how grand to be home. Thank you, Karel, for escorting me from the train.

KAREL It is my honor, Baroness.

AUGUSTA (*With grandeur.*) This solid entry bids me welcome and gives me strength. Indeed, no one would dare invade my portal. My, what lovely playing. Is that a new recording?

KAREL The Baron is giving a party and the American pianist, Gertrude Garnet, is the guest of honor.

AUGUSTA (*Somewhat disturbed.*) An American? How very interesting.

BARON (*Enters from the salon.*) Mother, you've arrived, looking splendid. We've missed you. (*Removes her cape.*)

AUGUSTA I arrived home a day early and a grand soirée is in progress.

BARON (*Gives cape to Karel.*) An intimate supper party, nothing more. Karel, you may go.

KAREL Yes, your excellency. (*Hangs cape in closet next to front door and exits.*)

BARON Now, Mother, tell me of your visit to Heidelberg.

AUGUSTA Who is this American piano player?

BARON Gertrude Garnet is a world famous artist. She is to perform at the Festspielhaus next Tuesday. Madame Garnet and her friend, the Countess de Borgia, will be staying with us.

AUGUSTA The Countess, an Italian?

BARON No, she too is an American.

AUGUSTA (*Thinking it over.*) Two Americans under our roof?

BARON Yes, and they are charming ladies. Come, Mother, you must hear Madame Garnet play.

AUGUSTA Two Americans under our roof? Willy, is this prudent?

BARON I see no reason why it should not be.

AUGUSTA My dear son, we shall be at war with their country at any moment. What could you be thinking of? I am astonished. The Führer will not find this to his liking.

BARON (*Exploding.*) Mother, I will not be bullied by you or the Führer, do you hear me? (*Stamps his foot.*)

AUGUSTA Wilhelm!!! Don't you dare raise your voice to me, not in my house!

BARON (*Meekly.*) Forgive me, Mother.

AUGUSTA After you have finished entertaining these creatures, you will find them accommodations in the village for the night.

BARON (*Quietly.*) Mother, that I cannot do.

AUGUSTA Willy, is there something you're not telling me? What is it? You and I have no secrets. We are partners, soldiers in arms.

BARON Madame Garnet . . . I am in love with her.

AUGUSTA Willy.

BARON I have met her but this morning and I am passionately in love.

AUGUSTA You cut a ludicrous figure. You are not a school boy with an idiotic infatuation. You are a commanding officer, serving the greatest leader in the history of the world. Now straighten your back and remember your duties. I shall telephone the Inn and find these women lodging.

She picks up the telephone on the mantle. The Baron stops her.

BARON You don't seem to understand, Mother. I plan to marry her. She shall be the next Baroness Von Elsner.

AUGUSTA (*Puts down the phone receiver. With great intensity.*) Wilhelm, if you persist in this foolishness, before all the servants . . .

BARON I do not wish to argue. Have you never fallen in love at first sight? Of course you have, my darling, beautiful Mutti. Surely with Father.

AUGUSTA Indeed not. The marriage was contracted at birth. You should know. For centuries the Von Elsners have married their first cousins.

The music ends, we hear applause.

BARON Please, Mother, do not be rude to her.

AUGUSTA I am never rude.

Gertrude enters in a magnificent evening gown. She is followed by Kitty, Erik and DR. MAXIMILIAN. *The Doktor is an elegant Nazi aristocrat in his forties. He, Kitty and Erik carry drinks.*

DOKTOR Brilliant, simply brilliant, so passionate and yet so effortless.

GERTRUDE This is, of course, the secret to playing Wagner. One must and I say, one must, read his score as one would read Shakespeare. The notes themselves always dictate the emotion. (*To Augusta.*) Dear, I left my drink on the piano. (*To the Doktor.*) When I first approach any score, I look . . .

BARON Madame Garnet, this is my mother, the Baroness Von Elsner.

DOKTOR Augusta, we did not expect you until tomorrow.

AUGUSTA Evidently, Doktor Maximilian. I see you have taken time off from your medical experiments.

DOKTOR It has been well worth it. I only wish you had arrived earlier to partake of Madame Garnet's genius.

AUGUSTA I am sure we will hear more from Fraülein Garnet before her visit is over.

BARON (*With a note of warning.*) *Mutter, Du hast versprochen, Dich gut zu benehmen.* (Mother, you promised you would behave.)

AUGUSTA (*Disgusted.*) *Was siehst Du in Ihr? Sie ist so vulgaer and buergerlich.* (What do you see in her? She is so vulgar and common.)

BARON *Mutter, beleidige Sie nicht. Ich warne Dich.* (Mother, do not embarrass her. I'm warning you.)

AUGUSTA *Drohe Deiner Mutter nicht.* (Do not threaten me.)

GERTRUDE (*Oblivious.*) Love your hair. What would you call that color?

KITTY Battleship grey.

BARON Mother, the Countess de Borgia and Professor Maxwell.

ERIK A pleasure.

AUGUSTA Another American. *Ach du lieber.* Has our country been invaded in my absence?

BARON Mother is quite comical. You know the German sense of humor.

Gertrude laughs gaily then abruptly stops when she realizes there was nothing funny.

AUGUSTA Madame Garnet, forgive my ignorance of your remarkable career. As chairwoman of the Reich Committee for the Preservation of the Teutonic Arts, I have devoted myself to the work of exclusively German artists. Do you include any Strauss in your repertoire?

GERTRUDE (*With charm.*) Indeed. His "Bein Schlafengehen" is a concert staple of mine.

AUGUSTA (*Appalled.*) An American playing "Bein Schlafengehen." No doubt you also perform his "Burlesque in D."

GERTRUDE (*Understands the bitchiness behind the remark.*) I sure do. I'm also quite adept with Liszt, particularly his "Weiner, Klager, Sorgan, Zagen."

AUGUSTA (*Topping her in bitchiness.*) Really, of course, a true test would be Schumann's "Warter, Warter, Wilder, Schiffsmann."

GERTRUDE (*The war escalates.*) I play it with my eyes closed. Honey, get me in the right mood, and I'll hit you with my "Faschingsschwank aus Wein!"

AUGUSTA I am sure you do quite a raucous "Freulings Fahrt!!"

GERTRUDE (*Mad.*) Oh, yeah!

LOTTE, *the Baron's teenage niece, appears at the top of the stairs. With blonde braids, elaborate traditional German costume, she is a twelve-year-old demon.*

LOTTE (*Scampering down the stairs.*) Uncle, uncle, why did the pretty music stop?

BARON Lotte, what are you doing up so late?

LOTTE Uncle Willy, I heard the music. It was ever so lovely.

BARON Madame Garnet, my niece Lotte.

GERTRUDE Perfectly charming.

AUGUSTA Madame Garnet and her friends are from America.

LOTTE America. That dreadful place, so dirty, so crowded. All the races mixed up. (*To Kitty.*) You have such a funny face. Doesn't she have a funny face? You must be a combination of a million races.

KITTY I sure am, honey, but you're pure bitch.

GERTRUDE Kitty, that's a terrible thing to say.

KITTY It must be this German firewater. I apologize, dear.

AUGUSTA You will find Lotte quite precocious. She has a great interest in history.

DOKTOR She knows far more than I do.

LOTTE (*With perverse enthusiasm.*) Oh yes, I practically live at the prison museum. Do you know they have a complete fourteenth century dungeon. They have a rare torture device whereupon four prongs are attached to the prisoner's face and then stretched in four different directions.

KITTY A totalitarian face lift.

BARON Shall we have coffee in the library? Cook brews an excellent cafe Viennese, and we will have some chocolates.

LOTTE May I come, Uncle? I love sweets.

BARON May she, Mother?

AUGUSTA All right, but do not overindulge. Chocolate gives you acne.

She exits, Maximilian follows.

KITTY (*To Lotte.*) Oh, don't worry, honey, tomorrow we'll find you a nice medieval pimple popper.

She exits, followed by Lotte, then Erik. The Baron stops Gertrude.

BARON Gertrude, this has been such a delightful surprise, meeting you.

GERTRUDE And you were a godsend. I really don't know what we would have done.

BARON I only wish I could spend more time with you. I have so many meetings and military obligations. I hope you won't find our little village too tiresome.

GERTRUDE Oh no, I adore *quiet* places.

BARON Away from the glamor of Manhattan?

GERTRUDE Rather.

BARON Away from the many stage door Johnnies. Isn't that what you call them?

GERTRUDE (*Amused.*) Yes, that's what we call them.

BARON I imagine a woman of your fame and beauty has many, how do I say, flirtations?

GERTRUDE Fewer than you may think. I'm completely devoted to two figures, the bass and treble clefs. (*Sits on sofa.*)

BARON Is there no place in your life for love? (*Sits beside her.*)

GERTRUDE I'm not too keen on love, never having known it. Besides, my spiritual advisor, the swami, has made me realize that I can't love others until I love myself first. I must be number one. And I can only make others happy after I have made myself completely happy, first and foremost. It may take years.

BARON You're very mysterious, Gertrude. As mysterious as a prelude by Debussy.

GERTRUDE Am I? (*She plays piano scales on her arm of the sofa.*)

BARON Such beautiful hands. Let me see them. Ah, lovely. So delicate. (*She displays her hands in a picturesque manner.*)

GERTRUDE Yes. Every finger is double-jointed and X-rays have revealed large airpockets in the bone marrow.

BARON So sensitive and yet so practical. Rather like myself. I feel as if we were two melodies that fit together in perfect counterpoint.

GERTRUDE I'm flattered, your excellency.

BARON Your excellency? Why so formal? You Americans are so famous for your nicknames. What shall you call me?

GERTRUDE (*Flirtatiously.*) Well, for Wilhelm, I could call you "Bill." And, of course, you are a bit older than I, I could call you "Popsie."

BARON No, I don't care for that. What about "darling?"

GERTRUDE Don't you think that's a bit too intimate?

BARON (*Rises. Intimately.*) No, I don't. And to demonstrate our intimacy, I shall let you in on a little secret. I'm going to show you something of mine I don't let everyone see.

GERTRUDE (*Dubious.*) Oh, yeah?

BARON You see that portrait of the Führer?

GERTRUDE An excellent likeness.

BARON (*Pulls, it away, revealing a safe.*) It conceals a safe. Most clever. Everything of importance is locked in that safe. Let me see if I can remember the combination. Now, close your eyes.

She does. He murmurs the combinations, she mouths it to remember.

BARON Turn right three times to zero, left all the way round to six, right back to twelve. Open sesame. Voila!

GERTRUDE (*Stands and crosses to Baron.*) Whatcha got in there, Billy boy?

BARON All sorts of goodies. This ring once belonged to the Grandduchess Mathilde.

GERTRUDE Ooh, daddy, emeralds.

BARON (*Gives her ring.*) It looks lovely with your hair. Try it on.

She puts on the ring.

BARON Most attractive. It's yours.

GERTRUDE I couldn't possibly . . .

BARON Please, it gives me pleasure, but for now, when you see Mother, turn the ring around.

GERTRUDE By all means.

BARON (*Silly.*) And there's more where that comes from, baby. But only for the girl that I marry.

GERTRUDE Mmmm, you're tempting me. And all in that safe?

BARON No, no, no, no. They are in a special vault. The most precious object in this safe is this set of keys. The keys to every room in the house and for the rooms off the catacomb.

GERTRUDE The catacomb?

BARON The house was built in the fifteenth century. My warrior ancestors built a mile-long network of tunnels leading away from the house as an escape route.

GERTRUDE And where does it end?

BARON A nasty place. Let's not speak of it, particularly when these keys lead to such nice places, such as the vault where we keep the family jewels. (*Returns the keys and locks the safe.*) Now, my darling, does that illustrate our intimacy and my trust?

Erik enters.

GERTRUDE I promise I won't betray it.

BARON Ah, Professor Maxwell, do come in.

ERIK I don't wish to intrude.

BARON You did, but you are forgiven. Gertrude, I must check on Mother. She was away for the weekend and I haven't even asked about her trip. She can be a real Tartar when she feels ignored. Will you miss me?

GERTRUDE Unendurably.

BARON My darling. (*Exits.*)

ERIK You two get along very well.

GERTRUDE He's sweet.

ERIK Like a tarantula.

GERTRUDE (*Warning.*) He is our host.

ERIK I must apologize for my rudeness this morning. I was a busybody and deserved the treatment I got.

GERTRUDE I, too, was at fault. But with my maid running off and the loss of our hotel reservation, I really was at sixes and sevens.

ERIK Then friends?

GERTRUDE Friends.

ERIK It sure is good hearing an American voice. I like talking to you, even beefing with you.

GERTRUDE A good fight does wonders for the circulation.

ERIK Then I must be in excellent health. I'm afraid I'm not adjusting very well to the German way.

GERTRUDE Really, I wonder why. It couldn't be more lovely. And the people are so warm, so friendly, so, how do they say it, "gemutlich."

ERIK Haven't you noticed the fear in everyone's eyes?

GERTRUDE Fear? What are they afraid of?

ERIK Miss Garnet, surely you read the newspapers. Germany is in the grip of an evil dictator. The whole country's gone mad. Such arrogance. I tell you, I've had it up to here. (*He raises his arm in a "Heil Hitler" salute.*)

GERTRUDE I never, never discuss politics. I am an artist, the world is my stage. Now what else can I do for you?

ERIK I can't help feeling we've met before.

GERTRUDE When you're a great celebrity, you find this happens quite often.

ERIK It was on the stage, but not in a concert hall. Where could it have been? My God, it was in a beer hall . . .

GERTRUDE (*With forced gaiety.*) A beer hall?

ERIK . . . a beer hall in . . . Sandusky, Ohio . . .

GERTRUDE I hardly think . . .

ERIK . . . Nearly fifteen years ago. You weren't wearing much either . . .

GERTRUDE (*Indignant.*) Now really . . .

ERIK Now I remember, didn't you used to be Barrelhouse Gertie, the Kissing Kitten on the Keys?

GERTRUDE (*With vulgar roughness.*) Oh, shut up.

ERIK Then I am correct?

GERTRUDE (*Tough and common.*) So what of it? I never said I was an overnight success. Okay, Charlie Chan, what's your angle?

ERIK I'm hoping to find underneath your glamorous facade, the real woman.

GERTRUDE What for?

ERIK Because I must ask her a deep favor.

GERTRUDE (*Irritated.*) Now it comes. How much do you want?

ERIK I don't ask this favor for myself, but for someone I love very much; my mother. It's dangerous for me to speak to you here.

GERTRUDE Spill it now.

ERIK My mother, my mother is also a great artist, an actress, her name is Raina Aldric.

GERTRUDE (*Impressed.*) Raina Aldric is your mother? I saw her on the stage when I was very young, a great actress. How can I be of any help to her?

ERIK (*Bitterly.*) As we speak, she lies dying in a Nazi prison only a mile away.

GERTRUDE A prison so near by.

ERIK A prison for political prisoners. My mother was arrested for appearing in a play that dared speak against the new order. For this hideous crime, she is sentenced to death.

GERTRUDE That poor woman.

ERIK But in a mad world, sometimes one can succeed with a mad act.

GERTRUDE (*Nervously.*) What are you saying?

ERIK I have friends here, brave wonderful people who have planned her escape tomorrow. I can't tell you the details now, but there is one fatally missing link. We need an ally here in the Baron's home.

GERTRUDE (*Breaking away from him.*) You mustn't ask me this.

ERIK I beg you, please help me.

GERTRUDE I dare not.

ERIK Please. Please.

GERTRUDE (*Frightened.*) I'm a simple, ordinary woman, extraordinarily talented, perhaps, but in every other way, ordinary. I am not capable of such heroism.

ERIK Then you're a coward, a selfish, egocentric, opportunistic, vulgar, manipulating cunt!

GERTRUDE Vulgar! Now that did it. Look here, you. I don't owe you or your old lady anything. I pay my own freight, never asking for a handout. Now, you must excuse me. I must join my host, the Sacher torte is said to be divine.

ERIK Yes, gobble down their Nazi food, guzzle their Nazi wine, and try to sleep tonight.

GERTRUDE You go too far.

ERIK (*Grabs her.*) Please help me, I don't even know what I'm saying anymore. I'm desperate. You are our only hope. If you don't help us, Raina Aldric will die on Friday. Please, please help me! (*She breaks away from his grasp.*)

BARON (*Enters.*) I seem to be interrupting a passionate scene.

ERIK I was demonstrating a new method to save someone from choking.

BARON She will have no need of that. I hope you have enjoyed yourself, Professor Maxwell. I have done my best to be hospitable. Food and intelligent conversation, my favorite pastimes.

ERIK And at times, equally hard to swallow.

BARON Not in my house. We all tend to think the right ideas.

ERIK Or rather, forced to think the right ideas.

GERTRUDE (*Alarmed.*) Erik!

BARON (*Intrigued.*) Erik? You have become quite intimate.

A Strauss waltz is heard in the salon.

BARON Professor, I don't think I like you. I shall remember this evening. (*To Gertrude.*) My darling, they are playing a Strauss waltz. Will you indulge me in a spin, if my impudent friend will permit?

Terribly torn, Gertrude looks first at Erik, then at the Baron. They form a triangle. She makes her choice and crosses vivaciously to the Baron.

GERTRUDE But, of course. A waltz can be marvelously diverting.

The music swells, the Baron leads Gertrude in a waltz. He moves her in a circle but as she spins around to face the audience, the look on her face is one of agonized guilt.

Lights fade to black.

ACT ONE

Scene 3

The music fades out. Lights up and we are in the catacomb below the Schloss. It is morning. A backdrop is in that shows the catacomb in its creepy, black, dank state. Heidi is garbed as a prison guard. With her in a wheelchair is the legendary RAINA ALDRIC. *Raina is a beautiful woman in her fifties, fragile but still dramatically vibrant. She lives on drama and speaks in the manner of a wildly flamboyant stage actress.*

HEIDI That was close. I was sure the guard saw through my disguise. You may rest now, Madame Aldric. For the moment, you are safe.

RAINA Safe. The most beautiful word in any language. But where am I? What time of day is it? I'm so bewildered.

HEIDI You poor darling. It's early morning. A short while ago, I moved you out of the prison infirmary, took you through the secret door and we came down that very long tunnel. We are now in a room off that tunnel and directly underneath the home of the Baron Von Elsner.

RAINA A baronial home. I do not understand.

HEIDI The Baron's ancestors built two fortresses, one they lived in and the other was a prison. They linked them together with a long series of catacombs in case of enemy attack. That door leads to the interior of the Baron's home and to freedom.

RAINA Why are we waiting? We should go through it now.

HEIDI The door is locked from the outside. We must wait till my father or Erik opens it and escorts us through the house late tonight.

RAINA (*With great theatricality.*) Freedom! I shall never be free. I have seen too much and I shall never be free of the memories. They have destroyed me. I no longer even have the will to walk.

HEIDI You are a great actress. You have so much more to give.

RAINA I once was a great actress. "The shining beacon of the European stage" was what Brecht once called me. "Aldric's Hilde Wangel sang with a poetry Ibsen could only hint at," *Munich Bugle,* September 9. 1934. "Raina Aldric's Ranyefskaya ranks with the Cathedral of Chartres as one of the world's great artistic treasures," *Lisbon Daily News,* May 12, 1937. But now I'm old, weak, my legs are worn-out pipe cleaners. You should have let them execute me. My soul died the night they shot my lover, Gebhardt. "Don't shoot him, don't, don't shoot!" Bang, bang, bang. "Then kill me too, kill me!"

Heidi bursts into tears.

RAINA (*Concerned.*) Forgive me, I didn't mean to upset you.

HEIDI No, it's just that I, too, was once in love.

RAINA Is he dead?

HEIDI He might as well be. His name was Karel, the most wonderful boy in the world. It seems a century ago that we lay in the weinerwald and he taught me the names of all the birds and flowers that gathered about us.

RAINA What happened?

HEIDI He came under the influence of the Baron Von Elsner. They have turned his brains to sauerkraut. When I look into his beautiful eyes, I only see swastikas. (*Weeping vulnerably.*) Madame Aldric, tell me, help me understand why he has turned against me. (*With fierce, hardened vengeance.*) Oh God, how I hate them. They've made this whole goddam world LOUSY! Well, something has changed in Heidi Mittelhoffer and I'm gonna make those bastards pay for what they've done. They've butchered my dreams!!!

Kitty and Gertrude, laughing, are heard Offstage, unlocking the door.

GERTRUDE (*Offstage.*) Kitty, this has got to be the right key.

KITTY (*Offstage.*) Gertie, give it a break.

GERTRUDE (*Offstage.*) I wanna see those family jewels if it's the last thing I do. I didn't open that damn safe for nix. (*Opening the door.*)

HEIDI Someone's coming.

KITTY I gotta sit down. This tunnel is as long as Gary Cooper's . . .

They see Raina and Heidi.

KITTY Oh, I'm so sorry.

GERTRUDE We're guests of the Baron. We were having a marvelous time exploring his lovely home.

KITTY We didn't mean to intrude.

GERTRUDE (*To Heidi.*) You were at the train yesterday, weren't you?

HEIDI Yes, I was meeting my father.

KITTY Your friend looks ill.

HEIDI No, she's quite all right.

KITTY She's pale as a ghost and trembling. She should see a doctor.

RAINA Thank you for your concern. I'm recovering from an illness.

KITTY Your voice is so familiar. Are you an actress?

RAINA Oh no, never.

KITTY Of course you are. Why, you're Raina Aldric.

GERTRUDE (*Shocked.*) Raina Aldric. But I thought you were . . .

HEIDI Please, please, you must pretend you've never seen us.

KITTY What do you mean?

GERTRUDE Kitty, we should leave this place and do as she says.

KITTY Are you a guest of the Baron's? But why are you in this drafty, cold room? Come, we'll take you upstairs where it's warm.

HEIDI No, you mustn't.

RAINA Please, I am quite all right. (*She has a sudden attack of pain in her heart.*) A toothache.

KITTY This is silly, you must come with us.

GERTRUDE Kitty, Madame Aldric is a prisoner of the Nazis. I believe this young woman has engineered her escape.

KITTY This is utterly mad. How do you know of this?

GERTRUDE Eric Maxwell told me and he . . . he is her son.

RAINA Erik, you know my Erik?

GERTRUDE Yes, I do.

RAINA You must be the one. The ruby red hair. A gift from heaven.

GERTRUDE It's actually a gift of henna.

RAINA You are the one in my dream. I have a recurring dream that my Erik is walking through the snow with a beautiful young woman with long red hair. I know in my heart, she is the woman he shall marry.

GERTRUDE I hardly know him.

RAINA I feel it in my heart. (*She has another heart attack.*)

GERTRUDE He's really quite a guy. Come, Kitty, we should return before our absence draws attention.

KITTY Was Erik enlisting your help? He was, wasn't he?

GERTRUDE Yes, he was.

KITTY (*Very gung ho.*) Why didn't you tell me? What do we do? How do we proceed?

HEIDI You must forgive me. I didn't know you had agreed to help.

RAINA You are both most gracious.

KITTY Forget that. Just fill me in.

HEIDI This morning, disguised as a guard, I moved Madame Aldric out of the prison, through the tunnel and into this room under the Baron's Schloss.

GERTRUDE (*It all dawns on her.*) Yes, of course.

HEIDI We are to remain here for eighteen hours, at which time, one of you will unlock this room and usher us through the house.

KITTY Yes, and then?

HEIDI At precisely midnight, a car will be waiting at the servants' entrance to drive us to the airfield and a plane which will fly us to Switzerland.

KITTY Well, count me in.

GERTRUDE Kitty, we must talk. You will excuse us.

KITTY Let's run upstairs, and rustle up some blankets, hot coffee and crullers. Then we can . . .

GERTRUDE Kitty, stop it.

KITTY Gertie, what's wrong?

GERTRUDE Nothing.

KITTY (*The light beginning to dawn on her.*) Gertie, I don't know, but I'm beginning to believe you refused Erik. You refused to help his mother. Tell me I'm wrong.

GERTRUDE (*To Raina.*) We'll get you some crullers . . .

KITTY You did refuse him, didn't you?

GERTRUDE Please, Kitty, let's go upstairs.

KITTY No, answer me. I want the truth.

GERTRUDE Yes, I refused him. I'd botch it up. I'd be a hindrance.

KITTY (*Quietly.*) That's not the reason, and you know it. (*Painfully.*) You're selfish, Gertie. All your life you've thought of no one but yourself.

GERTRUDE This is hardly the time for a character analysis. (*Turns away from Kitty, her face obscured.*)

KITTY I'm seeing you as if for the very first time. Oh, Gertie, your face has a terrible look to it.

Gertrude turns around, her face looks like a grotesque version of Ma Barker. She realizes this and tries to restrain it.)

KITTY Go ahead. I'm going to stay.

GERTRUDE Kitty, you fool, this is serious business. This isn't a madcap caper with your Palm Beach eccentrics. If the Nazis catch you aiding the escape of a prisoner, you'd be lucky merely to be shot.

KITTY We just won't fail. Besides, I'm not a citizen of Germany.

GERTRUDE No, but all your finances are tied up in Italy. I've read enough to know that Germany and Italy are allies. You could lose your entire fortune.

KITTY Sister, with this face, I'll never starve. Now, are you going to help?

GERTRUDE No, I can't. Nothing personal, Madame Aldric, but I'm scared. Scared to death. I'm not courageous. I like a warm, comfortable bed, a fur coat, dinner and dancing at the Stork Club. I'm not cut out for self-sacrifice. I'm leaving. I must put in my three hour's daily practice, I have a concert at the Festspielhaus on Tuesday. I shall pretend I never opened this door. Kitty, will you join me? Kitty?

Kitty leaves Gertrude and goes over to Raina and Heidi.

GERTRUDE Very well. But please, do be careful. *She exits and we hear a door close.*

KITTY Madame Aldric, do not fear, we shall bring you to safe harbor.

Music comes in, tender and somewhat sad. It slowly builds as we watch the three women in tableau. The lights fade to black.

ACT ONE

SCENE 4

The Schloss. An hour later. Kitty enters, looks around furtively, and goes to the telephone. She takes a cigarette from a box on the mantle and lights it with a lighter.

KITTY (*To the operator.*) *Hallo, Telephonistin, sprechen Sie Englisch? Koennten Sie mich bitte mit jemandem verbinder, der die Sprache spricht?* (Hello, operator, do you speak English? Could you connect me with someone who does?) Thank you. Operator, please connect me to Felsenkirk. The number is Bitburg eight, four thousand. Thank you. Hello, is this the Professor? This is the Countess de Borgia.

From her room at the top of the stairs, Lotte comes out and quietly watches.

KITTY (*Unaware of Lotte.*) I'm calling from the Schloss of the Baron Von Elsner. I have seen Raina Aldric, and Heidi has told me all. I am willing to do anything I can to help . . . Yes . . . yes . . . But of course . . . Yes, I can do that. Goodbye. (*She hangs up, thinks for a moment, she picks up the phone again.*) Operator, the overseas connection . . . Hello I would like to place a transatlantic trunk call to the United States . . . Yes, thank you.

Very softly we start hearing scary music. Lotte now starts down the stairs very quietly and slowly to hear better. She gets all the way to the bottom of the stairs before Kitty senses her.)

KITTY Hello, New York, please. The number is Trafalgar six, five one hundred . . . Walter Winchell, please. The Countess de Borgia, and make it snappy . . . Walter, darling, it's Kitty. I'm calling from Germany and, darling, the Deutschland is as dreary as a rotten bratwurst. I've got a scoop for you, but you've got to promise to keep it under your hat for a few days. Remember the

German actress, Raina Aidric, well, I've just . . . (*For the first time, Kitty feels Lotte's presence. Into phone.*) I've just . . . I've just remembered that I left the number in my room. I'll . . . I'll call you later. (*Puts out her cigarette.*)

Kitty hangs up the phone as Lotte comes into the room. Slowly Kitty turns and sees Lotte. Both smile at each other.

KITTY Hello, Lotte.

LOTTE I like your scarf. It's so pretty.

Scary music builds. Lotte starts moving toward Kitty slowly as the lights fade to black.

ACT ONE

Scene 5

The Schloss, an hour later. Lotte is onstage holding Kitty's scarf from the last scene. She hears someone knocking and hides it in the cushions of the sofa. Karel enters, looking for someone.

KAREL Good afternoon, Fraülein Von Elsner. (*Turns to leave.*)

LOTTE Who were you looking for?

KAREL The Countess. I am to drive her to the beautician in the village. (*Looks at slip of paper.*) Fritzi's Chalet of Beauty.

LOTTE Well she changed her mind. She won't be needing the services of a beautician.

KAREL Thank you, Fraülein, for the information. (*Turns to leave.*)

LOTTE (*Blocks him.*) Don't go, Karel. I want to talk to you.

KAREL Yes, Fraülein.

LOTTE Why don't you call me Lotte? I've asked ya a dozen times.

KAREL It would not be fitting. I am a soldier under your uncle's command.

LOTTE Screw him. I want you to be my best friend.

KAREL (*Nervously.*) I am your friend. . . . uh . . . Lotte.

LOTTE (*Caressing his chest.*) You know, you're not that much older than me, Karel.

KAREL You're growing up very fast.

LOTTE (*With dead seriousness.*) Very fast. I'm bleeding regularly.

KAREL (*Trying to be encouraging.*) Congratulations.

LOTTE (*Perversely flirtatious.*) I have a confession. I've never seen a man's weiner. Take it out, I want to see it.

KAREL (*Appalled.*) No, Lotte.

LOTTE Then give me a kiss.

She kisses him, he wipes it off unconsciously.

LOTTE Why did you do that for?

KAREL What?

LOTTE You wiped off my kiss.

KAREL I didn't.

LOTTE (*Moving into hysteria.*) You did. It's as if I repulsed you. You hate me, don't you?

KAREL I don't.

LOTTE You hate and despise me. Well, you'll be very sorry you wiped off my kiss. (*Viciously.*) Very sorry indeed!

The Baron and the Doktor enter.

BARON Karel, are you waiting for me, what can I do for you?

KAREL (*Panicked.*) I was to drive the Countess to the village, but I hear she has changed her mind. If there is nothing else, may I go?

BARON But of course. Heil Hitler.

KAREL Heil Hitler. (*Exits.*)

BARON (*Furious.*) Those blundering idiots! How could a sick, old woman be allowed to escape?

DOKTOR That sick old woman has strong allies. Do not worry, Raina Aldric's friends shall be rounded up and executed.

LOTTE Uncle, I have already done . . .

BARON Death will be too mild. First, in the name of science, they will all be volunteered as subjects for your most extreme medical experiments.

DOKTOR Science must be served.

LOTTE Uncle . . .

DOKTOR Herr Baron, why is this case of such importance to you?

BARON To the liberals, Raina Aldric is a great symbol of artistic conscience. That symbol must be crushed. Art must serve the nation.

DOKTOR But, Herr Baron, who is to judge what is good or bad art?

BARON (*Intrigued.*) Such questions, Herr Doktor. You are beginning to sound like a liberal.

DOKTOR (*Alarmed.*) No, Baron, call me anything but not a liberal.

BARON Decent people can judge what is obscene. All of the arts are mired in decadence. And the theatre is the worst. I am sick of effeminate neurotics parading their warped fantasies across our stages.

LOTTE Uncle, listen to me. I have taken care of the little matter you spoke of. One of Raina Aldric's cohorts has indeed been disposed of.

BARON (*Pleased.*) Lotte, my little bulldog. You have done well.

He roughhouses with her. She barks like a dog.

BARON Bite the Doktor, bite the Doktor. Sic him, Lotte. Sic him.

She attacks the Doktor like a pit bull.

DOKTOR Lotte, stop!!! Please stop!!!

Gertrude enters from the front door in riding clothes, brandishing a riding crop.

GERTRUDE (*Amused by the spectacle.*) Oh dear, I knew I should have packed a muzzle.

BARON Liebchen, have you had a brisk canter?

GERTRUDE (*Full of vigor.*) Bracing, invigorating. Have you seen Kitty? We're having our hair done together in the village.

BARON I have not seen her.

LOTTE I saw her this morning. She did not seem quite herself.

GERTRUDE (*Placing her knee on the back of the sofa jauntily.*) Really, in what way?

LOTTE She mentioned something about an albatross around her neck, choking her. What could she have meant?

DOKTOR A most stimulating young woman.

BARON We are going to the beer garden in the village. Care to join us?

GERTRUDE No, thank you, I think I'll wait for Kitty.

BARON You should not be alone. But, I imagine loneliness is a cloak worn by all artists.

GERTRUDE It would take a special man to strip it off me.

BARON (*Tantalized.*) Most provocative, Gertrude. Before long I shall find the key to your mysterious nature.

GERTRUDE (*Suspicious of his intentions.*) The key?

They stare at each other for a beat.

BARON Yes, the key. Till later. Auf wiedersehen, my sweet.

Baron, Doktor, and Lotte exit into library.

GERTRUDE Auf wiedersehen. (*She nervously takes the keys from her pocket, checks kitchen door, and tiptoes over to the safe. She swings the* *portrait open and attempts to open the safe.*) Turn three times to zero. Then the opposite way round to twelve and then back to six. (*It doesn't open.*) Oh, boy. It must have been left. Round to twelve . . . no, it was six . . .

AUGUSTA (*Offstage from kitchen.*) No, Elsa I said "sauerbraten for six," not at six.

Gertrude quickly closes the portrait and puts keys back in her pocket and looks up at portrait as Augusta enters, carrying a large book. She is surprised to see Gertrude.

AUGUSTA Gertrude?

GERTRUDE I can gaze at this portrait for hours. Those eyes, so sensitive and yet so virile.

AUGUSTA (*In rapture.*) What an honor to serve such a man. My only regret is that I am too old to bear him children.

GERTRUDE There are other forms of volunteer work. Please, don't let me disturb whatever it was you were doing.

AUGUSTA I was consulting my astrological charts. I find astrology a cruelly neglected science. What is your birthday, Gertrude?

GERTRUDE August twenty-third. The cusp of Leo and Virgo.

AUGUSTA A most revealing horoscope. (*Pronounced whore-scope.*)

GERTRUDE (*Laughs.*) That's horoscope, Baroness.

AUGUSTA (*Laughs.*) My English. Do forgive.

GERTRUDE Of course.

AUGUSTA I would imagine you are far closer to the lion than the virgin.

GERTRUDE (*Catching her drift.*) No, I think I'm right in the middle.

AUGUSTA A combination is rather interesting. One could be a ferocious prude or a methodical *tramp*.

GERTRUDE (*Hardboiled to the core.*) Enough with the digs. You don't like me, do you? Why? (*She crosses to Augusta confrontationally.*)

AUGUSTA (*Calmly.*) Because you are from a hateful, enemy nation. You are cheap and common, are using my son and embody everything I loathe in the human race.

GERTRUDE (*Beat.*) Gimme another reason.

AUGUSTA Fraülein Garnet, you are a guest of my son. I am doing my best to be gracious to you and your friend. By the way, where is the Countess?

GERTRUDE (*Concerned.*) I don't know but I should like to find her.

AUGUSTA (*Going upstairs.*) Do not worry. I am sure you will find her shortly, my dear. I suppose she could be almost anywhere. Good day.

Exits—Lotte's room.

Feeling great anxiety, Gertrude sits on the sofa. She stretches her arms out and flings them down wide on the sofa. Accidentally, she touches Kitty's scarf tucked behind a pillow. Tense, suspenseful music underscores the rest of the action. Confused, Gertrude picks up the scarf. Determined to get to the bottom of Kitty's disappearance, she puts down the scarf and crosses to the State Left arch. She calls out "Kitty!" When there's no response, she crosses Center Stage and looks up to the landing and calls out "Kitty!" Still no response. Resigned, she slowly crosses to the Down Stage Right door, lost in her thoughts. She opens the door and to her horror, Kitty swings out, hanging from a noose, her face hideously contorted. Gertrude screams. "What have those fiends done to you!" As Kitty continues to swing back and forth, Gertrude runs to the mantle to steady herself. In hysteria, she crosses back to Kitty and then collapses to the floor in a faint as the music builds to a climax and the lights fade quickly to black.

END OF ACT I

ACT TWO

SCENE 1

The Schloss, several hours later. Erik is comforting Gertrude. She suffers beautifully in a luxurious full length velvet dressing gown.

GERTRUDE It was horrible. Her lovely face, so twisted, her eyes bulging.

ERIK Here, take my handkerchief. Where is she now?

(*He gives her his handkerchief, she uses it and returns it to him.*)

GERTRUDE I must have fainted. When I came to, her body was gone. Thank you for rushing over so quickly. You must think me totally mad.

ERIK I believe every word you've said.

GERTRUDE How could they do this? She, who was so kind, so gentle.

ERIK They'll stop at nothing until the whole world is filled with their evil.

GERTRUDE (*Rises from the sofa.*) I must see the swami. He'll make sense of this. He says everything happens because we choose it. I must take comfort in that.

ERIK (*Challenging her.*) Then Kitty somehow wanted to die?

GERTRUDE (*Cries out in confusion.*) I don't know! She couldn't. No one loved life more than Kitty. Erik, I'm so confused. It's as if the ribbon that's kept my world together has untied. You see, Kitty and I fought. She said I was selfish, that I think only of myself . . . and Erik, she was so right. I've lived a terrible life and now, now I'm so ashamed.

ERIK I'm sure she would have forgiven you.

GERTRUDE That I shall never know.

ERIK I imagine you'll be on the next plane.

GERTRUDE No, I'm staying on.

ERIK What do you mean?

GERTRUDE I must avenge Kitty's death. She was my friend. I must finish the work she died for, saving your mother. The Baron and his henchmen knew of Kitty's pledge to aid your mother. That's why they killed her. Raina Aldric must leave Germany alive.

ERIK Then you're with us?

GERTRUDE If you'll have me. I'll cancel my concert at the Festspielhaus. I'll whip up some excuse, but first I must see the Baron. I'll have it out with him. Force him to admit they murdered Kitty.

ERIK No, you must pretend you never found Kitty.

GERTRUDE (*Aghast.*) But Erik . . .

ERIK (*Forcefully.*) Listen to what I say. You can do us more good if the Baron continues to trust you.

GERTRUDE You're asking me to pretend I'm in love with him. Aren't you?

ERIK Yes, I am. It will act as a smokescreen to mask our true plans. Will you do this? Can you do this?

GERTRUDE (*Revolted but game.*) Yes. You can depend on me. I shall carry out this deception to its very end. Can you ever forgive me for my foolishness? (*Tender, romantic music underscores the scene.*)

ERIK Of course. You're so unbelievably beautiful at this moment. The way the sunset catches your face and hair.

GERTRUDE Oh, you mean like this? (*Composing her face into an unforgettable image.*)

ERIK (*With deadpan thoughtfulness.*) No, like this (*Adjusting the position of her head.*) I know it's madness to feel this way after so short a time and with so much at stake, but I love you, Gertie.

GERTRUDE Please, don't say it.

ERIK I love you. From the first moment I met you.

GERTRUDE (*Tenderly.*) I believe you, and the strange thing is, I feel the same. For the first time, something has burst inside me and I feel what the poets call love. But do I trust it?

ERIK You must and you will.

GERTRUDE (*Tremulously.*) Erik, hold my hands.

ERIK Really? I know how you feel about your hands.

GERTRUDE It doesn't seem to matter anymore. Today, we all need as much tenderness as we can find. (*She takes his hands.*) Hold my hands like any American boy would do with his girl. They won't win, will they, darling, the Nazis?

ERIK (*With inspiring fervor.*) We won't let 'em. God is on our side. Yeah, he's a regular Joe who won't let the bad guys get away with just a kick in the pants. You'll see, this time the krauts will be smashed to smithereens forever.

GERTRUDE And will we be fighting alone?

ERIK No, ma'am. All of Europe will join together. Uncle Sam'll come in swinging, and Russia too. Sure, the Nazis fooled 'em for awhile, but they've wised up. I met Joe Stalin once, at a seminar in Moscow. He wasn't so bad. Believe me, kiddo, he won't let old Schickelgruber into his backyard.

GERTRUDE I love hearing you talk this way.

ERIK I love holding you this way. (*He gently kisses her.*)

GERTRUDE Darling, we have so little time. Do you see that portrait? Behind it lies a safe. This morning, Kit . . . Kitty and I opened it and found the keys to all the rooms in the house.

ERIK Good going.

GERTRUDE Unfortunately, when I tried to return them, I forgot the combination. I'm terrified the Baron will notice the keys are missing . . .

ERIK We can only hope he doesn't go near the safe for (*Looks at his watch.*) the next six hours. Let's fetch Mother from the catacombs.

GERTRUDE I've seen to that already. I've hidden your mother and Heidi in the butler's pantry.

ERIK You're a genius.

GERTRUDE (*Radiantly.*) Go to her, darling.

ERIK Mother on the other side of that door. It's been so many years since I've seen her. I've got the willies.

Heidi wheels Raina in from the kitchen.

RAINA Erik?

ERIK Mother?

RAINA My darling. (*They embrace.*) I thought I'd never see you again. Look at you, so big, so handsome. You were a little boy when last I saw you.

ERIK From now on, you'll never be alone.

RAINA My heart can't take such happiness. My dear, too many years have been wasted. Perhaps it was wrong of me to pursue the career I did, traveling around the world.

ERIK You're a great artist.

RAINA Yes, but I had a child. You must believe me, I wanted to take you with me, but your father, the son of a bitch, he thought it best that you grow up in a more normal, stable household. You don't hate me?

ERIK Hate you? I worship you.

HEIDI Come, we best hurry.

RAINA Where do we go now?

GERTRUDE Erik, you and Heidi leave. I'll take care of your mother for the few hours until the car arrives at midnight.

HEIDI But I couldn't possibly leave her.

RAINA Heidi, darling, you must do what Madame Garnet says. She knows best.

HEIDI (*Near hysterics.*) But what if she has another attack, or starts to shake, or falls into a coma, or what if she . . .

RAINA Heidi—

HEIDI Yes, ma'am.

GERTRUDE I'll bring Madame Aldric upstairs to the attic. There is to be a supper party tonight and that should divert attention.

ERIK It's like you're a different woman.

GERTRUDE I am a different woman. (*With a swift gesture, she lifts Erik's coat and hat off the back of the sofa.*) Come, hurry.

ERIK Mother, this shall be our last goodbye for a long time.

RAINA God bless you.

They kiss.

HEIDI Goodbye, Madame Aldric.

GERTRUDE Godspeed.

She gives coat and hat to Erik. He kisses her on the cheek. He and Heidi exit.

RAINA He loves you, Madame Garnet.

GERTRUDE (*Embarrassed.*) Oh.

RAINA And you love him.

GERTRUDE Oh.

RAINA You're blushing.

Gertrude, blushing, makes a raspberry sound and puts her face against the wall.

RAINA I'm a worldly woman. I know a great deal about love, particularly how to squander it.

GERTRUDE We hardly know each other. What we may say now, in a moment of . . .

RAINA It can happen in an instant. Two people meet and their past and future are one. Don't end up like me, old, sick, alone. Look at this face, look at it. There's a lot of mileage on this puss. Every role I played, every dirty dressing room, every mile I traveled is etched on this map. Look at it, my girl, this could be you.

GERTRUDE (*Horrified.*) No! No!

They hear Lotte barking from salon.

GERTRUDE Oh my God, someone's coming. Hide behind the sofa.

RAINA But I can't.

GERTRUDE Get down. (*She pushes her out of the wheelchair and behind the sofa. The Downstage Right door to the salon opens, obscuring Gertrude as she pushes the wheelchair out the swinging kitchen door.*)

LOTTE (*As she enters from the salon followed by the Baron.*) I hate her. I hate her.

BARON (*Follows Lotte.*) But, Lotte, you will learn to love Madame—(*Turns as Gertrude shuts salon door.*) . . . Ah, Gertrude! Are you alone in here? I thought I heard voices.

LOTTE There were two female voices, Uncle.

GERTRUDE I suppose I'll have to confess. I've been involved in a top secret project.

BARON Indeed?

GERTRUDE (*Madly improvising.*) I'm composing an opera. I was acting out all the roles. It's a very contemporary opera.

LOTTE She's lying. Don't believe her.

BARON Lotte, that was ill-mannered. Apologize to Madame Garnet.

LOTTE (*Crosses to her.*) I love stories. Tell us the story of your opera.

GERTRUDE Never you mind. It's very sophisticated, and I wouldn't want your hormones to go haywire. You're liable to wake up in the morning, full breasted and with a moustache. No, I'm dreadfully tired. I think I'll lie down here for awhile.

BARON Wouldn't you be more comfortable in your own room?

LOTTE (*Very bitchy.*) Uncle, I think Madame Garnet would like to be alone in this room. It's so dusty! That new servant girl is so incompetent. Let me do a quick cleanup of the *entire* room.

GERTRUDE (*Rushing to Lotte.*) No! It was rude of me not telling you the story of my opera. Let's see. I'll act out the whole thing for you. Lotte, you sit over here. (*She pushes Lotte down on the sofa with such force that Lotte's skirt flies up reducing Lotte to a flurry of pink petticoats. To Baron.*) And you, darling, you sit over here. Nice and comfy. (*She gently seats him also on the sofa.*) This shall be the stage. (*She indicated the Downstage area.*)

She moves down near fireplace as Raina's head pops up behind sofa.

GERTRUDE It all takes place in Greenwich Village. That's part of New York. Downtown. (*She sees Raina.*) No, what am I saying? I've changed it. It takes place in Harlem. That's uptown. Up, up, uptown.

She points for Raina to go upstairs.

GERTRUDE It's the upper corner of Manhattan Island. The upper right corner.

Raina drags herself up the stairs.

GERTRUDE That's right, folks, Harlem. The home of Jelly-roll Morton, The Cotton Club, Satchmo.

She sits on arm of sofa next to the Baron, as Raina starts up to the first landing.

GERTRUDE It's about the wild, bohemian set. Grasping at everything life has to offer, one step at a time. This woman, Annabella, is a painter. A painter of large murals and loose morals. Isn't that funny? Sometimes I just come up with these little . . . (*No one is laughing.*) She falls in love with a nobleman, kind of like you.

BARON Like me?

GERTRUDE Oh yes, handsome, debonair.

BARON This nobleman; he makes her happy?

GERTRUDE (*Near hysteria.*) Oh honey, she's downright slaphappy!

BARON (*Amused.*) Then it must be, what you call, escapist entertainment.

GERTRUDE You might say.

LOTTE (*Standing up.*) I'm bored.

Raina hides around corner of first landing, as Gertrude stands up and runs to Lotte holding an imaginary knife.

GERTRUDE (*Screams.*) A crazy lady runs out of a building holding a knife. She sings "I can't, I can't. I can't go on much longer like this."

During this she has "stabbed" Lotte back down on the sofa again. Raina falls from her hiding place onto the newel post of the second landing.

GERTRUDE The music gets faster and faster. It speeds up, accelerato!

Raina falls onto second landing stairs.

GERTRUDE It slows down.

Raina drags herself up to second landing.

BARON (*Starting to get up.*) It's chilly in here. Let me close the window.

GERTRUDE (*Pushing the Baron back onto the sofa.*) I didn't tell you, Annabella also works as a part-time chiropractor. She met the Baron while cracking his neck.

She sits between the Baron and Lotte and with one arm grabs the Baron around the neck to keep him from seeing Raina.

BARON Ow!

LOTTE It *is* cold in here. I'll close the . . .

GERTRUDE (*With her other arm, grabs Lotte around the neck.*) She's also a part-time lesbian.

BARON This sounds like decadent art.

GERTRUDE Oh, it's madly decadent. Annabella seduces the Baron and his niece. She takes them to her artist's garret and forces them both to strip naked.

Behind them on the top landing, Raina realizes she simply can't walk another foot to get to the door. She does a full somersault that gets her to the exit.

GERTRUDE Slowly she caresses their nude bodies and . . .

Gertrude looks up and Raina gives her the okay sign, and exits.

GERTRUDE And that's all I'm going to tell you. I'm fairly tingling with inspiration. I must go to my room and compose. (*She runs up the stairs at a clip.*)

BARON But, Gertrude, what happens next?

GERTRUDE I'm concentrating, darling. (*She sings strange atonal phrases as she ascends the stairs and exits.*)

LOTTE The whole thing was a lie.

BARON Lotte, you must not be so suspicious. Come, Lotte, let us go to the freezers and choose the best steaks and sausages for tonight's supper.

(*They cross to the mantle. The Baron moves Hitler's portrait revealing the safe.*)

LOTTE Oh, Uncle, this is an honor. You've never let me see the freezers before.

BARON I keep my special keys in the safe behind this portrait. (*Does the combination.*) Now that you are a young woman, I shall trust you with these keys. (*Opens the safe, sees keys are missing.*) That's strange. The keys are missing.

LOTTE (*Gasps.*) She took them! She took them! I thought I saw her sneaking around here this morning.

BARON Who, Lotte?

LOTTE The piano player, Miss Gertrude Garnet!

BARON But why should she do this? She is in love with me. True, her friend was a conspirator, but not Gertrude, I don't believe it.

LOTTE Uncle, only an hour ago I heard her arrange to meet the other American, Erik Maxwell. Are you aware that Erik Maxwell is none other than the son of Raina Aldric?

BARON (*Screams and starts to strangle Lotte.*) This is not true!!! (*Controls himself.*) Is true. What a great fool I am. What have I done?

AUGUSTA (*Enters with basket of apples.*) Good afternoon, my liebchen. Why so glum? It is a gorgeous day.

BARON Mutter, I have done a terrible thing. We must talk.

AUGUSTA (*Fearing the worst.*) What have you done, Willy?

BARON It is hard for me to say.

AUGUSTA First, bring me a cigar. Then you will sit here and tell me what you have done. (*She sits on sofa, basket of apples to floor.*)

BARON Mutter, I have fallen in love. (*Lights cigar.*) I have fallen in love with an American agent.

AUGUSTA Is she with a big agency like William Morris?

BARON You don't understand. She is a spy. Gertrude Garnet has helped Raina Aldric to escape.

AUGUSTA (*Fiercely.*) Swine!!! (*Slaps him.*) Dumpfkopf!! Why do you not listen to me?

BARON Mother, please.

AUGUSTA You are weak, Wilhelm, weak. This is the eternal curse of the Von Elsners.

BARON Please, Mother, not in front of Lotte.

AUGUSTA No, she must stay. She is more of a man than you. Let her know of her heritage and the cross she must bear. All of the men in your ancient line have been weak, infantile. It is the women who have led the family to greatness.

BARON That is not true. My father died a hero in battle.

AUGUSTA Your father died in a madhouse. I should know. I placed him there. They all go the same way. First they display childlike stupidity, then impotence, and then madness.

BARON (*Spooked.*) I am still not mad. I will show you, Mother. I will show you I am not weak. Fraülein Garnet!!!

AUGUSTA Don't! I gather she does not know you know that she knows that we know.

BARON Uh uh.

AUGUSTA Then let us wait a bit longer.

LOTTE And then I will strangle her myself.

AUGUSTA No, Lotte, that would not look good. Such an important personage must not be found murdered. It must appear far more natural. I shall take care of the lady in question.

Baron cries, head in hands.

AUGUSTA Do not worry, my little Wilhelm, Mother will take care of everything.

Bright Viennese waltz music comes in as the lights blackout and continues into the next scene.

BLACKOUT

ACT TWO

Scene 2

The Schloss, that evening. Gertrude, Doktor, Baron and Lotte enter from dinner. Gertrude carries an evening bag. A small side table has been added against the Downstage Right wall.

GERTRUDE Dinner was absolutely superb. The weinerschnitzel and sauerbraten were perfection and the potato dumplings, so delectable. I will not leave without your mother's recipe. (*Sits on the sofa.*)

BARON I am so happy you enjoyed your last supper . . . before you leave us. Is there no way, my darling, I can persuade you to stay? (*Sits next to Gertrude on the sofa.*)

GERTRUDE I'm afraid not. When MGM calls, one lifts one's skirts and runs. Just imagine, me starring as myself in my own musical biography, "I Love a Piano." Of course, I am heartbroken I had to cancel my concert at the Festspielhaus. All those poor little burghers who camped out all night to buy their tickets.

LOTTE But what of your friend, the Countess, what if she returns and you're not here?

GERTRUDE (*Holding herself together.*) I'm sure wherever she is, she will understand.

BARON She left without saying goodbye.

DOKTOR An enchanting creature. (*Crosses to fireplace and lights a cigarette.*)

BARON But you, Gertrude, when will I see you again?

GERTRUDE I shall be in Los Angeles through December. I'm sure by then, darling, you and your men will be marching down La Cienega Boulevard.

DOKTOR I am so disappointed. I did so want to show you my laboratory. I am just beginning with human experiments.

GERTRUDE I am fascinated by science. Music is, after all, closely allied to the field of physics.

BARON Perhaps, Herr Doktor, Gertrude will stay if we, how do you Americans say, twist her arm.

LOTTE I'll twist her arm, uncle.

GERTRUDE Dear Lotte, I do hope some day you'll realize that you have a special kind of beauty, the kind which comes from within, my precious little monkeyface.

Augusta enters with a tray of strudel, through the kitchen's swinging doors. She places it on the small table against the Downstage Right wall.

AUGUSTA I have a surprise for our lovely guest. I have baked my famous Von Elsner strudel.

BARON Oh, Mother, you haven't. Gertrude, we have a great treat in store for us.

GERTRUDE Oh, dear. Had I but known. The sauerbraten did me in.

LOTTE This strudel will really do you in.

GERTRUDE My girdle is way too tight already.

AUGUSTA Just a small piece, a sliver.

GERTRUDE I couldn't.

BARON Mother shall be quite offended.

AUGUSTA I shall be furious.

GERTRUDE I'll take a sliver.

AUGUSTA The pieces are already cut, so you just eat as much as you can. (*Puts powdered sugar on Gertrude's strudel.*)

DOKTOR Augusta, *I* am furious. Never once have you baked me your famous strudel.

AUGUSTA (*Serving everyone.*) Tut, tut, tut, Herr Doktor. When your first human experiment survives, I shall make you my all-butter pound cake. (*Gives Gertrude her specially prepared piece of strudel.*) Eat up, dear. See if it is to your taste.

GERTRUDE (*Innocently perplexed.*) Why is mine the only piece with powdered sugar?

AUGUSTA I . . . I understood all Americans liked things sweet. Should I take it off?

GERTRUDE No. It looks divine.

They all stare at her.

GERTRUDE (*Takes a bite and grimaces with revulsion then tries to be polite.*) Mmmm, light as air.

BARON Mother, you must have worked hours on that strudel.

LOTTE And I helped.

AUGUSTA Indeed she did. Lotte was my chancellor of ingredients. And she was most precise, everything according to measure.

Gertrude is gradually growing sicker.

DOKTOR That powdered sugar looks good.

BARON Careful, Max. You don't want a potbelly.

DOKTOR I don't care. Madame Garnet, if you don't mind, I shall be quite boorish and take a little of that powdered sugar.

Gertrude holds out her plate and the Doktor's fork is going for the sugar . . .

BARON
(*Alarmed.*) That's for Ger . . .

AUGUSTA
(*Fiercely.*) No, Max . . . sweets are not good for you.

The Doktor pulls back his fork and Gertrude realizes there's poison in the sugar. She looks at the Doktor.

GERTRUDE (*Elegantly.*) Excuse me. (*She gives her plate to Baron.*) Excuse me. (*She leans over the back of the sofa and violently throws it all up. The others quickly get out of the way.*)

GERTRUDE I guess it didn't agree with me.

AUGUSTA You have not fooled us, Fraülein Garnet.

Doktor crosses to a lever against the Upstage Left wall and pulls it up. A strong "interrogation" light hits Gertrude on the sofa.)

BARON Mother, let me handle this. Gertrude, you will tell us everything you know about Raina Aldric.

GERTRUDE She's a great actress.

BARON Tell me more.

GERTRUDE I believe she made a silent film in 'twenty-six.

BARON (*Barks.*) Do not be flippant! You have taken me for an idiot, but no more. Your life is in my hands. Raina Aldric has escaped her prison. You have helped her. Who are your confederates?

GERTRUDE (*Terrified.*) I don't know what you're talking about.

AUGUSTA Your friend, Kitty, she knew, didn't she?

GERTRUDE (*Emotionally.*) You tell me, since I'm sure you were the last to see her alive.

BARON Where is Raina Aldric now? Tell me the truth!

GERTRUDE (*Fighting for composure.*) I don't know where she is. Never met the dame.

DOKTOR Where is Raina Aldric?

GERTRUDE (*Assuming a tough facade.*) Don't you guys listen? I told you I know nothing about that old lady. Got my own troubles, and if Goering, Goebbels and Himmler asked me, I'd tell 'em the same. And get that light out of my eyes. What are you fitting me for, glasses?

AUGUSTA We will be fitting you for a coffin if you do not comply.

GERTRUDE Testy.

BARON Why should you be so loyal to your country? I thought you considered yourself a citizen of the world, Madame Gertrude Gar*net* (*Gar-nay.*)

GERTRUDE The name's Gertie Garnet (*In the American pronunciation.*) I'm a citizen of Brooklyn, New York.

DOKTOR Brooklyn?

GERTRUDE Yeah, what's it to you?

BARON This Brooklyn, it will soon be part of the Third Reich.

GERTRUDE (*With defiant pride.*) Brother, you may take the Maginot Line, but you'll never take the Canarsie Line.

AUGUSTA Your bravado is quite pathetic.

GERTRUDE I give as good as I get.

DOKTOR You will tell us the truth. I have several medical methods that can be most excruciating.

GERTRUDE All right, I'll give you some truth. This whole set up in Germany stinks. And your Führer, Herr Hitler, has only one nut to his name.

AUGUSTA (*In a rage.*) Damn you! Damn you!!!

BARON Mother, control yourself.

AUGUSTA (*With mad fervor.*) That is a filthy lie. The Führer has two enormous testicles!!

BARON I believe this is time to call in our next subject. Doktor Maximilian, have Karel bring in the young lady.

GERTRUDE Please don't.

The Doktor pulls down the lever, killing the light. He calls for "Karel!" Karel enters with Heidi and pushes her towards the fireplace. Karel stands behind the sofa.)

BARON Good evening, Miss Mittelhoffer. So happy you could join us. Please answer a few questions, and then we shall release you. Where is Raina Aldric?

HEIDI (*Lying very badly.*) I know nothing. Please, believe me.

BARON Come, child, do not fear us. We will not harm you. Where have you taken her?

HEIDI I know nothing. Please let me go.

BARON You are guilty of hideous crimes against the Reich. You will tell us everything.

AUGUSTA Let me. (*She crosses for a cigar.*) Miss Mittelhoffer. Do you mind if I call you Heidi? Pardon my indulgence. There's nothing I like better than a good after-dinner cigar. So fragrant. So satisfying. (*Holds the lit cigar close to Heidi's face.*) Tell me, girl, where is Raina Aldric?

HEIDI Believe me. I don't know where she is.

AUGUSTA You are very pretty. I can make it so no man will ever love you.

HEIDI (*Near hysterics.*) Please believe me. I don't know anything.

(*Augusta, frustrated, crosses the stage growling animal-like.*)

LOTTE Karel, you're very quiet. Karel and Miss Mittelhoffer are very old friends. Perhaps Karel will have some influence on her.

KAREL We are mere acquaintances.

LOTTE (*Viciously.*) That's not true. I believe they were once sweethearts.

BARON Who is your allegiance to? This tramp or the Führer?

KAREL The Führer, Herr Baron.

BARON Then rip off her blouse. Rip it off, I command you.

(*Karel rips off her blouse, revealing her chemise.*)

BARON Mother, the whip.

(*Augusta gets whip from table and gives it to the Baron.*)

BARON Doktor, please escort Mother to the library. Lotte, go to your room. This is not for your eyes.

LOTTE Oh drat, just when the fun starts.

(*Augusta and the Doktor exit Upstage Left. Lotte runs upstairs and exits.*)

BARON (*Handing whip to Karel.*) Karel, give her five lashes and perhaps her memory will serve her better.

KAREL (*Tortured.*) Yes, Herr Baron.

GERTRUDE (*Rushing to the Baron.*) Please! The girl is innocent. She has been told nothing.

BARON Silence!!! Proceed, Karel.

Karel places Heidi's hands on the mantle of the fireplace to steady her and hesitantly starts to whip her. Each time he hits her the Baron yells, "Harder." Although she screams at each strike, she is being very brave. On the last one she falls to the floor sobbing. Karel is in a state of shock.)

BARON Once more, tell me, girl, where is Raina Aldric?

HEIDI (*With raw, ugly power.*) You can all rot in *hell!!!*

BARON How defiant and most entertaining. I am in the mood for more entertainment. Karel, I would like to see you and this young lady have sexual intercourse. Here, before us. Karel, rape her.

KAREL Please, Baron, do not force me to do this.

BARON You must do this for the Führer.

KAREL I can't. I won't! Have you no respect for human life?

BARON Karel, watch yourself.

KAREL (*Takes out a gun and points it at the Baron.*) No, watch yourself. I though you were a great man. How wrong I was, you are a monster. Heidi, put on your blouse, we're going.

Lotte enters from upstairs.

BARON Where are you going? You fool, traitor!

LOTTE (*Runs down the stairs.*) Karel, you're leaving. You're leaving together. You can't do that. You can't do that! I won't let you!

KAREL Don't come any closer!

LOTTE (*Feverishly.*) I'm the one you desire.

BARON (*Aghast.*) Lotte, what are you saying?

LOTTE Ravage me, impale me!

KAREL Get out of my way.

LOTTE Fuck me, Karel, fuck me! (*Insane.*) You don't want her. I'll get her out of the way. I'll kill her for you. This will be the test of my love.

She pulls out a knife and is about to stab Heidi when Karel shoots her and she falls dead.)

KAREL (*Drops the gun on the sofa in disgust.*) Come, Heidi.

They run out the front door.

BARON (*With mad vengeance.*) The traitors, they will not go far. I shall phone the Gestapo and put an end to this ridiculous love story.

GERTRUDE (*Picks up the gun on the sofa and points it at him.*) Put down that phone.

BARON I certainly will not.

GERTRUDE Put it down, I say.

BARON Give me the gun. You do not have the courage to fire it.

GERTRUDE Oh, don't I? (*Defiant music comes in.*) What a joy it will be to kill you. Yes, joy. But first I shall torture you as you have tortured thousands. You thought I loved you. I never loved you. I pitied you because you were a pathetic, mother-fixated fool. Imagine my happiness when I execute you and escape with my lover. Yes, my handsome, young lover. You, who hounded an innocent actress nearly to her death. You, who cruelly humiliated a pair of young lovers. You, who murdered my friend. The Lord God in Heaven may forgive you but I never shall. Now die, your excellency, die.

BARON Gertie, perhaps I was a trifle brusque.

She pushes him up the stairs.

BARON (*Pathetically yellow.*) You are a great artist, artists should be above such nonsense as politics. Gertie, don't shoot. I beg of you. I don't wanna die. I'll do anything. I'll make any phone call. I have money. You want cash? How much, take it, a hundred marks? Don't, Gertie, don't. Mother! Mother! Don't shoot.

She impassively shoots him twice, then once more as an afterthought. The music fades out.

GERTRUDE (*With bitter irony.*) And to think, before you, once trembled all of Schauffehausen.

ERIK (*Runs in from the library.*) Gertie, are you all right? What happened?

GERTRUDE (*Terribly shaken.*) I killed him. I killed him.

ERIK We must get Mother out. The car will be here any minute.

GERTRUDE What about the Baroness and the Doktor? Shan't they hear us?

ERIK Dr. Maximilian saw me climbing in through the window. We thrashed it out and I've got him tied-up in the basement.

GERTRUDE And the Baroness . . . ?

ERIK (*Lights a cigarette at the mantle.*) She heard us fighting and came after me with a shovel. I belted her in the stomach, got her in a half-Nelson, and wrestled her to the ground. Then I grabbed her by the hair and dragged her across the room and slammed her against an old chifferobe. When she was knocked out cold, I tied her to the Doktor. They'll keep for awhile. Professor Mittelhoffer!

The Professor comes in from the front door. Erik puts out the cigarette.

PROFESSOR I heard shooting. Was Heidi here? (*Sees the bodies.*) Ach du lieber.

GERTRUDE They brought her in and tortured her. You'd have been proud. They couldn't break her spirit. Karel saved her and got her out of the house. He's on our side now.

PROFESSOR She is a smart girl, she knows to meet us outside the servants' entrance at midnight. It's almost time.

ERIK Let's go get Mother.

Raina enters from the upstairs right room, walking slowly. She is wearing a fur coat and looks radiant.)

ERIK Mother, you're walking. (*He starts for her.*)

RAINA (*With great courage.*) Don't help me. I must walk to freedom on my own two legs!

They embrace on the stairs.

PROFESSOR Oh dear, with Karel along, we don't have enough letters of transit. What should we do?

GERTRUDE Then you must take mine. (*Gets her purse from sofa.*)

ERIK We couldn't. You'd never get out.

GERTRUDE I'd find a way. I always do.

ERIK (*Crossing to the mantle.*) We're close to the Swiss border. We could possibly make it by foot.

GERTRUDE But you, you have a letter of transit.

ERIK It means nothing without you. I'll take my chance with you in the mountains.

PROFESSOR It's midnight. I think I hear the car.

RAINA Bless you, Gertrude. You have given me back my life, my son and my art. "Gallop apace, you fiery-footed steeds . . ."

PROFESSOR Come, Raina, the plane leaves promptly in ten minutes.

GERTRUDE Here is your letter of transit, Madame Aldric, and you can't greet your public without this. (*Gives her a lipstick.*)

RAINA A lipstick, and such a lovely color. (*Puts it on, kisses Gertrude's hands.*) Thank you, thank you, thank you.

Gertrude gives her the handbag.

ERIK Mother, I'll meet you across the border.

They kiss.

ERIK Professor, good luck.

Raina and the Professor exit.

GERTRUDE Darling, there's still time. You should have gone with them. I'll never forgive myself if you . . .

ERIK Shhhh.

They listen to the outside. We hear the car drive off.

ERIK They're on their way.

GERTRUDE What do we do now? How do we find Switzerland?

ERIK We have very simple directions. I'll show you.

He takes her hands and leads her to the open door. They look out.)

ERIK We just follow that brightest star. Are you game?

GERTRUDE I love an adventure.

ERIK Let's go.

FADE TO BLACK

Lush, romantic music redolent of courageous adventure comes in and eventually underscores the following voice over.

ACT TWO

Scene 3

In the blackout, we hear . . .

VOICE OVER Flash. Flash. Dateline Bavaria. Famed U.S. piano virtuoso, Gertrude Garnet, is missing and feared dead after aiding the escape of German stage actress, Raina Aldric, from a Nazi prison. Miss Aldric and companions have landed safely in Zurich but fear Nazi retaliation against Miss Garnet and against Miss Aldric's son, Erik Maxwell. Stay tuned for further reports.

The large screen from Scene 1 is across the stage. Lights come up on the Right side of the screen detailing a mountain landscape. On grooves carved into the screen, two small figurines representing Gertrude and Erik are seen skiing down the mountain. The effect should be that of a movie 'long shot." This is accompanied by thrilling, adventure music. The lights fade down and rise on the Left side of the stage where Gertrude and Erik are seen in person skiing on a small slope. Snow is falling on them and loud gunshots are heard in rapid succession.

GERTRUDE (*Skiing.*) Faster, darling, faster!

ERIK Where'd you learn to ski?

GERTRUDE San Moritz, Vail and Aspen. They're shooting at us!

ERIK Don't look back! When we get back to the states, will you marry me?

GERTRUDE Of course, darling. I think I'd make a divine professor's wife. And when I go on tour during summer vacation, will you join me?

ERIK I'll carry all the luggage.

GERTRUDE Then you've got yourself a deal. Are we almost there?

ERIK I can't tell in this darkness.

A shot rings out and hits Erik in the back. He falls to the ground. Gertrude stops skiing and joins him on the ground. The music and snow fade out.

GERTRUDE Erik! Erik!

ERIK Keep going!

GERTRUDE I will not. You're hurt. Hold onto me!

ERIK (*Through his pain.*) No, go ahead. I'll catch up with you.

GERTRUDE (*With great emotion.*) Darling, if this is the way it ends, so be it. During these past few days, you've taught me more than most people learn in a lifetime.

ERIK (*Fading away.*) I can hardly see your face.

GERTRUDE (*Desperately.*) Hold onto me, darling. (With great determination.) No one's going to harm you.

The end seems to be near. Wistful, quietly sad music is heard.

GERTRUDE Erik, what a fool I've been. All these years I've been obsessed with myself and called it a philosophy. (*Very simply and with great restraint.*) This is what matters. This is real. Fighting for something I believe in. Loving someone. Why must we always come to our senses when it's too late? (*She pauses and realizes there is silence.*) Listen, the shooting has stopped. Do you hear?

Erik lifts himself up to a somewhat seated position. He's going to live. The music becomes hopeful.

ERIK Yes, the night is suddenly peaceful.

GERTRUDE (*Pointing to the sky.*) Look, darling, the brightest star. It's directly over our heads. We must have crossed the border! (*Elated.*) We're free, darling, we're free! (*Eyes full of tears, she's the embodiment of bravery as she cradles Erik in her arms Her voice rises in emotional rhythm and cadence.*) And soon that bright star will shine above all of Europe, and the whole world will glow in radiance, brighter and stronger than we've ever, ever known!

The music builds triumphant as the lights fade out on Gertrude and Erik's upturned, enraptured faces. Above them, we see the snow-capped mountains and the title "The End" appears as if through the clouds.)

FADE TO BLACK

RED SCARE ON SUNSET

Charles Busch as 1950s star Mary Dale in *Red Scare on Sunset*. Photo Credit: T. L. Boston.

The Cast

Red Scare on Sunset was originally produced by Theatre-in-Limbo (Manny Kladitis, Drew Dennett, Shaun Huttar) on April 24, 1991, at the WPA Theatre (Kyle Renick, Artistic Director). Directed by Kenneth Elliott, with set design by B.T. Whitehill; costumes, Debra Tennenbaum; lighting, Vivien Leone; and sound, Aural Fixation, it was performed with the following cast, in order of appearance:

Ralph Barnes .... Mark Hamilton
Jerry .... Roy Cockrum
Pat Pilford .... Julie Halston
Frank Taggart .... Arnie Kolodner
Mary Dale .... Charles Busch
Malcolm .... Andy Halliday
Marta Towers .... Judith Hansen
Salesgirl .... Mark Hamilton
Mitchell Drake .... Ralph Buckley
Bertram Barker .... Roy Cockrum
R.G. Benson .... Mark Hamilton
Granny Lou .... Mark Hamilton
Old Lady .... Andy Halliday

The Characters

Ralph Barnes
Jerry
Pat Pilford
Frank Taggart
Mary Dale
Malcolm
Marta Towers
Salesgirl
Mitchell Drake
Bertram Barker
R. G. Benson
Granny Lou
Old Lady

Place:
Hollywood, California

Time:
1951

RED SCARE ON SUNSET

Prologue

Setting: The stage where The Pat Pilford Radio Show is broadcast. An "on the air" sign hangs above. The year is 1951, the place: Los Angeles.

At Rise: JERRY, *a technician enters SR with a cigarette in his mouth, carrying a mike stand and a script folded in his jacket pocket. He sets mike DSC, exits SR and returns with doorslam unit and sets it SL. He adjusts mike.*

RALPH BARNES *enters. Ralph is an actor playing the folksy Uncle Sven on the radio show and is wearing a fake moustache and porkpie hat.*

RALPH (*Looking over his script.*) Hey there, Jerry.

JERRY Afternoon, Mr. Barnes.

RALPH Have you read this script?

JERRY Nah, I never read 'em.

RALPH Smart fella. You know they pay people to write this stuff?

DIRECTOR (*V.O.*) Ralph, please. The studio audience.

RALPH Just kidding, folks, Just kidding.

DIRECTOR (*V.O.*) Has anyone seen Pat?

RALPH Can't say that I've had the pleasure.

DIRECTOR (*V.O.*) It's thirty seconds to air.

JERRY I'll check her dressing room. (*Exits SR.*)

RALPH Would you like me to read her part? (*No response.*) There goes my big chance.

JERRY (*Reentering SR.*) She's coming.

DIRECTOR (*V.O.*) Fifteen seconds. Where is our star?

PAT PILFORD *enters SR. She's an attractive blonde in her thirties the quintessential movie wisecracking, loyal sidekick, a clown who can't resist a doubletake or a pratfall. She's also a fierce right wing red baiter. Pat is both unlovable but impossible to dislike. She enters wearing an outrageous hat covered with fruit.*)

PAT I'm coming! I'm coming! I'm coming! You try running in this corset. (*To the audience.*) Believe it or not, I have a terrible weight problem. I always have to be on a diet. My old boyfriend, Herman, gave me a present. It didn't fit. And it was a Buick.

DIRECTOR Five, four, three, two . . .

ANNOUNCER (*V.O.*) The Veedol Motor Oil Program with Pat Pilford . . .

Applause/Music.

ANNOUNCER . . . makers of Veedol Motor Oil, found wherever fine cars travel, present Miss Show Business, Pat Pilford. With Ralph Barnes, Emmaline Crane, Jimmy Stall and special guest stars Tony Martin, Dagmar, Slapsy Maxie Rosenbloom, Les Paul and Mary Ford. Yours truly Bill Simmons and Victor Arnold and his chiffon orchestra. (*Music Tag.*) . . . And now your fabulous femme-cee, Pat Pilford.

PAT Hello sweeties. Boy oh boy, do we have a show for you. I get so excited. I can't help it. I suppose I've always been stage struck. I'm the type of gal that when I open the refrigerator and the light goes on, I do twenty minutes. Now I simply must tell you . . .

Jerry slams door.

RALPH (*Using a comical Swedish accent.*) Patty dear, may I speak to you for just a minute?

PAT Oh Uncle Sven, (*Applause.*) I'm about to start my show. Is something the matter?

RALPH I apologize. How would you like to go with me Saturday night to the Swedish folk dance marathon? What suspense? Can Olaf and Hildy dance the Glog and Shpickle for forty-eight hours?

PAT I'm afraid I'll have to pass. Hold onto your chair. I've got a date Saturday night.

RALPH Oh yumpin' yimminy. I'm as yolly as a yune bug dancing a yoyful yig. Is this a serious romance?

PAT Sure is. His first glimpse of me was at the Beverly Hills Hotel when I was lying by the pool. I was being real seductive. He was desperate to meet me. I heard him whisper to his pal "get her."

RALPH Now darlin', be careful. Sometimes I just worry about your choice in men.

PAT Oh, you're thinking about Herman. He wasn't what you call "husband material." He was addicted to horse racing. When I took him to church, I had to keep telling him "It's Hallelujah, not Hialeah."

RALPH I apologize for interfering, but I just have your best interests . . .

PAT (*Putting down her script.*) I have to stop here.

RALPH (*Still acting.*) I just have your best interests at heart . . .

PAT I said stop. I cannot continue this show.

RALPH (*Retaining his accent.*) Patty, dear, is there something I can do?

PAT Yes, you can can the accent. You're not Uncle Sven. Fortunately you are no relation to me at all. You're Ralph Barnes, an actor, and as of now, an unemployed actor.

RALPH (*Dropping the accent.*) I don't understand.

PAT Then I shall make myself clear. You're fired. I will not perform another minute with anyone whose politics jeopardize . . .

RALPH Pat, I'd be very careful choosing my next few words if I were you.

PAT How are these words? I'm giving you the pink slip, bub.

RALPH I can't believe this is happening. Pat, we are on the air.

PAT I don't care if we're in the air, I will not continue until you leave this studio. I'm waiting.

RALPH (*Mortified.*) I will. I will leave. I can't believe this. This is unbelievable. (*He exits SR bewildered.*)

PAT My dear audience. I apologize for what must seem to you cruel and unprofessional behavior. Sometimes in life, drastic measures must be taken. A long time ago, I devoted my life to bringing you, the American public, wholesome, clean entertainment for the entire family and I will be darned if I'll let some cynical, agitating New York actor come between me and that pledge. Now I say this to you, not as Pat Pilford, funny lady but as a concerned citizen and long-time friend, the time has come for all of us to clean house.

BLACKOUT

ACT ONE

Scene 1

The beach house of movie stars Mary Dale and Frank Taggart. There is a chair SR and a small settee SL with a coffee table in between. On either side of the stage are platforms that can be used as table surfaces.

Late afternoon, tea time. Pat Pilford is seated with FRANK, *a handsome and intense man in his mid-thirties.*

FRANK I'm surprised to see you. That was some havoc you created on your show this afternoon. The whole town must be talking about it.

PAT You should have seen the press buzzing around. It was like they had Mexican jumping beans in their jockstraps. All I did was fire an actor.

FRANK On the air and nearly denouncing him as a communist.

PAT And I should have but I could see my producer was about to have a coronary. I'm sorry. I just hate phoniness. Anyway, Frank, what's done is done, no looking back, tomorrow's another day.

FRANK But this is serious. You've destroyed a man's career.

PAT You dramatic actors get so histrionic. He can always get a job with the Moscow Art Theatre. Look, I don't want to talk about it. *C'est la vie*. Frank, I am very impressed with this house. It is just too, too, too, too, toooo . . . I'm so glad Mary wouldn't let me see it till it was finished.

FRANK Well, it's not my taste but you know Mary. She always wanted a real movie star beach house in Santa Monica.

PAT Mary has such style. Did Billy Haines help her with the decor?

FRANK Natch. Can I fix you a drink? Pat, you're a Rob Roy girl if I recall.

PAT A shot of hootch would be tempting but I better say nix. I'm Mary's guest for tea and that girl's a walking breath test.

FRANK If it's all right with you, I'll fix myself one. (*He goes to a small liquor tray SL and makes himself a drink.*)

PAT Starting rather early these days, aren't you Frank?

FRANK These are tough days.

PAT They sure are, boy, they sure are. Everything's topsy turvy. Hollywood ain't the boom town it once was. Not the way it was when I landed here in '35. It's the big T, television. Every actor in town is looking at his bank book and sweating. I applaud your confidence in building this dream house. I don't want to be rude but I've seen the numbers on your last few pictures. My little nephew has crayon drawings that have been more widely seen.

FRANK I appreciate that, Pat. I could have told the studio those films would flop. The public is sick of that same romantic crap the studios have been feeding them for years.

PAT That's right. You're from the old Give-the-folks-a-message-and-ram-it-down-their-throats school of entertainment. Well, not me, brother, I like to leave 'em laughing. That's what the name Pat Pilford stands for. That's my message and here's how I send it. (*She makes a wild comic face.*)

FRANK I imagine you weren't laughing when you lost the SAG election last month.

PAT No Frank, I wasn't. In fact, I wept and not for me, Frank. I wept for the union. To think that I could lose the Presidency of the Screen Actors Guild. Oh, and I bet I didn't have your vote.

FRANK I'm sorry Pat. I just didn't think you were experienced enough for the position.

PAT Experience! I have been in this business since I was four years old. Vaudeville, the chorus, the Follies, radio, forty-two films and believe you me, I know why I lost that election. It's the red influence of Mr. Stalin and Mr. Lenin that has infiltrated every corner of our industry!

FRANK Pat, I really don't want to discuss politics with you. It upsets Mary and she should be down any minute.

PAT You don't seem to mind discussing politics with others.

FRANK What's that suppose to mean?

PAT Oh nothin'. It's just that you have a reputation for having passionate political beliefs. Weren't you quite active in liberal causes in your New York theatre days?

FRANK We all were. It was the spirit of the times. We suffered so during the depression.

PAT You're going back to New York soon, aren't you.

FRANK You *are* well informed. Perhaps I *should* have voted for you. Yes, I'm going back to do a play.

PAT Will Mary be joining you?

FRANK I doubt it. She's got a string of pictures lined up. The studio's giving her the big star treatment.

PAT It's the old "Star is Born" scenario. One goes up and the other goes down.

FRANK (*Matter of factly.*) Pat, fuck you.

MARY DALE *enters SL Door. Mary is a gracious woman, a star who is also the perfect wife. She is wearing a magnificent green chiffon dress covered with pink roses. She is Scarlett O'Hara at the barbecue circa 1951.*

MARY My darlings. Pat, precious. (*She crosses to her and kisses her.*) Frank, darling. (*She starts cross to him, notices him drinking, makes a horrified face but then tries to put on a bright expression. She crosses to* *him and kisses him.*) Forgive me for being late. When one has tea with the girls, one dresses to the nines.

PAT Well, honey, you're dressed to the ninety nines. There is no one in Hollywood with more tone.

MARY (*With a gentle mocking tone.*) You're sweet, but Pat, that hat . . .

PAT Leave my hat alone. I'm a low comic. I'd be more at home in baggy pants.

MARY I heard you fired Ralph Barnes.

PAT Well you heard right.

MARY (*With true sincerity.*) Poor darling, I know how hard it is for you to fire people.

PAT (*Very grateful.*) Thank you Mary, I appreciate that. It's always hard and I shed tears. Now please, let's not say another word about it. Frank was telling me about the play he's doing in New York.

MARY (*Suddenly sad.*) He could be gone for months. Don't know how I'll bear it.

FRANK You'll be busy filming.

MARY (*Suddenly happy.*) Yes, a biography of Lady Godiva. I've always felt such an affinity for Eleventh Century England. It's a marvelous script. Really illuminates those troubled times. And we have terrific musical numbers. I wanted the studio to cast Frank as the Lord of Coventry but . . . he didn't think the role was right for him.

FRANK You mean the studio didn't think we had the right chemistry on screen.

MARY What am I to do with my brooding young man?

FRANK I just hate this town and everything it stands for.

PAT Be careful Mary. He may go to New York, and not come back.

MARY I'll get him back. When I told that preacher "till death do us part," believe me I never spoke dialogue with more conviction. (*Takes Frank's arm.*) Pat, I found myself a man, do you hear, a *man* and I'm not going to let this one get away, ever.

FRANK (*Draining his drink.*) Well, you're gonna have to let me go for a little while. I'm due at the photo gallery in forty five minutes. I'll be glad when I'm an old character man and don't have to take these phony glamour photos. Give a kiss, baby.

They kiss.

MARY Oh darling, remember we're having dinner with the Gradys this evening. Cocktails at seven.

FRANK Oh boy. I'm really gonna catch heck from the big boss. I can't Mary.

MARY Why not? We've had this planned for weeks. They're counting on us.

FRANK You'll have to go without me. I'm meeting with my agent to discuss a new image for me. He says it's urgent.

MARY But surely you could have told me this earlier.

FRANK It came up very suddenly.

PAT Sort of from left field, so t' speak.

FRANK (*Glares at Pat.*) Look, I've gotta run. I'm sorry Mary. I am. (*He exits SR door.*)

MARY I worry about him, Pat. I worry about him.

MALCOLM, *the houseboy, enters SL door. Malcolm is a good looking fella in his late twenties, though high-strung and pale.*

MALCOLM Mrs. Taggart, should I serve tea now or would you prefer waiting till your other guest arrives?

MARY (*To Pat.*) Are you famished or shall we wait?

PAT Oh, it don't matter. A cup of tea is a cup of tea. How're things going, Malcolm?

MALCOLM Quite well, Miss Pilford. You're looking in full bloom.

PAT Can't complain.

MARY Weren't you both working at Republic at the same time?

PAT Oh yes. Malcolm was in the make-up department when I did a picture there.

MALCOLM (*Matter of factly.*) Indeed. Miss Pilford is the reason why I'm not working at Republic anymore.

MARY Pat, did you have Malcolm fired?

PAT Let's just say that I didn't care for the shade of red he was pushing.

MARY Malcolm, I'm glad you're free to work for me. I don't know what I'd do without you.

MALCOLM That's very kind of you, Mrs. Taggart.

MARY Miss Pilford knows our little secret that Frank has something of a drinking problem. You don't know how grateful I am to Malcolm. How many nights he's had to strip Frank naked and hold him under the shower. I owe Malcolm a lot.

MALCOLM Think nothing of it Mrs. Taggart. It was my pleasure. Will that be all for now?

MARY For the moment.

MALCOLM Excuse me. (*He exits SR door.*)

PAT (*Sighs.*) I suppose some women have a passion for pansies.

MARY What are you talking about?

PAT Surely you know that Malcolm is that way. (*She licks her pinky and wipes her brow.*)

MARY Because he isn't married. Really Pat, haven't you ever heard of a bachelor? My Uncle Maurice lived with his best friend Cyril for thirty-two years. They had the most beautiful home in Indianapolis. You've never seen such gardens and they were definitely not that way. (*She licks her pinky and wipes her brow.*)

PAT (*Irritated.*) Mary Dale, you are just too good to be true.

MARY Besides it's none of our business what people do in the privacy of their own homes.

PAT Mary, you are so wrong. We must know who's boffing who.

MARY Pat, such language.

PAT (*Getting all riled up.*) It's time to grow up and smell the lavendar. That kind of behavior undermines the core of our entire system, the sanctity of the American family. Girl, there's strange sex going on in homes throughout this fair city and it's my duty as a citizen to expose it. People are sodomizing each other at the drop of a hat. The government must have this information. We must drag them out into the light!

MARY Next you'll be wanting FBI cameras in our bedrooms.

PAT Why not? I've nothing to be ashamed of. Roll film! Cut! Print it!

MARY (*Sincerely.*) Pat, I do envy your grasp of the issues challenging our world.

PAT (*Takes her hand.*) You are just a darling little kitten with a heart as big as the Hollywood Bowl. I'll do the big thinking for both of us. So Lambikins, who's our mystery guest for tea?

MARY Marta Towers.

PAT Marta Towers! Are you crazy?

MARY Why? Do you know her?

PAT Marta Towers is the most notorious pinko in Hollywood.

MARY Oh Pat. She has a few liberal friends.

PAT Marta Towers has had more Russians in her than the Kremlin.

MARY (*Covering her ears.*) Pat, please.

PAT Well, I won't speak to her. Imagine inviting me here along with that woman. She holds everything that Pat Pilford stands for with contempt.

MARY She's a fine actress and a lovely girl. I've only met her a handful of times and for a housewarming gift, she sent us a complete set of silver bar equipment.

PAT An ice bucket, a shaker and a hammer and sickle.

MARY Stop that. (*Doorbell rings.*) And none of that pink talk when she's here. That's just nasty gossip, you'll see.

Malcolm enters SR door.

MALCOLM Mrs. Taggart, Miss Towers has arrived.

Malcolm exits SL door and MARTA TOWERS *enters SR door. Marta is a pretty woman in her thirties, demure and ladylike but with an inner fire.*

MARY Marta dear.

MARTA Mary, your house is exquisite. Makes my little place look like a shack.

MARY I can't believe that. Let me guess your style. French provincial?

MARTA I have no style. It's just a mish mash of furniture I've picked up around the world on my travels. I do have one prize possession. A genuine nineteenth century Russian samovar.

MARY I'm green with envy. Oh, I'm so rude. Do you know Pat Pilford?

MARTA Who doesn't? You're an institution like Southern California Gas.

MARY Pat, you were awfully funny at the Hollywood Women's Press Club Awards.

PAT I was so nervous. I thought I'd go wee wee in my panties.

MARY You nervous?

PAT Oh I always get stage fright. I'm yellow as a sunflower.

MARY (*Laughs.*) Isn't that funny?

MARTA What Mary?

MARY Oh I was just thinking. Here I'm green with envy, Pat's yellow with cowardice and you're pink . . . (*Mary fumbles about stuttering over her faux pas. Finally she lets out "Oh Boy" and sits on the settee.*)

Malcolm enters SL door with a tray of tea and crumpets.

MALCOLM Tea, ladies.

MARY Over here, dear. There's nothing like a spot of tea on a cold Los Angeles afternoon.

PAT Aren't we terribly grand. I knew this dame when she was Dale Evans' stand-in.

MARY I never was.

MALCOLM (*Offering crumpets to Marta.*) Would you like one Miss Towers?

MARTA They do look delicious, but alas I just started a diet.

MARY (*Pouring tea for Marta.*) You, you're as thin as a rail.

MARTA Well, perhaps I will have a nosh.

MARY A nosh?

MARTA That's a Yiddish expression. A bite to eat.

PAT What kind of roll is this?

MARY An English crumpet. (*To Marta.*) Cream and sugar dear.

MARTA No thank you.

MARY (*Handing Marta her cup.*) You know I'm currently filming a biography of Lady Godiva and when I take on a role, I like to immerse myself totally in that world. England, England, England, that's all I think about. (*Laughs.*) Poor Frank, I've been serving him nothing but Yorkshire Pudding and Toad in the Hole for weeks. You should have seen his face when I served him his first Spotted Dick. (*Pours Pat's tea. To Pat.*) Cream and Sugar.

PAT One lump.

MARTA I suppose all actors are a little meshuganuh.

Mary pauses for a beat not quite comprehending Marta but then shrugs it off.

PAT Marta, were you born in this country?

MARTA Indiana born and raised.

MARY (*Relieved.*) Really. I'm a fellow hoosier. I should have known. There's nothing foreign about you. You're as fresh and wholesome as an Indiana corn field. (*Hands Pat her tea, pours her own cup and lifts it to sip.*)

MARTA It's been a problem. I long to play an exotic vamp but each time I do, I fall flat on my tuchis.

Mary nearly chokes on her tea.

MARTA My these are scrumptious.

MARY Are you much of a cook?

MARTA Yes, I adore cooking. As a matter of fact, I've been volunteering my services at a soup kitchen downtown.

MARY Really?

MARTA It's a terrible sight to see these once proud men reduced to poverty by a system that's failed them.

PAT (*Holds two crumpets over her breasts.*) Hey Mary, who's this? Gypsy Sara Lee.

MARY (*Laughs.*) Oh Pat . . .

PAT (*Holds crumpets like earmuffs.*) Sonja Henie. (*Puts crumpet halves over her eyes.*) Little Orphan Annie.

MARY (*Laughing.*) Pat stop. You're incorrigible. Marta, you were saying . . .

MARTA Yes. Only last week at the soup kitchen, I met a man, a former GI who risked his life for this country and yet found himself a pariah, unable to get a bank loan, unable to find a job. He told me his wife . . .

PAT Hey Mary. (*She puts the crumpet in the center of her forehead like a doctor's light.*) Calling Dr. Kildare.

MARY (*Hysterical with laughter.*) Pat, please. Marta, the GI told you what?

MARTA Well he . . . he said his wife left him because . . .

PAT (*Pulls her sleeve over her hand and holds the crumpet in front of the end of the sleeve.*) Mary, Harold Russell. (*She holds two crumpets sideways over her ears.*) Clark Gable.

MARTA He said she . . .

PAT (*Stands up and holds the two crumpets on her crotch like testicles.*) Hey Stella!

MARY (*Bent over with laughter.*) Pat, please . . . (*Wiping tears of laughter from her eyes.*) Pat, you are the funniest woman alive. (*To Marta.*) Marta, you've really given me food for thought. Terribly disturbing. Girls! I just got back my snapshots from Bermuda.

You must see Frank posing with all the little natives. It's darling. (*Mary exits to the bedroom.*)

PAT (*Sipping her tea.*) I hear in Russia they drink their tea out of a glass.

MARTA Yes.

PAT Ever been there, Marta?

MARTA A few years ago I did visit the Soviet Union. It was fascinating experience.

PAT (*With false sincerity.*) I bet. Inspirational.

MARTA In its way.

PAT Sort of inspired you to want to see their way of life over here?

MARTA We could learn some things from the Soviets.

PAT Such as denying the freedom of speech?

MARTA I wonder if we really have that freedom.

PAT You bet your bootie we do. Every crackpot in the land has his say. And the government supports it. That's the problem. Why must everyone have a voice? And the commies are using our media to put their message across.

MARTA Are you advocating censorship?

PAT Yes! Ideas *must* be censored. Why can't people *understand* that concept?

Mary enters looking very perplexed holding a passport.

PAT Mary, what's wrong?

MARY I was looking for the snapshots in Frank's sock drawer and I found this passport.

MARTA Is it Frank's?

MARY I don't know. It's an old passport, outdated and it's Frank's photo.

PAT So?

MARY Only the name isn't Frank Taggart born in Minnesota. It says this person was born in the Ukraine and his name is . . . Moishe Nisowitz.

BLACKOUT

ACT ONE

SCENE 2

That evening. The pier at Playa del Rey. Frank is seen waiting for someone on the lonely pier. He lights a cigarette. A woman appears in a trenchcoat and approaches him. It's Marta Towers.

FRANK I was afraid you wouldn't come. I had a helluva time getting out of the house. Mary thinks I'm with my agent. Marta, you looked very mysterious coming out of the fog. Mysterious and beautiful.

MARTA Not by Hollywood standards. I've been told that the camera brings out odd things in my face.

FRANK What does a cold metal thing like a camera know about a beautiful woman.

MARTA Frank, we're not shooting a scene. You don't have to seduce me. I came to this dreary pier in God forsaken Playa del Rey because I wanted to. Now I want you to kiss me.

FRANK Request granted.

They kiss.

MARTA Have you thought about my proposition?

FRANK Yeah, I have. I can't get it out of my mind.

MARTA And?

FRANK I . . . I don't know. It's what I'm starving for. I suppose deep down I'm just chicken.

MARTA Take the leap, Frank. We both know it's what you crave.

FRANK It's my every fantasy but do I have it in me? Can I really go that far?

MARTA Frank, dive in, get wet, get yourself dirty and do as I say, take a method acting class.

FRANK You've got to understand, Marta. I was trained in light Broadway comedies. It was drummed into my head over and over, technique and timing equals talent.

MARTA A cheap bourgeois simplification. There is no art without the soul, without the gut. Study Tolstoy and Turgenev and they will tell you the same.

FRANK I've never been with a woman like you before.

MARTA You mean with half a brain.

FRANK You mustn't talk about Mary that way.

MARTA Loyalty is admirable when it's directed at the right people and the right ideas. Misguided when it's wasted on idiots and tired clichés.

FRANK Mary is a wonderful girl, the perfect wife.

MARTA I'm sure she is but you've outgrown her, Frank. I'll admit she's not malicious but in her innocent way, she's dangerous. She's holding you back from becoming the artist we know you can be.

FRANK Can an actor really be an artist?

MARTA Oh yes, Frank. But you can't be content with superficialities. You must dig and search within yourself. I see in you such possibilities. I hope you won't think I'm being too pushy but I see us as a great acting team.

FRANK You do?

MARTA Oh yes, Frank. I see us returning to the theatre, away from all this silliness and act great roles in great plays. Think of how much fun we'd have doing "The Lower Depths," "The Weavers," "Saint Joan of the Stockyards."

FRANK (*Getting excited.*) "The Weavers," yes. (*She tries to kiss him, he breaks away.*) No, I can't do this. I can't betray Mary.

MARTA (*Wrapping her arms around him.*) "The Wild Duck," "Baal," "When We Dead Awaken," "Blood Wedding," "The Ghost Sonata," "No Exit."

FRANK I'll do it. Where do I go?

MARTA The Yetta Felson Studio. Sunset at La Brea. Tomorrow at eight. Frank, trust me, you'll never be the same.

BLACKOUT

ACT ONE

SCENE 3

Late that night. Mary and Frank's home. Frank stumbles in drunk. He sits down and struggles to take off his shoe and can't. Malcolm enters in his bathrobe.

MALCOLM Mr. Taggart, I thought I heard you come in.

FRANK (*Focused on his shoe.*) I can't . . . this thing's . . . I . . .

MALCOLM Here let me. (*Malcolm kneels down and unties Frank's shoes and takes them off.*)

FRANK Sorry I woke you up.

MALCOLM That's all right. I was just worried that you'd hurt yourself. Here, let me massage your foot. You like when I do that.

FRANK (*Relaxing.*) Oh yeah . . . like that. Were you in bed?

MALCOLM It's after two in the morning. It's not unusual for a person to be in bed. Actually I was reading. I won't tell you what I was reading. I wouldn't want to shock you.

FRANK Didn't we give you that robe?

MALCOLM Yes you did. Last Christmas. From you and the missus. You're a very generous man. It's pure silk, see? (*He lifts up part of the robe exposing his bare thigh.*) It feels really good cause you know, I'm nude under here.

FRANK (*Not really listening.*) Is that so?

MALCOLM Yes I am. (*Gets up and massages Frank's shoulders.*) I always sleep in the raw. It's handy since I never know when I'll have to throw you in the shower.

FRANK Malcolm, you're all pal, a real guy.

MALCOLM I'm also part woman.

FRANK (*Sobers up for a moment.*) Whaaa?

MALCOLM (*Sifting gears.*) I said "You've been with a woman." I can tell.

FRANK Shhhh. And what a woman. Brains, brains, brains.

MALCOLM I've got an idea. I'm going to take you to my room so we don't disturb the missus and I'm gonna give you a complete alcohol rub down. It's gonna feel so good.

FRANK No, too messy.

MALCOLM Don't worry. I'll take off my robe so it won't get ruined. We're just two guys. You won't mind if I'm also nude.

FRANK No rub down.

MALCOLM Don't give Malcolm a hard time. Bad boys get spanked. These pants are coming off, now. (*He begins unfastening Frank's pants.*)

Mary enters in pajamas and marabou trimmed mules. "Hers" is inscribed on her pajama top pocket.

MARY Frank?

MALCOLM (*Standing up.*) Mrs. Taggart, he's done it again.

MARY (*With true sympathy.*) And awakened you from a sound sleep. I'm so sorry, Malcolm.

MALCOLM That's all right, Mrs. Taggart. Better me than you.

FRANK Malcolm, my friend, fix me a scotch.

MARY (*To Malcolm.*) No, you don't. Frank, you're drunk.

FRANK Don't be upset, Mary.

MARY Malcolm, you can go back to bed.

MALCOLM Are you sure you don't need me? It can be hard getting those clothes off him.

MARY I can undress him myself. Goodnight Malcolm and thank you.

MALCOLM Well . . . goodnight then.

He starts to exit. Mary turns her back to him and Malcolm makes an ugly face frustrated that she interrupted his possible seduction of Frank. He exits.

MARY Really Frank, how many times must you wake up the servants and force them to handle you in this drunken state.

FRANK Lay off, will ya. I only had a few beers. I'm not that tight. Don't make me feel like I'm being watched by the FBI. Go back to bed, Mary.

MARY Well, since you're as sober as a judge, perhaps it's a good time to show you this. (*She takes out the passport.*)

FRANK What is it?

MARY A passport belonging to one Moishe Nisowitz.

FRANK (*Frank explodes and shakes her furiously by the shoulders.*) Where did you find that? Give that back to me! (*About to strike her, then catches himself in horror.*) Good God.

MARY You wanted to strike me.

FRANK I wouldn't have. I couldn't.

MARY (*With great dramatic intensity.*) Frank. I'll believe anything you tell me. But please give me some explanation of what this means and why my discovery of it would cause you to nearly harm me. (*She hands him the passport.*)

FRANK What can I say? I'm a louse. This passport does belong to me. I am Moishe Nisowitz and it's true I was born in the Soviet Union.

MARY Then everything you told me is a lie.

FRANK I was afraid if you knew the truth you wouldn't marry me. My parents escaped to this country when I was two years old. We settled on the lower east side of New York. I loved this country and I always felt I belonged more to it than to my parents. So when they both died, I gave myself a new American name and a new past.

MARY (*Rushing into his arms.*) Darling, I love you so. Despite everything. But please, let's not have any more secrets. You do love me, don't you? That isn't a lie, is it?

FRANK Of course not. I love you so very much.

MARY Because you know, if I ever found out you didn't love me, I think I'd kill myself.

FRANK Mary, don't say such a thing.

MARY I would, I would kill myself. When I love, I love completely. It's my life. It's who I am. Hold me darling. Hold me tighter. I like it like this. How did your meeting go with your agent?

FRANK Not bad. He wants to lean me more towards comedy. But it's a tough sell. The studio doesn't think I'm funny. I hate comedy. How was your tea party with Pat and Marta. Did they come to blows?

MARY They seemed to hit it off fine. But I don't know, there's something about Marta that bothers me. I don't know what it is. I'm tired. Let's get to bed.

FRANK What's wrong with Marta? She's certainly been a friend to you.

MARY She gave us lovely bar equipment although considering your proclivities, I would have preferred a blender for milk shakes. No, I wouldn't call her a great pal. Coming to bed?

FRANK Shortly. I just don't see where you come off criticizing a woman who's done nothing more than want to befriend you.

MARY I simply said there was something about her that bothers me.

FRANK It's just that in this town everyone passes quick judgements on people. This guy isn't funny, this woman should be shunned.

MARY I didn't say Marta should be shunned. But truth to be told, I find her humorless. And that certainly shows in her comedy playing.

FRANK I know she can't compete with the glittering wit of a Pat Pilford.

MARY Pat Pilford is a comedy legend and my best friend. I had no idea you were so devoted to Marta Towers.

FRANK (*With mounting anger.*) I don't like your tone, Mary. But it's my opinion that Marta Towers is one of the finest dramatic actresses gracing this artistic wasteland we call motion pictures.

MARY The studio only signed La Divine because she was sleeping with the head of publicity.

FRANK (*Shouting.*) Did Pat tell you smutty gossip?

MARY Frank, listen to us, we're nearly arguing. Now, please, let's end this conversation and go to bed. After all, tomorrow is a rather important day.

FRANK Tomorrow?

MARY January seventeenth. The anniversary of the day we first met.

FRANK Oh yes.

MARY Now I hope you haven't forgotten we have reservations at Ciro's tomorrow night.

FRANK Mary, I . . .

MARY Frank, you haven't . . .

FRANK I know it's awful but Marta said tomorrow night she could get me into her method acting class at the Yetta Felson Studio. They're very fussy about who they let in to observe. It's a great opportunity for me, Mary.

MARY (*Quietly.*) I see. Of course, I am disappointed but I know how much this means to you.

FRANK You're a great girl, Mary.

MARY Couldn't I come with you? Surely they'd let me observe too.

FRANK I don't think so.

MARY But why not? I could hardly be called an amateur. I've made twelve pictures in three years.

FRANK That's not the point, Mary.

MARY What is the point, Frank? I'm not good enough. Do they look down their noses at your little wife who last year had two films on Variety's list of top moneymakers. Should I be ashamed of that?

FRANK Mary, don't get worked up. It's just that they do a different kind of acting.

MARY My kind of acting comes from the heart. My high school dramatics coach, Miss Helen Phipps, said I acted with the simple pure belief a child. I'll compete any day with those pretentious intellectuals with their grunting and sweating.

FRANK Mary, you sound foolish. Great acting is uncovering depths of emotion that dare to be ugly, even repulsive. It's the exposure of the self in all of its raw truth.

MARY Can I help it if I'm pretty and have a flair for fashion. I'm terribly serious about my acting. I know everything about Lady Godiva, what she thinks, feels, wears. I swear if I was konked over the head this minute, her life would pass before my eyes.

FRANK Mary, just face it. You're a movie star, not an actress. You wouldn't know Chekhov from Chill Wills.

MARY Well, that does it! That does it! (*She runs into the bedroom.*)

FRANK Mary, forgive me. It was a terrible thing to say.

MARY (*Enters carrying his pillow and blanket.*) Tonight Frank Taggart or Moishe Nisowitz, whoever you may be, you sleep on the sofa. As of this moment, our twin beds are off limits.

FRANK You don't have to worry. (*He grabs his coat.*) And another thing, if you've read your history books, your precious Godiva was nothing but a two bit whore. I'll amend that. All women are whores.

MARY Buster, Godiva was a lady and so am I. Now get out!

FRANK With pleasure.

Frank exits leaving Mary alone, forlorn and confused.

BLACKOUT

ACT ONE

SCENE 4

Bullocks Department Store, the next day.

Pat is revealed DR when lights come up. Mary is in the changing room. SALESGIRL *enters SL door. She crosses to Pat.*

SALESGIRL Miss Pilford, is anyone waiting on you?

PAT Yes thank you. My friend is in the try on room.

SALESGIRL You really ought to take a gander at some of our new cashmere sweaters. They are simply to die for. There's one with a collar covered in gold paillettes that screams out your name.

PAT Oh honey, tell it to pipe down. My friend is trying to make me more refined.

SALESGIRL I listen to you on the radio every week and you are the only one with courage to speak out on the red issue. Those commies get me so mad. (*Giggles.*) Now if you'll excuse me Miss Pilford, I can see brassieres pointing at me. (*She exits SR door.*)

MITCHELL DRAKE *enters SL door. He is an attractive, dark-haired man in his late thirties, an odd mixture of the intellectual, the macho and the dangerous.*

MITCHELL Ah, then it is you, Pat.

PAT Mitchell Drake.

MITCHELL (*Charming.*) I saw the legs. They're still better than any race horse and then I recognized the voice. Once heard, never forgotten.

PAT What are you doing here in the ladies department at Bullocks? Oh, the perfume counter. A special gift for a special lady. I should have known better.

MITCHELL You've got all the answers, don't you Pat?

PAT I've got a helluva lot on you.

MITCHELL I could say the same.

PAT What brings you here to the Pueblo?

MITCHELL There seems to be a demand for my services here in Hollywood. Perhaps the boys upstairs are starting to realize great screenwriters don't grow on orange trees.

PAT I thought the great playwright would never leave New York.

MITCHELL The great playwright needed a change of scenery.

PAT Well, what sort of purchase do you have in mind? A large bottle of French perfume or a small vial of toilet water?

MITCHELL Oh, something small. The lady is just a passing fancy. And she's passing quicker every second.

PAT Oh, so you think we're ready for a second act, Mitch?

MITCHELL I think we've had a long enough intermission, yes.

PAT I nearly didn't survive the first act curtain.

MITCHELL It wasn't all drama. We had fun. Those were exciting days for us in New York. Me writing sketches for the Follies and you wringing every laugh out of them. You were great. Great at everything. I'm going to be in town for awhile. Shall we take advantage of the situation?

PAT Taking advantage are good words to describe an affair with you. No, Mitchell, edit me out of any of your second act ideas.

MITCHELL Oh, that's right. You're a great believer in censorship. You'll come around, Pat. Why fight it. You know you'll enjoy it. You always do.

Salesgirl enters SR door holding a foolish hat with pompoms jutting into the air.

SALESGIRL Sir, is there anything I can help you with?

MITCHELL No, I don't think so. I'll wait on that. Goodbye, Pat. (*He exits SL door.*)

SALESGIRL Miss Pilford, I thought this little chapeau might intrigue you.

PAT Oh, I don't know dear. It's a bit too "Mary Pickford on a bender."

Mary enters SR through curtains carrying garments and boxes.

MARY This is terrible, Pat. Here we are giving you a fashion makeover, and I go on a spending spree. (*She notices the hat in the salegirl's hand.*) Ah, that hat. It's so delectable. How much? Don't even tell me. Pat, this is your day.

PAT We should just forget it I'm never going to be chic. It's like putting a Dior on Plymouth Rock.

SALESGIRL (*Laughing.*) Oh, Miss Pilford. Miss Dale, shall I charge these to your account and have them delivered? (*Salesgirl takes packages and garments from Mary.*)

MARY That would be lovely. Thank you.

SALESGIRL (*Sighs, looking at hat.*) And I suppose this poor little orphan goes back to Millinery. (*Laughs. She exits SL door.*)

MARY After this I thought we'd look at slacks.

PAT No. We're going to talk. What's wrong, Mary?

MARY Nothing's wrong.

PAT Quit stalling. I'll get it out of you.

MARY Am I so transparent?

PAT Like a silk stocking without a run. It's Frank, isn't it?

MARY Yes, it's Frank. Pat, I really don't want to discuss it and certainly not here in Bullocks.

PAT Mary, this is Pat, you know Pat, P-A-T, zany, warm hearted, bad dye job, your best friend.

MARY I think Frank may be seeing another woman.

PAT Anyone we know?

MARY Oh yes. Marta Towers.

PAT (*Speechless.*) Don't even ... Did you catch them in flagrante delicto?

MARY What?

PAT Did you catch them in the act? The Soviet version of the old ooh la la.

MARY No, nothing like that. It's only a suspicion, mind you. But I'm scared, Pat. Frank's growing away from me. It's as if I hardly know him anymore.

PAT What's your evidence?

MARY Marta's convinced him to join her method acting class.

PAT Mary, if you let him walk through those doors, you'll never see him again.

MARY What can I do?

PAT You're so helpless. How did you become a star? You must have some steel in your girdle.

MARY He's moved out of the house. I can't very well throw myself in front of his car.

PAT Then you'll have to follow him there.

MARY I couldn't. He'd be furious.

PAT Better angry now then divorced later. Don't you see, Mary, it's not Marta that he loves, it's what she stands for, high art and all that crap. If it was sex he was after, he'd be hottailing it with some carhop with big bazooms, not some eggheaded pinko. Face it girl, your enemy isn't pussy, it's Stanislavsky! Want me to play sidekick?

MARY No, I must do this alone. If only I could be sure this was the right thing to do.

PAT Trust Pat. How many times must I tell people. Ideas are dangerous. Squash 'em!

MARY Pat, you're so vehement.

PAT Maybe it's just that . . . well I knew a woman once who loved a man, desperately. He too became infatuated with an idea and the little fool did nothing and lost him. Well enough of that malarkey. Hey, what do you say we look at them hats and get you a spiffy one for your entree into the academy of dramatic art.

MARY Well perhaps there is method in your madness. (*She laughs.*)

PAT Shakespeare, ain't it? And who says we ain't highbrow.

They link arms and exit through SL door.

BLACKOUT

ACT ONE

SCENE 5

That night. The administrative office of the Yetta Felson Acting School. BARKER, *a heavyset man with a cigar is seated behind the desk, SR.* R.G. BENSON, *an elegant director is seated in a swivel armchair smoking a pipe. Mitchell Drake, standing at the DS side of the desk is lighting his cigarette, and Barker's cigar as the lights come up. Malcolm is pacing.*

BARKER Don't be a nervous Nellie, Malcolm.

MALCOLM Mr. Barker, I wish you wouldn't speak to me like that.

BARKER You're too sensitive. Sit down. I looked in on Yetta's class. Taggart's buying the whole megillah.

MITCHELL Taggart's hooked on the method like a rug.

BARKER (*Snickering.*) Actors and their craft.

R.G. La Felson most certainly has a messianic quality.

BARKER I love the way this guy talks. Class all the way. Scene Study should be over any minute. Marta will bring Taggart to the office and before you can say "Charlie Chaplin," he'll be signed, sealed and delivered.

MALCOLM You will be gentle with him? He's a very vulnerable kind of guy.

BARKER What do you take me for, a bully? You hurt my feelings, Malcolm. I have a great respect for artists. What other organization can boast a famous New York playwright such as Mitchell Drake and an oscar-winning film director like the great R.G. Benson.

R.G. You're most flattering, Mr. Barker.

BARKER R.G., we would be greatly honored to display your oscar here at the Felson school.

R.G. I wish I could comply but my aged mother has it prominently displayed in her den in Black Hills, South Dakota and I couldn't possibly . . .

BARKER Are you refusing me?

R.G. I'm merely saying that . . .

MITCHELL (*Crudely.*) Get this straight, Benson. We don't take too kindly being turned down by some Hollywood hack who can't keep his pecker out of every female child star on the lot.

R.G. I would be delighted to donate my oscar.

BARKER Donation accepted.

MARTA (*Offstage.*) This way.

BARKER Box up! Here they come.

Frank and Marta enter SL door. Marta is wearing a black strapless cocktail dress.

BARKER Well, well, well Mr. Taggart. A great pleasure. I've so admired your work. It's almost like magic the way you can turn the most trivial formula picture into a penetrating character study. I'm Bertram Barker, the President of the Yetta Felson School.

FRANK You're more than kind, Mr. Barker. Malcolm?

MALCOLM I work part-time in the office. I hope you don't mind that I'm moonlighting.

FRANK Of course not. I just sat in on the scene study class. Yetta Felson is a genius. Such insight. I'd love to meet her.

BARKER In due time, my boy, in due time.

FRANK (*Passionately.*) I can't wait to roll up my sleeves and get to work. I have so many demons needing to be released.

BARKER Well, young man, just sign here on the dotted line and you can start releasin' them demons tomorrow night. (*He hands Frank a sheath of papers.*)

FRANK A thick contract. I suppose I should take it home and read it.

MITCHELL It's a standard acting school contract.

MARTA Darling, don't waste your time reading the fine print.

R.G. Most definitely migraine inducing.

MALCOLM There's no harm in him taking it home overnight.

MITCHELL Malcolm, stick to filing and light typing. Taggart, trust me, it's strictly standard stuff.

FRANK Hell, why not. Where do I sign?

BARKER At the bottom of the page here. All four copies. You'll be getting your card in three weeks.

As Frank signs the contracts, Barker gives a cynical wink to Mitchell.

BARKER Shall we have a drink toasting our new member?

Malcolm passes out shot glasses.

FRANK Thank you sir, but I think I'll pass.

BARKER Drink. Drink. Have a snort. It's a crime to pass up good Russian vodka. I knew from the first second I saw him up on the screen he was one of us.

MITCHELL We're in the presence of a true artist.

Frank takes a shot, his hand betraying an alcoholic's tremor.

BARKER That'a boy.

MITCHELL Congratulations.

All drink.

MARTA (*On upper level.*) Welcome aboard, darling.

BARKER Drake, you're the genius writer. Tell Frank more about our operations . . . I mean our artistic manifesto.

MITCHELL To us, acting is more than just making faces. It's a way of looking at life. That's why we're making every effort to make message films that expose society's corruption. The kind of performance we develop here at the studio can be painful but as Spinoza says "pain and pleasure are merely transitions to a greater state of perfection." It's a revolutionary approach.

FRANK (*In rapture.*) Yes, yes, revolutionary.

BARKER First we take over Hollywood and then the nation. Nostrovya!

ALL (*Except Frank.*) Nostrovya!

MALCOLM (*Enthusiastically.*) After the revolution, sex roles will be undefined. We'll accept that we're all part male and female and that human nature is meant to be bi-sexual.

BARKER Oh ho ho, wait just a minute. Don't get carried away, son. There ain't no place in the revolution for that kind of thinking.

MALCOLM What do you mean? You told me when I joined the party, that you were all for sexual freedom.

BARKER No siree, you weren't listening. I never said that. I meant free love between men and women.

MALCOLM But I thought Marxism meant that all workers were one, all equal.

BARKER That's right, kid. All equal and all normal. In the American communist society, all bedrooms will be monitored. Those who don't conform will be dragged into the light.

MALCOLM I'm finally coming to my senses. What could I have been thinking of? You're not my friends. You people are dangerous.

MARTA You're the one who's dangerous. You'd destroy the revolution with your decadence.

MITCHELL Deviationist!

R.G. Trotskyite!

FRANK Hey, wait just a minute. Malcolm was just saying . . .

MARTA Shut up! Wrong thinkers must be weeded out and destroyed.

R.G. There can be only one voice and that belongs to the state. Hail Big Brother!

ALL Hail Big Brother and Mother Russia!

MALCOLM This has been most enlightening. I think it's time for me to leave. I'll have you know I'm ripping up my membership card.

MITCHELL You insignificant worm. You think you can fight the party? Not a chance. We'll bury you.

R.G. What do you suppose you'll do for a job?

MALCOLM I have a job with Frank Taggart.

BARKER I happen to know your employer and you've just been fired.

FRANK Hey, I never said . . .

BARKER Shut up! (*To Malcolm.*) Kid, you'll never work in this town again.

MALCOLM Then I'll move to another city. I'm competent. I've got skills. There's always a position for a good hairdresser.

MARTA You fool. After we start our whispering campaign, no first rate salon would ever hire you. Eventually they'll revoke your operator's license. Perhaps you could get a job as a hairburner in some flea-bitten perm parlor off the highway but even there, after a few weeks, your employer will receive a copy of your membership card. Then see how fast they'll snatch away your perm rods.

R.G. I'm afraid there's no place you can hide. No place to run.

MALCOLM I'd rather take that chance. Dear Lord in heaven, forgive me for losing my faith.

MITCHELL Can it with that Bible junk!

MALCOLM Mother Mary, full of grace, how wrong I was to denounce my country, sweet land of liberty, of thee I sing . . .

MARTA (*Hands over her ears.*) Shut up! Shut up! Shut up!

MALCOLM God save us all. (*He runs out. Exit SL door.*)

BARKER Benson, follow him. The little twirp wouldn't dare sing to the FBI with all the dirt we've got on him. Still, I want you to monitor his every move. Marts, start the whispering campaign.

MARTA (*Whispering.*) Yes sir.

R.G. I'll be on him like a hound dog after a fox.

BARKER Yeah, yeah, yeah, just beat it.

R.G. Exits SL door.

FRANK It's late. I should be going.

MITCHELL You're not getting cold feet, are you?

FRANK To be honest, I am. I signed up for a class in Stanislavsky's method, not a political organization.

BARKER Oh you didn't, huh. (*Picks up contract.*) You should have read the fine print. "I Frank Taggart, am hereby a loyal sworn member of the Communist party and dedicate my life to the downfall and destruction of the American way of life."

FRANK You fat tub of lard, you conned me.

He springs at Barker, Mitchell belts him in the stomach. Frank doubles over and sinks back into the chair.

MITCHELL Should we have the goon squad toss him into the Pacific?

BARKER No. I think Mr. Taggart has gotten that little demon out of his system. Eh Nisowitz?

FRANK How did you know that was my name?

MARTA The party knows everything about you. We've got a dossier on Moishe Nisowitz three inches thick.

MITCHELL We know where you came from and why you had to leave. I don't think the fan magazines would like to hear how the young Moishe Nisowitz killed his childhood buddy.

FRANK It was an accident. Izzie and I were kayaking in the East River. We were horseplaying as teenagers do and he hit himself over the head with an oar and fell into the river. It was an accident.

MITCHELL The police would be very interested in hearing your side of the story since you ran away like a coward.

MARTA Darling, it doesn't look good. My prediction is definitely twenty years to life.

FRANK The studio would bail me out. They've got the top lawyers in . . .

BARKER Forget it, Nisowitz, you're in a bind. Swear your loyalty to the party. Swear it!

MITCHELL Swear it!

MARTA Swear it!

FRANK (*Grabbing his head with both hands in torment.*) I can't take anymore. Why are you browbeating me?

MITCHELL (*Scientifically.*) He's cracking.

BARKER We're your friends, Frankie. Not the government, not the studio. Just place your right hand on this here copy of Karl Marx and say "I swear loyalty to the Communist party."

From behind the file cabinet, we see Mary hiding. First we see her hat, then her eyes. She is wearing the silly hat the salesgirl carried in at Bullocks.

MITCHELL We don't have all night, Nisowitz.

FRANK (*Painfully.*) I swear . . . I swear loyalty to the Communist party.

Mary's eyes nearly pop out.

BARKER Let's get down to business. We must begin to implement our three step plan to take over the motion picture industry. Number one: All film scripts must promote the communist way of life. I see these films shot in a nice black and white. Number two: the termination of personal ambition. All starlets will be rounded up and shipped off to re-education camps. Number three and most important: the end of the star system. No person can be placed above the proletariat. All films will be ensemble productions with no star billing, no glamour wardrobe and definitely no special lighting or filters. (*Mary's eyes register total contempt.*) Any star who defies the system will be eliminated. (*Mary gasps.*) What was that?

MARTA It must be someone upstairs in the sense memory class.

BARKER Taggart, this is where you come in. The symbol of capitalist Hollywood is the Arthur Freed musical unit over at Metro. It must be destroyed.

FRANK But what can I do?

MITCHELL Your wife is shooting a musical about Lady Godiva. We want you to spy on her. Use her to get all the dirt on the Freed unit, who's boffing who, which men are fairies, who's on drugs.

BARKER We need you to get the dirt that women only discuss in the privacy of their homes.

MARTA And you'll get plenty from that loudmouthed Pilford dame. She's been flapping her trap about me since I got off the train at Union Station.

Mary in disgust, gasps and forgets to duck down. Mitchell sees her.

MITCHELL Hey look!

BARKER You get out here.

FRANK Mary, what are you doing here?

MARY I had to see for myself if my suspicions were true. This is far worse than I ever imagined.

MARTA So the good little wife finally wakes up.

FRANK Can it, Marta.

MARTA I'm not afraid of her.

MARY Marta, I feel very sorry for you.

MARTA Sorry for me?

MARY Because in your quest for love, you've allowed yourself to be manipulated into a world of corruption. Now that corruption is showing in your face and that's the kind of ugliness even the House of Westmore can't repair.

MARTA She can't talk to me that way. Mr. Barker, do something.

MARY (*To Frank.*) Don't you see darling, that everything they're feeding you is a lie. All of these people are embittered failures who couldn't make it within the system so now they seek to destroy it. Look at Marta, spinning her wheels in B-movies. She didn't have what it takes to be a true star, beauty, glamour, drive. There always have been stars and there always will be. It's the reason one kitten stands out in a litter. It's part of the great cosmos around us. Politics come and go but the star system is eternal.

MARTA (*Viciously.*) It's a lie! A lie! You're not an actress. There's no interior life behind you're eyes. You have a dead face. Dead! Blank! Dead!

MARY Come to your senses, darling. It's wrong. It's all wrong. Jamison has the car waiting for us around the block. Take me home, darling.

Frank moves towards her.

BARKER Trailing after the little woman. You're weak, Taggart, you're weak.

FRANK But she's my wife.

BARKER No wonder your audience laughs at your love scenes. Pathetic.

MITCHELL (*With great vulgarity.*) Be a man. Grow some hair on your balls.

MARTA Remember Izzie in the East River.

FRANK (*Tortured, makes up his mind.*) Go home, Mary.

MARY Frank!

FRANK I told you to go home. This is where I belong.

MARY I don't believe you. You've been brainwashed.

MITCHELL You heard what the man said. Get lost.

FRANK Yeah, beat it. Get out of here. If you thought you could lead me around on a leash, you were very much mistaken. I'm not one of your flunkies who jump at your every command.

MARY Darling, what are you saying?

FRANK I'm saying we're through. I'm not coming home again.

MARY Say it so I'll believe it.

FRANK Go home!

MARY I don't believe you.

FRANK Go home!

MARY It's the party speaking. I want to hear from your own lips that you want me to leave.

FRANK (*As loud as he can shout.*) GO HOME!!!!

MARY (*Quietly.*) Very well, I'll leave. Good luck Frank. You'll need it.

MARTA Dead Face!

(*Mary starts to exit but decides to prove to Marta that she doesn't have a dead face. She proceeds to look wistfully, then hurt, then vengeful, then tormented. She sneers, curls her lip and generally gives Marta every look that could kill. When she finishes this display of facial pyrotechnics, she matter-of-factly says:*)

MARY Good night. (*Exits SR.*)

BARKER She knows too much. Something must be done.

FRANK What are you saying?

MITCHELL Something must be done about Mary Dale.

BARKER (*To Frank.*) And you're going to do it.

FRANK (*Panicked.*) No! No! You can't ask me to do that. Please!

MARTA Frank you wouldn't want us to tell the FBI that we've found Moishe Nisowitz. They're very anxious to know more about that nasty little crime which may or may not have been a murder. Either angle won't look good on your resume.

MITCHELL Here's the situation, Taggart. Mary's life and we cover it up most efficiently or your previous crime is revealed and you're sent up the river on first degree murder. It's your choice.

BARKER Quite a pickle you're in, Taggart. Quite a pickle.

FRANK Please. There must be another way. Please. Please.

The three communists close in on the pleading Frank.

BLACKOUT

END OF ACT I

ACT TWO

Scene 1

The next morning at the studio. The set of "Godiva Was a Lady."

R.G. Benson enters SR. Stagehands set up R.G.'s directing chair and a klieg light. RUDY, *the assistant director, enters with a clapboard. Mary enters dressed as a musical comedy Lady Godiva, with a long switch of hair attached to her short 1950s coiffure.*

R.G. Mary, are you ready?

MARY Yes, darling.

R.G. Quiet please. We're ready to shoot. (*BELL rings.*) Lights! Camera! Rudy, slate it.

RUDY (*Snapping the clapboard.*) "Godiva Was a Lady" Scene 23. Take 1.

R.G. Roll playback

VOICEOVER Rolling tape.

Music starts.

R.G. Action!

(*MARY begins lipsynching to playback. The song is a cheerful upbeat tune suitable for a musical about Lady Godiva. Midway through the number, she falters.*)

R.G. Are you all right?

MARY I'm sorry. I got lost.

R.G. Darling, you must sit down for a spell.

MARY But R.G. I know time is money.

R.G. Not on a R.G. Benson picture. (*To the crew.*) Everyone, break for ten!

MARY You're awfully kind. I can see why every actress in town longs to work for you. (*She sits in the director's chair.*)

R.G. I must tell you, dear, I am concerned. There's something troubling you. I can see it in the dailies when I watch your closeups. Trouble at home?

MARY Don't you read the fan magazines? My life is perfect. The perfect career, the perfect house, the perfect marriage . . . (*She breaks down.*) Oh R.G., it's far from perfect. I can't lie to you. Your eyes are too honest.

R.G. Go on, dear, tell me everything.

MARY I'm afraid I can't. It's too awful. Frankly R.G., I don't know how I can go on.

R.G. I have faith in you, Mary. You're from good strong stock, with all the right values. You'll endure and survive.

MARY Strange you should say that. I was brought up on the simple values taught to me by my grandmother who was taught by her grandmother that life could be beautiful. One married, had children, worked hard and made a profit. Now I find my every belief shattered and exposed to ridicule.

R.G. Mary, you're tired. You've shot five pictures back to back.

MARY Oh, I am tired. I can't sleep. I lie in bed wondering where I went wrong. I feel so helpless. So small.

R.G. Mary, I think I can help you. (*Reaches in his pocket and takes out a vial of pills.*) I'm going to give you these sleeping pills. Take one a night and you will find your restful sleep.

MARY All in a little pill.

R.G. Promise me you won't be foolish and take too many.

MARY I promise, Dr. Benson.

R.G. I have one other prescription. Lose yourself in work. Whatever your private hell is, use it in this role. Expose yourself. And be the great actress we know you can be.

MARY The great actress. I wonder.

R.G. Mary, don't do this to yourself.

MARY Let's be honest, R.G., we both know I'm not really an actress. I'm a glamorous personality. I've never appeared in a real role, in a real play. You can't call what I do, acting.

R.G. Mary Dale, you stop this at once! Do you hear me? If you want to be a real actress, then act! I've got a script that would be perfect for you. It's a serious drama that sends home a powerful message, it's a blistering indictment, never shirking from it's ugly truths.

MARY (*Vulnerably.*) You'd really want me?

R.G. What a challenge to reveal to the public a new Mary Dale, devoid of make-up.

Mary's eyes pop open wide with alarm and suspicion.

R.G. Now mind you, it's not a star vehicle. It's an ensemble piece. You wouldn't be over the title. It'll be shot in black and white on a very low budget. No glamorous wardrobe or flattering lighting, or filters.

Mary listens to him with mounting horror. He's spouting the radical plans she overheard at the communist cell.

R.G. I can see it intrigues you.

MARY Indeed. R.G., I've always meant to ask you, what is that marvelous cologne you wear? I know I've smelled it somewhere else.

R.G. Oh, it was given to me as a gift a long time ago. You can't even get it in this country. It's called "Moscow Breeze."

MARY I believe I met a girl who wears the perfume.

R.G. You must mean Marta Towers. A lovely girl. Really unfair, the scandalous rumors that follow . . .

R.G. continues to talk but his dialogue is drowned out by cacophonous music and Mary's thoughts.

MARY (*Voiceover.*) He's in on it. Part of the conspiracy. A communist. Unspeakable. Unspeakable.

The music fades out. Mary's face instantly switches from hysteria to a calm facade.

R.G. Feeling any better, Mary?

MARY Oh yes. Everything is much clearer now. I think I'm ready to resume the number.

R.G. Good girl. Shall we begin our new realism now and have the cameraman remove some of those filters?

MARY (*Archly.*) Let's not be hasty.

R.G. (*Laughs.*) You're quite a gal, Mary. Quite a gal. (*He exits.*)

Mary returns to the set, the playback begins again and she stares at R.G., his back to her, with great suspicion.

END OF SCENE 1

ACT TWO

Scene 2

The Radio Station. Pat Pilford is standing before the mike.

PAT Hey, has Mary Dale arrived yet? Hello? Can anybody hear me? My guest today, Mary Dale . . . Forget it.

TECHNICIAN (*Voiceover.*) Miss Pilford. Could you give us something for a sound check?

PAT C*oi*tenly.

Mitchell Drake enters.

PAT One, two, three, four. (*She sings to the tune of "Over the Rainbow."*) Somewhere over my boobies, Bluebirds crapped. (*In a stuffy British accent.*) Thank you, Lord and Lady Mumsford. (*As herself.*) That's it, kids. Anymore of Aunt Patty's ditties you pay for.

MITCHELL (*Applauds her.*) The same old Pat. The funniest gal in the world. You really ought to visit my psychiatrist-friend, Dr. Hans Mueller. His theory "Dirty jokes as a sexual deterrent" fits you like Dotty Lamour's sarong.

PAT I'd like to know how you got in here.

MITCHELL Doors have a way of opening for me.

PAT If you're here for the broadcast, we won't be starting for several minutes.

MITCHELL You can knock off the great lady schtick. I told you I'd be seeing you.

PAT You really are the most contemptible . . .

MITCHELL I said knock it off.

PAT And now?

MITCHELL That's better. (*Picks up her hand.*) Yes, you had beautiful hands. I'd forgotten that. (*Kisses her fingers.*)

PAT (*Afraid she'll give in.*) Please, Mitch, please don't do that.

MITCHELL Why? Because you'll forget you're the slapstick Statue of Liberty. You miss me, don't you?

PAT I miss the fellow who wasn't so twisted with hate.

MITCHELL Yes, I hate. I hate those who would deny me my right to build a better world.

PAT And I hate those that seek to destroy everything I hold sacred. But you don't frighten me, Mitch. Your automatons can infiltrate all of our industries but the American people will never capitulate their freedoms.

MITCHELL You really believe this crap you dish out on the radio every week.

PAT Of course I do.

MITCHELL That's too bad because you're about to switch sides.

PAT You're out of your mind.

MITCHELL No, but very lucky. I have in my possession some entertaining photographs taken fifteen years ago of a nubile Pat Pilford, America's own, performing some of the most disgusting, degrading sexual acts imaginable.

PAT Acts you made me do.

MITCHELL And you loved every minute of it.

PAT What are you planning to do with those photos?

MITCHELL I could be persuaded to lock them away forever. If and I say *if,* you cooperate with the party.

PAT You really are out of your mind. Besides no publication would ever print such filth.

MITCHELL We wouldn't need to publish them. They'd be distributed by our network of followers to every town and city in the old U.S. of A. And with that memorable mug of yours, there would be no doubt as to the frisky model's identity.

Pat breaks down in tears.

MITCHELL I hate seeing you cry, Pat. (*He tries to hand her his handkerchief, she flinches.*) You had to be stopped.

PAT (*With rising egomania.*) I suppose this order came from party headquarters in Moscow.

MITCHELL Don't flatter yourself. I have a creative mind. I have after all, won a Pulitzer prize. I can certainly figure out how to shut up one gabby comedienne.

PAT All right. You've silenced my voice. Now get out of here.

MITCHELL We're not quite finished yet. You're going to fire your writing staff.

PAT But why? They're the best gagmen in the business.

MITCHELL You're all ready going to be gagged, baby. The party has new writers for you and will deliver you a polished script every week, starting with this one. (*He hands her a script.*)

PAT I'd never read this garbage. You won't make me a commie tool.

MITCHELL Remember the night you said "cheeze."

PAT I'm a famous conservative. The public will never believe I'd turn around so completely.

MITCHELL It'll be subtle at first. A gradual coming to your senses. You better go over your lines. We want you to be convincing. Oh, look, you've got a nice big studio audience coming in. Pat, you always were a sell out. See ya, kid.

As Mitchell exits, Mary enters carrying her script.

MITCHELL Hello Mary.

MARY Mr. Drake, I have nothing to say to you.

MITCHELL If only Gogol could have written about you. So lovely and so absurd.

MARY (*Smugly.*) Who's this Mr. Gogol? A fellow traveler?

She walks past him to Pat. Mitchell shakes his head in disbelief and exits.

MARY Pat darling. I'm sorry I'm late. What was Mitchell Drake doing here?

PAT Was that Mitchell Drake? I've never met him.

MARY What's wrong, Pat. You're as white as this paper.

PAT I always get the willies. We should be on the air any minute.

MARY Pat, you won't believe what I've been through. What I've seen, what I've heard.

PAT Shhhhh, we can't talk now.

MARY I know, we can't . . . it's just that . . . Pat, I'm in the middle of a communist conspiracy. Frank, Marta, R.G. Benson, Mitchell Drake. I need your help. You're so strong. Tell me what to do.

PAT (*Urgently.*) Do nothing.

MARY What?

PAT Do nothing. You don't know these people. How far they'll go.

MARY That's so unlike you.

PAT You wanted my advice. Well, that's it. Whatever happens, keep silent.

DIRECTOR (*Voiceover.*) Ladies, we'll be starting in thirty seconds.

MARY Pat, something's bothering you. What is it?

PAT I told you nothing's wrong.

MARY You're trembling.

PAT (*Sharply.*) Mary, I'm about to do a show. Be a professional and stop wasting my time with your silly paranoia.

DIRECTOR (*Voiceover.*) Fifteen seconds to air.

PAT Oh Mary, the script has been rewritten somewhat. Just a few of my lines. Nothing major. It doesn't affect you.

DIRECTOR (*Voiceover.*) Five, four, three, two.

PAT Here we go.

ANNOUNCER (*Voiceover.*) The Veedol Motor Oil Program with Pat Pilford. (*Applause/Music.*) Makers of Veedol Motor Oil, found wherever fine cars travel, present Miss Show Business, Pat Pilford. With Emmaline Crane, Jimmy Stall and special guest stars Mary Dale, Olson and Johnson, Helen Traubel, the Ames Brothers, Yours truly Bill Simmons and Victor Arnold and his Chiffon Orchestra. And now your fabulous femm-cee, Pat Pilford.

PAT (*Reading from the new script.*) Welcome comrades.

Mary is startled but tries to ignore it.

PAT For the sake of variety, I'd like to skip my usual opening and bring out my special guest, lovely film star, Mary Dale. Besides, I know I've been boring you to tears these past months with my idiotic red baiting. I don't know a fool thing about politics. Please ignore anything I may have said. Believe me, I was wrong, wrong, wrong! Mary, come on out here Mary. Mary Dale. (*Applause.*) How are ya, darlin'?

MARY (*Reading from her script.*) Marvelous. I'm so glad we could finally get together on your show. Pat, you look fantastic, but if you get any blonder, the studio won't need light bulbs.

PAT (*Reading from the new script.*) Interesting that you should mention that, dear. I've decided today to let my hair go back to it's natural mousey brown color. I'm beginning to realize that hair dye and make-up are simply capitalist tools that blind women to ideological realities.

MARY (*Reading her script, very perplexed.*) Thank you Pat. I loved making that picture. When are we going to do one together? I'm dying to do a wild slapstick comedy but it will be in my contract that I throw the pies.

PAT That would be such a waste of good food. Food that could be divided equally among the working class. The more I think about it, darling, bakers should unite and deny the rich their decadent cakes and cookies.

MARY (*Realizing that none of her lines make sense in this context.*) I love this dress too. It's a Don Loper original.

PAT Mary, if you don't mind, I'd like to take this moment to tell my listeners what exactly is going on in this country. My dear comrades, we are in the grip of a . . .

Mary looks at Pat aghast as Pat reads her communist propaganda. Threatening music overpowers Pat so we can no longer hear her. Over the music, Mary's thoughts are heard.

MARY (*Voiceover.*) This can't be real. Not Pat. She couldn't be one of them. All of them pinkos, all of them red.

The music fades out.

PAT My, it feels good getting that off my chest. Now Mary, tell us about . . .

Mary starts to move away from the mike.

PAT Mary, come a little closer, dear. We're losing you.

MARY (*Distraught.*) I'm sorry. I forgot something . . . I . . . I . . . I've got to run. (*Mary runs out of the studio.*)

PAT Mary!

END OF SCENE

ACT TWO

Scene 3

The beach house. A short time later.

Frank is waiting for her. He's reading a book. A small gift box is on the coffee table next to him.

Mary enters SR door, holding her purse.

MARY Frank, you're home.

FRANK (*Puts the book on the coffee table open.*) I've been here for hours, waiting, hoping you'd come back soon.

MARY (*Puts her purse down on the SR level.*) You look tired.

FRANK Please take me back, Mary. I'm so miserable. How could I have been such a fool to think what they had to offer was real. It was all an illusion.

MARY Marta Towers is hardly an illusion.

FRANK I hate her. I wish she were dead. Believe me, Mary, I was never unfaithful. I couldn't go through with it. I love you so.

MARY (*Very confused.*) Frank, I'd like to believe that. (*Giving in.*) Oh darling, come here. (*They embrace.*) How can two people who love each other as we do be so silly.

FRANK Is it possible for you to forgive me? They don't come lower than me.

MARY (*Emotionally.*) Of course I forgive you. You're my husband. I made a vow.

FRANK (*Passionately.*) It's this town. Come away with me, Mary. New York, London, anywhere.

MARY I will darling. Anywhere. My poor lost boy.

FRANK It's going to be different. I'm going to change. I will. Starting tonight.

MARY Tonight?

FRANK Do you smell something cooking?

MARY Yes.

FRANK It's called dinner. And I'm cooking it myself. I gave Selina and all the servants the night off. Wanted you all to myself. I have so much to make up to you.

MARY (*Playfully.*) You were awfully confident that I'd forgive you.

FRANK I wasn't confident. I got on my knees and prayed.

MARY Did you, Frank? And to what God?

FRANK Your Lord, Mary. Now, madame, if you'll excuse me, I must return to the kitchen to check up on my sauce reductions. (*He clicks his heels like a butler.*)

MARY (*Laughing.*) Oh my. Taggart, you may go.

FRANK Yes, mum. (*He exits SL door.*)

MARY (*Lighting up a cigarette.*) They may all be communists but not my husband. Not my Frank. (*Calling to the kitchen.*) Will we be eating soon, darling?

FRANK I can't hear you, dear.

MARY (*Calling offstage.*) How soon will we be eating? Do I have time to call my aunt in Indiana?

FRANK (*Offstage.*) Darling, I'm sorry I can't understand you. I'll be right out.

MARY (*Laughs, sits in the chair SR and picks up phone on the SR level to dial.*) Hello . . . Hello . . .That's odd.

FRANK (*Enters SL door.*) Darling, what is it you asked me?

MARY The telephone's dead. I can't even get an operator.

FRANK Give it to me. (*He takes the phone.*) You're right. Dead as my last picture. I'll go next door and report it on the Stewart's line.

MARY No, no, no. You're busy cooking. I suppose for ten hours we could do without the blasted telephone. It'll be a pleasure.

FRANK You're so pretty. (*He kisses her forehead. Exits SL door.*)

MARY This coffee table is a mess. (*She crosses to coffee table and picks up book.*) "Cousin Bette" by Balzac. Oh my. (*She opens it where Frank left the marker.*) Shame on him. Scribbling in the margin. ". . . poisoned by a prick of a needle in the clasp of her necklace." How ghastly. (*She closes book and puts it down on the coffee table.*) Give me Fanny Hearst any day. (*She picks up jewelry box from coffee table.*) What's this? (*She opens box.*) Oh, how lovely. (*She takes necklace out of box, crosses right and holds necklace up. Her face is away from the audience. Sound cue. She turns towards the audience, her face a mask of sudden fear and terror.*)

FRANK (*Enters SL door.*) Oh, you found it. I wanted to surprise you with it after dinner. They're exquisite, aren't they?

MARY (*Trying to compose herself.*) Yes.

FRANK They'll be even more perfect once they're around your neck. (*He tries to stroke her neck, she moves away.*) You pulled away.

MARY Did I?

FRANK I think we should put these on you now. Get a special preview.

MARY No, I don't think so.

FRANK Why don't you want to put them on, Mary? Pearls are your favorite.

MARY Is there a reason why I shouldn't put them on?

FRANK None in the world. They were specially designed for you.

MARY That's what I thought.

FRANK I can put them on for you. It's a simple clasp. (*He moves closer to her.*) Why are you moving away, Mary?

MARY Darling I really don't want to put them on. Please dear. Put them down.

FRANK (*With a quiet urgency.*) I can't Mary. I have to do this. I don't want to. They've made me. They're bigger than we are. We can't fight 'em. This is the way it has to end. Please, darling, don't fight me.

MARY Darling, there must be another way. You love me. You must have loved me once. Please, Frank, it's me, Mary. Frank! Don't. Don't.

Frank grabs her. She tries to fight him off. She bites his hand but he continues to try to put the necklace around her neck. In their struggle, he drops the necklace and finally grabs her around the throat and starts to strangle her. When she appears to be on the brink of death, Frank suddenly wakes up and realizes he's about to murder his beloved wife. He breaks away in horror.

FRANK What am I doing? What have I become?

Frank staggers and runs out. He exits SR door. Mary is panting for breath. The cacophonous music starts again and Mary in her hysteria hears threatening voices.)

MARY (*Voiceover.*) Frank, what's happened to us?

FRANK (*Voiceover.*) We can't fight 'em. This is the way it has to end.

PAT (*Voiceover.*) Whatever happens, keep silent.

MARTA (*Voiceover.*) So the good little wife finally wakes up.

BARKER (*Voiceover.*) Stars who defy the system will be eliminated.

MARY Stop! Stop!

R.G. (*Voiceover.*) It's called "Moscow Breeze."

FRANK (*Voiceover.*) We can't fight 'em. (*ECHOES over and over.*)

MITCHELL (*Voiceover.*) Grow some hair on your balls!

PAT (*Voiceover.*) Keep silent! (*ECHOES over and over.*)

MARY (*Collapses on the steps. Hysterical.*) Trapped. Desperate. In a trap. No exit . . . No exit.

Mary runs over to find her purse. She rummages through it until she finds the vial of pills that R.G. gave her at the studio. She empties the pills into her hand and tosses them into her mouth. She then grabs the bottle of whiskey off the bar tray and chases down the pills with liquor. She stumbles and staggers to center stage, the pills kicking in. The music underscoring her hysteria reaches a pitch of dissonance and the lighting becomes distorted and full of swirling shapes. At last she collapses to the ground unconscious. The music turns dreamlike and the lighting covers everything with a golden hue. Two young pages in medieval garb enter with gold banners. They place the banners above the two doorways SR and SL and exit. Marta enters SR dressed in medieval costume. In Mary's dream, she is LADY PRUDWEN, *lady-in-waiting to Lady Godiva. She enters carrying a voluminous gold robe and cone-like medieval headdress. Mary rises in her dream confounded by the spectacle before her.*)

LADY PRUDWEN (*Dressing Mary in the gold robe and headdress.*) Milady Godiva, we must make haste and dress you in your ceremonial robes. The very same robes you wore to last years Academy Awards governors ball.

MARY But I'm not Lady Godiva!

LADY PRUDWEN Shhh, Milady.

PAGES *cross DS steps and strike props, both side units, and flip in SR chair. Settee remains.*

Enter SL: ARNOLPH (*Mitchell*), BALDRIC (*Barker*), *&*
LEOFRIC (*Frank*) *all in medieval costume.*

ARNOLPH The king must die! He shall ride to the cathedral to hear his Sunday mass and there upon the Cathedral steps, he shall meet his assassin's sword.

BALDRIC And by the following morn you, Leofric, will be crowned King of all England.

LEOFRIC (*Panicked.*) But good sirs, the people do love King Edward. They will not be pleased to see him replaced.

BALDRIC (*Sneering.*) The people! What do the people know?

ARNOLPH The peasants are cowlike in their ignorance. They shall be taxed heavily and their gold will fill our coffers.

LEOFRIC (*To the men.*) I cannot in good faith be a part of this treason.

ARNOLPH Be a man. Grow some hair on thy fertile orbs.

MARY (*Joining the scene.*) Frank, don't listen to them!

LEOFRIC I can't fight 'em, Godiva. I can't fight 'em.

MARY I'm not Lady Godiva. That's a role that I play. I'm Mary Dale Taggart. No, that's not me. I'm Mary Dale. No, that's my stage name. I'm Mary Louise Hofstetter.

PRUDWEN She babbles. Leofric, tis your destiny to be king and I to be your queen. (*She caresses and kisses him. Mary is shocked.*)

FRANK (*Trying to fight her off.*) But I love Godiva.

They continue to kiss.

MARY (*In horror.*) I've got to get out of here.

(*Malcolm enters SL as* THOMAS, *a monk.*)

THOMAS Shall I hear your confession, Lady Godiva?

MARY Yes, this is my confession. I'm not Lady Godiva. I'm a movie star and a homemaker. And I can prove it. I have a parking place on the MGM lot.

All laugh.

ARNOLPH And where do we find this mythical spot?

MARY It's called Culver City.

BALDRIC She's mad.

MARY Listen you, I want to send a telegram, I mean a carrier pigeon to Dore Schary. He's the head of the studio. That's Dore Schary. S-C-H-A-R-Y. Get it?

PRUDWEN She's as mad as the poor Thane of Cawdor's late wife, Irma.

BALDRIC It's the age old story. Man becomes king, wife goes nutso.

ARNOLPH Reminds one of the tragedy of poor Lady Olivia de Havilland in the 20th Century Fox feature "The Snake Pit."

All laugh. Smoke.

MARY I am not mad (*To herself.*) Now what was that last rewrite? (*To Frank. In classical Shakespearean tones.*) Shrive me sir, slubber not this calamitous venture. Tho I may be but a croff and woosel, enfranchised to a clog, suckled with a posset. I possess by Circe's cup, a wisdom not to be dismissed like some cankered malt horse drudge. This murrian flock that serves your ancestral crest must not be tossed twixt and tween your humors and conceits. They trudge from Aurora's harbinger to the collied spheres' shadow. Nay! Swinge me soundly for I must clagger thee as would Judas' daughter. My heart cleaved with the blind bow boy's butt shaft and enscrolled with a Tyrian throstle!

Pages enter to strike banners.

ARNOLPH She speaks as a traitor! Send her to the tower for execution!

BALDRIC Her head must be stricken from her body!

THOMAS Heretic!

PRUDWEN Put her on the rack!

FRANK No! Please! Don't!

ARNOLPH Seize her!

All exit but Mary. Pages strike banners.

MARY (*Sobbing.*) Pat, where are you when I need you so desperately. Pat!

Pat enters SL door. She is dressed as a court jester, except for fishnet stockings and spike heels.

PAT Darling I can't chat, I'm so late. I was emceeing a bear-baiting down the road. I went over well. I invented the first hemorrhoid joke.

MARY Listen to me, Pat.

PAT Sorry, darling. I can't help you. I gotta run! I suggest you hie thee hither! There's a warrant out for your head. I'm coming! Goodbye Sweetie. (*Kiss. She exits SL door.*)

MARY There's no escape! I must throw myself into the moat! Farewell, my beloved. (*She exits SR.*)

The ghost of Mary's GRANNY LOU *enters SR door, Granny Lou is a simple farm woman, gentle but firm, holding a dish towel.*)

GRANNY LOU Mary-Godiva, don't you go near that water. You come over here . . . That's right, child, it's me, Granny Lou. You're looking at my hair. Honey, it's not hair dye. The minute you get up here, your hair goes back to it's old color. Pretty isn't it. Dear (*She sits on settee.*) I wish I could invite you inside but I can't. It's not your time yet. I'm afraid I've gotta keep you on the other side of this screen door. There's a whole slew of us watching over you. Maudie, Aunt Olive. We sure do love you.

But honey, we're a bit disappointed, seeing you giving up like that. We know you've got that Hofstetter gumption in you. Now use it, honey. Save yourself and save your husband. He's not a bad man, just so very scared. Save him, darlin'. One little person can make a difference, you know. But sometimes you gotta do something—oh do something kind of crazy to make people stand up and take notice, You'll know what it is honey. We don't need to tell you. My dear one. You shall prevail. You shall prevail. (*Granny Lou exits.*)

Pages enter, strike settee. Thomas enters.)

THOMAS Look out the window! The Lady Godiva is riding naked through the streets of Coventry! All the peasants are covering their eyes. None will gaze upon her nakedness. Oh, my eyes. My eyes. They burn with pain. Oh, the agony. I can't see. I've gone blind! Blind! History shall know me as Peeping Tom. (*He exits.*)

From behind a scrim we see Godiva (Mary) riding naked upon her steed as offstage voices cheer. Fade to black.)

GRANNY LOU (*Voiceover.*) One person can make a difference. But sometimes you gotta do something crazy to make people stand up and take notice. You shall prevail. You shall prevail . . .

ACT TWO

Scene 4

The hospital.

Mary is lying in a hospital bed, unconscious, Frank by her side, worried. On the SL level lies a Bible.

MARY (*Murmuring.*) You shall prevail. You shall prevail.

FRANK Come back to me, Mary. Please don't die.

Mary opens her eyes.

FRANK Mary? Mary?

MARY Am I naked?

FRANK No, my darling. You're alive. You've come back.

MARY Am I in a hospital? Have I gone mad?

FRANK You tried to kill yourself and it was all my fault.

MARY Yes, you tried to murder me. That was no dream.

FRANK There's so much to explain.

MARY Tell me now. The truth.

FRANK The communist party found out I'd accidentally killed my childhood friend. They threatened to expose me unless I . . . Unless I murdered you. It was as if they hypnotized me. I should have killed myself.

MARY No, Frank, that's the cowards way out.

FRANK I can never atone for what I did to you. Mary, you'll never see me again.

MARY No, Frank, that's not the answer either. I want to save our marriage.

FRANK You would do that?

MARY There's good inside you. I'd be willing to nurture it if you are.

FRANK I've given up drinking. Last night, I poured all the booze down the sink.

MARY Last time you told me you prayed. That was a falsehood. This time, I must ask you to pray before me. Hand me that Bible, Frank. (*He gives her Bible.*) Kneel. Kiss the Bible.

FRANK Lord, please help me.

MARY Forgive us our trespasses as we forgive those who trespass against us. Lead us not into temptation but deliver us from evil.

PAT (*Enters SL door.*) Mary, you're yourself again.

FRANK (*To Mary.*) My beautiful one.

PAT Mary, the last time I saw you at the radio station. It was so hideous.

FRANK Tell the truth, Pat. Tell us why you're suddenly spouting the party line.

PAT I can't. You mustn't ask me that.

MARY Then I want you to leave.

PAT (*Horrified.*) Mary . . .

MARY I want you out of here. This is my party line. No communists are welcome in this room.

PAT (*Crying.*) Please don't throw me out. I'm so alone.

MARY I mean it Pat. I'm not afraid anymore. (*Listens to herself.*) "I'm not afraid." "I'm not afraid." (*With great strength.*) I'm not afraid.

PAT (*In awe.*) Mary, what's come over you?

MARY I never believed that dreams could change one but mine has. While I was in the coma, I journeyed to another world and what I saw there has given me new hope. (*With great intensity.*) For the last time I demand to know, are you now or have you ever been a member of the communist party?!

PAT (*Breaks down.*) NO, no, no, no, no. I hate the communists. I'd like to see them all exterminated. It's Mitchell Drake . . . He's blackmailing me.

FRANK What's he got on you?

PAT Years ago in New York, I was very much in love with the son of a bitch. Love. Whoever thought love could be a dirty word. I was obsessed with him. I was no longer a woman of achievement, but a thing. I abandoned all sense of decency. I was in his thrall. Always that penis staring at me, taunting me! Mocking me! One night he got me drunk and took photos of me performing some of the most repugnant acts a woman could do.

MARY (*With genuine interest.*) For instance?

PAT To even tell you would be to insult you. Now he intends to distribute them nationally unless I remain a commie tool.

MARY Then we must find the negatives.

PAT (*Vulnerably.*) We?

MARY Friend, we're in this together.

PAT (*Sobbing.*) Oh Mary, it's been so awful.

MARY They must be tucked away somewhere in the bowels of the Yetta Felson Studio. Girl, we must go there tonight.

FRANK You mustn't. It's too dangerous. Don't forget Mary that they want you murdered. They tried to get me to do it, the monsters.

PAT What?

FRANK They think Mary knows too much.

MARY I overheard their plot to destroy the Freed Unit.

PAT Over my dead body.

FRANK I'll get those negatives for you.

MALCOLM (*Enters SL door furtively.*) Please, may I come in?

MARY Malcolm, where've you been? I was out of my mind with worry. You left with my fine washables still in the sink.

MALCOLM I've been many places but they follow me everywhere.

MARY Who Malcolm?

MALCOLM The party. I thought I could break away but they were right. There's no dark corner to hide in.

MARY Stop this Malcolm and tell us everything.

MALCOLM No, Mrs Taggart, you were the only one who was ever nice to me in this whole stinkin' town.

PAT How did it all go wrong?

MALCOLM I came here from Secaucus, New Jersey, an idealistic young cosmetologist with a dream. Hungry to change the world and invent a new form of hair weave. The party promised to fight for tolerance for my people and supply me with human hair. It was all a sham.

FRANK You're young. You've got your whole life ahead of you.

MALCOLM I gave that up the day I walked into that building on Sunset. I just wanted to say goodbye. (*Slightly mad.*) This is a lovely hospital room, so high above the ground. The fifth floor, isn't it? I guess I finally made it to the top.

FRANK Malcolm, what are you thinking of?

MALCOLM The end, Frank, the end.

Malcolm runs off SR. We hear him jump out the window. The glass breaking, the body crashing to the pavement, passersby screaming below.)

PAT (*Covering her face.*) Horrible! Horrible!

MARY Dear sweet Malcolm.

FRANK Poor little guy.

MARY (*With great compassion.*) I suppose in a way it was the only end for Malcolm. He lived with such sorrow all his life, existing in that bizarre lonely netherworld of half-men.

FRANK (*Sensitively.*) Perhaps then it is best this way.

MARY But not for you Frank or for you Pat. I won't let them destroy you. I'll die fighting. Lady Godiva defied her world and succeeded. And dammit, so will I!

BLACKOUT

ACT TWO

Scene 5

That night. The office of the Yetta Felson Studio. Frank is revealed at desk rummaging through drawers. Marta enters SL door.

MARTA Frank, what are you doing here?

FRANK I wanted to leave a note for Barker. I was looking for a pencil.

MARTA I don't believe you. You're indicating. The subtext is you're searching for something that you believe is hidden in that desk.

We hear a man screaming in agony.

FRANK What's that?

MARTA Jeff Patterson's working on a scene from "Life With Father." You know you let us down. Yesterday, you were supposed to start scene study class and then kill your wife. You did neither. Not a good political move, darling,

FRANK What if I told you I was sick and tired of political moves.

MARTA All art is political.

FRANK What if I told you Abbott and Costello are looking downright attractive.

MARTA Frank, you're still not giving us one hundred percent. You need a private session with Yetta Felson. Your ideology needs some serious reinforcing. Come along, junior.

Marta and Frank exit SL door. Mary and Pat enter SR door from behind the curtain.

MARY And to think I invited that creature into my home. Pat, you take the desk and I'll take the file cabinet.

They open drawers and look through them.

PAT (*Opens a file.*) Hey look, Mary.

Mary crosses to her.

PAT Here's a list of the student body. It's certainly an impressive star roster and not an ounce of glamour in the lot of them.

MARY Give it to me, dear. You never know when it might come in handy. (*Puts roster in her purse and returns to file cabinet.*) Pat, I think I may have stumbled onto something.

PAT What is it, Mary?

MARY A file marked "Project Pilford." Do I dare open it?

PAT Go ahead.

MARY (*Opens file and sees photos. Gasps.*) Ah! Oh! Ah!

PAT Remember I did a contortionist act in Vaudeville. Are the negatives in there?

MARY Everything's here. Now let's amscray before the Ams-hay get back.

MITCHELL (*Enters.*) Well, well, well, if it isn't Nancy Drew and her friend, Kama Sutra. You girls interested in signing up for a course in the method?

MARY I have my own method. "Learn your lines and don't bump into the furniture."

MITCHELL Find what you were looking for?

PAT Yes, we have. Negatives included. You can tell your writers they can go on permanent coffee break.

MITCHELL (*Laughs and takes out a sealed envelope from his pocket. While he talks he opens the letter with a letter opener from the desk.*)

So you found the nasty incriminating photos. You two ladies think you've got this problem all wrapped up. You got the dirty pictures. Well, what about the blue movie. I have in this envelope a document listing the contents of a Swiss safe deposit box including one sixteen millimeter pornographic home movie starring Pat Pilford.

Mary looks at Pat in disbelief.

PAT (*At the end of her rope.*) HE MADE ME!!! Damn you Mitchell. Damn you to hell!

MITCHELL (*Laughing.*) You can't win, Pat. You just never know where to draw the line. (*Puts letter opener back on desk.*) Mary, I'm very touched by your devotion to your naughty friend. I wonder how far you'd go to save her from exposure. I might be willing to forget about this list provided you two join me in a sexy partouze once a week at a hotel of my choice.

Pat in her hysteria, grabs the letter opener from the desk and stabs Mitchell. He writhes in agony and falls down dead. Pat stands over him in dumb shock.

MARY Thank you, Pat. He deserved to die. (*Rushes to Pat's side and holds her.*) Darling, don't you worry about a thing. We're going to hire you the best shingle in town and you're going to beat this rap. Remember, dear, I was a witness.

Marta and Frank enter. Marta sees Mitchell's dead body and screams. She rushes to the body.

MARTA You idiots! You blithering idiots. You've murdered one of the theatres' finest writers.

MARY Now he belongs to the ages.

FRANK (*Joining Mary.*) Mary, are you all right?

MARY I'm fine, darling, but we must get Pat out of here.

Barker enters, followed by R.G. Benson.

BARKER Nobody's movin'. (*To Marta.*) Is he dead?

MARTA Yes, Mr. Barker.

BARKER You three are in a heap o' trouble. The list of possible indictments boggles the mind. Taggart, you've been a thorn in my side from day one. I have goon squads to take care of the likes of you. Marta, call in Vladimir. It's time to lance these carbuncles.

R.G. For once I must contradict you, Mr. Barker.

BARKER But out, windbag.

R.G. Barker, this is one time you may want to listen. I realize you've dismissed me as simply one of your many artistic stooges, but I must inform you that I'm more than that (*Lifts his jacket, revealing a badge*) In fact, I've been placed here as an undercover agent by the FBI. How am I doin', Mary?

MARY Aces, R.G.

PAT Mary, did you know R.G. was a government agent?

MARY I figured it out just this morning. I knew in my heart that a great woman's director couldn't be red.

BARKER I commend you on your performance, Benson. Highly professional. Yes, you had me quite fooled. I toast you. Well, well, well.

Barker makes an awkward dash to the exit. Frank tries to block him. Barker grabs him and pushes him aside.

BARKER Out of my way, cretin! (*Barker dashes out.*)

FRANK He got away. Dammit, he got away.

MARY Don't you worry. Mr. Hoover's men are surrounding the building. The Fatman won't get far.

FRANK How do you know there are men outside?

R.G. Show them your badge, Mary. I appointed our girl an honorary G-man just a few hours ago.

Mary pulls back her coat and flashes her badge.

MARY My new favorite piece of jewelry.

A severe-looking OLD LADY *enters. She speaks in a vaguely European accent.*

THE OLD LADY Look at this office. I have never seen such a mess.

MARY I should say so. You're not much of a cleaning lady. This whole school should be fumigated.

THE OLD LADY My dear, I am not the cleaning lady. I am Yetta Felson.

MARY Well, Miss Felson, without even mentioning your communist activities, I think you're doing American actors a dreadful disservice encouraging them to wallow in self-indulgence and disregarding every tenet of discipline and professionalism.

YETTA First of all, my dear, I am not a communist. I am also an agent with the FBI. The United States government financed the Felson Studios as a front to ensnare communists in the film industry. Furthermore, I am sick of the Stanislavsky method. I've just signed to play the grandmother in the new Red Skelton picture.

MARY R.G., you must keep me abreast.

MARTA (*Fiercely.*) Comrade Felson, you have betrayed the Moscow Art Theatre.

MARY Marta, I'd suggest you not fling accusations. R.G., may I?

R.G. Mary, she's all yours.

MARY Ever since we first met at the "Young Man With a Horn" premiere, I found it curious, your extreme aversion to signing autographs.

MARTA There's nothing curious about that. Autograph collecting is a capitalist fetish encouraged to separate artists from the people.

MARY A rudimentary phone call to the girls in the studio contract department revealed that even those documents were signed by proxy.

R.G. We were both left wondering where we could find your signature.

MARY Certainly not in cement at Graumann's. No, it was I who finally discovered your Jane Hancock on this postcard from Tijuana. It perfectly matches the signature of one Olga Shumsky, a Soviet agent of the KGB. The message itself was also a tip-off. "Having a great time but wish I was in Odessa."

MARTA You're a liar! It's a frame-up.

MARY No, Miss Shumsky. It is you who have created an identity built on lies. The real Marta Towers was a lovely, aspiring young actress who was found murdered on a lonely dirt road outside Tijuana. We have also located Dr. Leon Beidemann, who performed extensive plastic surgery on you, enabling the dog-faced, moustached, piano-legged Olga Shumsky to successfully break into American show business. I charge you with the murder of Marta Towers.

MARTA (*Violently.*) Yes! I am Commissar Olga Shumsky! And yes, I killed Marta Towers, the simpering little fool. I shared a quesadilla with her at a truck stop, and endured her recitation of Juliet's potion scene in her revolting Oklahoma twang. It was simple slipping the arsenic that turned her tequila sunrise into a sunset. I became the respected actress she'd never be. The New York critics rhapsodized over my solo "Three Sisters." I should have become a major film star but the studios were too busy giving the big buildup to clap-ridden whores with dubbed voices!

Ominous music begins.

MARTA You think you've stopped us, but you haven't scratched the surface. We're everywhere, getting stronger, getting three picture deals and producer credit. Listen, hear the drums beating, pounding as we march down Hollywood Boulevard, trampling over the faded names of the soon-to-be-forgotten stars. March! March! Stamp on the infidels, the agents, the bloodsuckers, the columnists! March! March!

R.G. (*To Yetta.*) Send her to the psychopathic ward.

Yetta begins to lead Marta away.

MARTA (*Clearly insane.*) Who am I? I'm a soviet agent . . . No, I'm an actress. I'm a soviet agent . . . No, I'm a seagull. Squawk! Squawk! Masha, want a cracker? (*She lashes out at Yetta.*) Get away from me, Konstantin Gavrilovitch!

YETTA (*Grabbing hold of her arms.*) These nails have to be trimmed.

R.G. Outside, Yetta, not on the floor. (*Yetta leads Marta off.*)

MARY And now, Frank, what about you?

FRANK Well, I want to do what's right. But I'm not sure what that is anymore.

MARY Darling, I think you know what you must do. Come clean.

FRANK Admit everything?

MARY Only then can you enjoy your freedom. Pat knows how deadly a secret can be. Don't you, Pat? Don't you?

PAT Frank, listen to Pat. Secrets kill.

R.G. Frank, what do you say? You'll talk to the committee?

FRANK Yeah. Sure. I may have just joined the party but Hell, I've been pink for years. I'll turn myself in.

MARY Darling, that's marvelous, but don't you think it would be helpful if you gave the names of others we know to be disloyal?

FRANK Name names? Gee, I don't know if I could.

MARY My love, leave it to me. We'll think of something. I'm in your corner.

FRANK But what about my childhood friend, the one I killed? It was an accident. I swear it.

MARY There's no cause for worry. I looked into that too. Your wife has had quite a busy afternoon. The bureau knows you were innocent That's why they never chose to pursue you.

PAT But what about me, Patricia Maybelle Schmuckleberger? The blood on my hands?

MARY Oh, Pat, don't you concern yourself about a thing. You're an American. Remember that. And in our country, only the guilty need live in fear.

Mary holds both Frank and Pat in her generous embrace. R.G. watches with admiration.

BLACKOUT

ACT TWO

Scene 6

ANNOUNCER (*Voiceover.*) The Veedol Motor Oil Program with Pat Pilford.

Applause/Music.

ANNOUNCER (*Voiceover.*) Makers of Veedol Motor Oil, found wherever fine cars travel, present Miss Show Business, Pat Pilford. With special guest stars Kate Smith, Dr. Norman Vincent Peale, Music by the West Point Choir and Parker Jones and his Red White and Blue Orchestra, and yours truly, Bill Simmons in what will be my last introduction, since I was fired by Miss Pilford this morning. And now, your fabulous femm-cee, Pat Pilford . . .

Applause.

PAT (*In front of her mike DR.*) My dear audience. I must tell you what a very special day this is for me and really, employing the most grandiose terms, I'll just say it, for our country. I've made it no secret that the lovely film star Mary Dale is my closest and dearest friend. Through thick and thin, that's my Mare. Beauty, grace, talent, yes, those words spring to mind when we think of Mary Dale. Add to that recipe a dash of heroine. Mary Dale is a heroine of our time. As I speak, she is mounting the steps of Congress in Washington, D.C. to testify before the esteemed House Un-American Activities Committee. Some say it's a controversial move on Mary's part. What controversy? The girl's just trying to help. If we don't nip this in the bud, by golly, by next election day, our White House will be painted red. These people are getting away with murder! Don't get me started. Mary, I just want you to know our hearts and prayers are with you. God bless you, Mary Dale.

Mary enters SL in a lovely white dress and straw boater. She is the essence of magnificent American womanhood. She is radiant. She crosses to podium. Pat exits SR door. Behind Mary we see the Capitol Building.)

MARY (*Standing at podium with microphones U.C.*) Senators, gentlemen, I stand before this august body terribly humbled. Only in America could a young girl raised by struggling farmers in Indiana grow up to be a movie star and able to speak to a distinguished panel of Senators and may I add, most handsome. I must tell you of a dream I had about Lady Godiva, which is my latest film and I cordially invite all of you to the premiere at the Pantages. And from that dream I learned to apply the simple answers of a bygone era to the complicated questions of today. And that is why I am here before this congressional investigation to provide you with a list of names to aid you in your noble hunt to route out the red menace. Together with God's help we can make sure that these people never work again. (*She opens envelope.*) My this is very exciting. (*She takes list out of envelope.*) I name Marta Towers, Bertram Barker . . . (*She pauses for a moment, hesitantly.*) and because I love him, Frank Taggart. (*Regaining her sense of purpose.*) From the student roster of the Yetta Felson Studio, I name Betty Foster, Jeff Patterson, Morris Kleiner, Mildred Pishkin, Lona Myers, Anthony Reaci, Rudy Abbotelli, Howard Mandlebaum, June Sycoff . . .

Patriotic music swells and eventually drowns out her speech. Behind the Capitol, a giant flag appears rustling in the breeze. On the SR side of the flag, a miniature of the Statue of Liberty appears and on SL of the flag, a miniature of the Liberty Bell. As Mary names names, both the music and lighting become dissonant, disturbing and threatening until both sound and lights suddenly blackout.)

THE END

THE TALE OF THE ALLERGIST'S WIFE

Tony Roberts, Linda Lavin, and Michele Lee in the Broadway production of *The Tale of the Allergist's Wife*. Photo credit: Joan Marcus.

THE CAST

The Tale of the Allergist's Wife was originally produced by Manhattan Theatre Club (Lynne Meadow, Artistic Director; Barry Grove, Executive Producer) at City Center Stage II and subsequently moved to the Ethel Barrymore Theatre, opening November 2, 2000, under the auspices of Manhattan Theatre Club, Carol Shorenstein Hays, Daryl Roth, Stuart Thompson, and Douglas S. Cramer. Directed by Lynne Meadow, with set design by Santo Loquasto; costumes, Ann Roth; lighting, Christopher Akerlind; and sound, Bruce Ellman and Brian Ronan, it was performed with the following cast, in order of appearance:

Mohammed .... Anil Kumar
Marjorie .... Linda Lavin
Ira .... Tony Roberts
Frieda .... Shirl Bernheim
Lee .... Michele Lee

The Characters

Mohammed
Marjorie
Ira
Frieda
Lee

Place: Manhattan

Time: Today

THE TALE OF THE ALLERGIST'S WIFE

ACT ONE

Scene 1

A two-bedroom apartment on Manhattan's Upper West Side. It's a post-war building and the apartment, cherished for its views, is decorated in an expensive contemporary style. A living room leads directly into the kitchen. A counter separates the kitchen from the living room, enabling people in the two rooms to converse with each other. It is late morning but the curtains are drawn.

MARJORIE TAUB *is lying in her robe on the sofa. She is an attractive, stylish woman but at the moment she's in her robe and feeling far from stylish. She speaks in a somewhat studied manner. It's a New York accent with a strange overlay of affected theatricality. She's in the throes of an epic depression. It's not quiet depression but raging frustration. She's a volcano that explodes, simmers down, and then explodes again. One of her wrists is bandaged.* MOHAMMED, *a boyish and very good-looking twenty-two-year-old doorman from Iraq, is attaching an elaborate chandelier into the ceiling. He's removed his jacket and shirt and tie and is wearing a white T-shirt.*

MOHAMMED Mrs. Taub, are you sure you want me doing this now? I can come back later. I'm on the door until four-thirty when Felix takes over.

MARJORIE Now, later, yesterday. Ce n'est pas le difference.

MOHAMMED Because if you have a headache—

MARJORIE How I'd relish a simple headache. This chandelier—I don't know. It's just not—I can't express it.

MOHAMMED Mrs. Taub, describe to me your vision once more.

MARJORIE It should be a feverish dream out of Baudelaire. Exotic, mesmerizing. This doesn't say "Extravagant decadence." This says "Lighting fixture."

MOHAMMED No it says "Romantic opulence."

MARJORIE (*Losing her patience.*) It says "Repro bought at cost." (*Flings herself down on the divan.*) I'm sorry I put you through all this. Take it down. Bring it back in the storage room.

MOHAMMED Perhaps you should give it a little time.

MARJORIE I want it out of here!

MOHAMMED (*Changing the subject.*) Oh, I meant to return your book.

MARJORIE You have a book of mine?

MOHAMMED Nadine Gordimer. I loved how she wove the politics of apartheid into the emotional lives of the characters.

MARJORIE Yes, she is an inspired artist.

MOHAMMED I can see why you loved it so much.

MARJORIE And yet, the more I think about it, the more facile and superficial it was.

MOHAMMED It was very subtle and thought-provoking.

MARJORIE Not compared to Tolstoy, Turgenev, Flaubert.

MOHAMMED But Mrs. Taub, they were giants.

MARJORIE They were. Weren't they? Everything today seems so—trifling. But what do I know. Who the hell am I? I have such respect for you, Mohammed. You can do things. With your hands. Plumbing, electric.

MOHAMMED My father is an architect. Very much respected. He didn't want us to be spoiled. He insisted that my brothers and I learn a great diversity of skills.

MARJORIE Skills are very important. I have very few skills.

MOHAMMED Did you not go to the university?

MARJORIE I was a business major. It's not what I would have preferred.

MOHAMMED And if you could have had your wish?

MARJORIE My wish? Philosophy. I would have loved to study the great works of Nietzsche, Kierkegaard, and Spinoza. I've tried to educate myself. Let's say I am no stranger to the New School for Social Research. (*She bursts into tears.*) Oh, I'm sorry.

MOHAMMED I wasn't on duty when they brought you home but I heard about it.

MARJORIE People are talking about me?

MOHAMMED You know what it's like. People gather in the lobby.

MARJORIE Well, if they're saying it was a suicide attempt, please tell them it was an accident.

MOHAMMED Is there anything I can do for you?

MARJORIE You're very kind but there's nothing anyone can do for me. Just finish putting up the damn thing. I don't know what I'd do if I had to depend on the rotten handyman in this lousy building. And I've enjoyed reading our books together. You're very perceptive.

MOHAMMED It's all done. Shall we try it?

MARJORIE That's all right. I'm sure it works.

He turns on the light. Like a vampire exposed to the light, Marjorie writhes on the sofa.

MARJORIE Turn it off, please! I never use the overhead!

Mohammed turns off the light and returns to move the ladder away. The front door opens and Marjorie's husband, IRA, *enters. He's a good-looking, highly energetic man, in his fifties. He's wearing his jogging suit and headband and talking on a tiny cellular phone.*

IRA (*On the phone.*) Take the prednisone as prescribed and listen to me, Renee. Forget "the show must go on." No talking for two days. And I have ESP so I'll know if you're cheating. There's no charge. You say that again and I'll be mad. Hugs to Steve and the children. (*He hangs up.*) Renee Elias. What a character but such God-given talent. It's an honor and a blessing to give that girl free samples of Humabid.

Ira crosses to Mohammed and pats him on the back.

IRA Hey there, kemo sabe. How's the skateboarding?

MOHAMMED Fine, Dr. Taub.

MARJORIE Mohammed attached the lighting fixture. I promised him forty.

IRA (*Thinking Mohammed can't see him, Ira grimaces that she went so high.*) And he certainly deserves it. The room is transformed. (*Takes the money out of the money pouch attached around his waist.*) Here you go, my friend. Don't spend it all in one place.

MOHAMMED Thank you. I shall see you both downstairs by the door. (*He exits.*)

IRA When I left this morning, you were sleeping on the sofa. Did you spend the whole night out here?

MARJORIE Apparently so.

IRA Was it my snoring? I don't know what to do.

MARJORIE It's not the snoring.

IRA Then what is it, darling? Please, tell me.

MARJORIE (*A long sigh.*) Perdu.

IRA What?

MARJORIE Perdu. Utter damnation. The loss of my soul.

IRA I'm opening these drapes. (*Ira pushes apart the curtains.*)

IRA Marjorie, you've got to rouse yourself from this perdu. You've spent how many weeks lying out here in the dark? I'm really worried. Perhaps you should see someone.

MARJORIE A therapist? My therapist died. I cannot replace that remarkable woman as easily as I would a dead schnauzer.

IRA Marjorie, I did not mean to disparage your relationship with Reba Fabrikant. But you cannot allow her passing to be a catalyst for a complete breakdown. Am I the problem? I know I'm far from perfect. It took me over thirty years to get the point that you hated my jokes. Have you heard a single joke from me in months, a play on words, a pun?

MARJORIE It was wrong of me to censor you. I should be ashamed of myself.

IRA No, you were right. People who constantly make puns aren't really listening. I'm glad you criticized me. I am grateful.

MARJORIE Please don't say that. Have you heard from the Disney Store?

IRA Yes. Good news. They're not going to press charges. They're being very understanding.

MARJORIE What do they understand?

IRA Well, that you had just left a memorial service for your beloved therapist and you had a—

MARJORIE The memorial service was nearly a month before.

IRA Doesn't matter. You were out of control.

MARJORIE It was an accident. People drop things.

IRA Within three minutes, you dropped six porcelain figurines. They tell me the Goofy alone was two hundred and fifty dollars.

MARJORIE And you had to pay for everything?

IRA Forget the expense. What is money but a conduit to help people? It's you I worry about.

MARJORIE It was an accident.

IRA I know but they thought you were making some kind of political statement about the Disney Corporation. You know what? I think you should get dressed and go outside. (*Eyes the calendar taped to the refrigerator.*) Let's see what you had going for today. Tuesday the seventh. One-thirty, lecture on the literary legacy of Hermann Hesse at Goethe House. "Hiroshima/Vagina," Multimedia landscapes, Landsberg Gallery, Soho. Five o'clock, Regina Resnik opera symposium, Florence Gould Auditorium. You've got quite a day mapped out for yourself.

MARJORIE I should be barred from all of those places. I'm of limited intellect. Never have I had even one original thought.

IRA That is not true. If I were half as intellectually curious as you.

MARJORIE Curious yes. Profound no.

IRA What do you call "profound"?

MARJORIE The ability to think in the abstract. Oh Ira, can't we just face it? We're Russian peasants from the shtetl. We have no right to be attending art installations at the Whitney. We should be tilling the soil, pulling a plow.

Ira's beeper goes off. He takes out his phone and dials the number.

IRA Jeffrey Krampf, one of my grad students. Brilliant, tortured mind. I think he's on crack. What can I do? Let him flounder? Now, the line's busy. You're so tough on us. You know, that last production of "Waiting for Godot" affected me deeply. I had the sense that I finally understood what that play was about.

MARJORIE You understood the story. You think it's about two guys who get stranded by the Tappan Zee Bridge. They're not waiting for Triple A. It's about—I can't even explain what it's about. That is my conundrum. I don't understand the play any better than you. I'm a fraud. A cultural poseur. To quote Kafka, "I am a cage in search of a bird."

IRA You're hungry.

MARJORIE Yes, I'm hungry. (*An agonized cry.*) Hungry for meaning!

IRA You need food, real food. You made that wonderful meat loaf and didn't eat a bite. You're gonna lose potassium. I'm cutting you off a square of this Entenmann's. Just to nibble. You'll end up in the hospital with an I.V. at this rate. (*Hands her the piece of cake.*)

MARJORIE Thank you, Ira. (*Eating a bite and yielding a bit.*) It is good.

The doorbell rings.

IRA You want me to let your mother in?

MARJORIE I have a choice? You're gonna go "poof" and she'll turn into Simone de Beauvoir?

Ira opens the door and Marjorie's mother, FRIEDA, *enters. Frieda is a small, shrunken eighty-year-old woman with a cane but tough as cowhide.*

FRIEDA Ira, my love. The greatest son-in-law in the world. (*He kisses her.*) Give me another kiss. (*Frieda sees Marjorie eating.*) You should be ashamed of yourself. It's Yom Kippur. Why aren't you fasting?

MARJORIE In my entire life I have never fasted on Yom Kippur.

FRIEDA That is not true. When she was growing up, we always fasted.

MARJORIE Never. Not once. There were times when you didn't even know it was Yom Kippur.

FRIEDA Marjorie, your memories of your childhood are so distorted with bitterness. If you could see yourself with that farbisseneh face.

MARJORIE "Farbisseneh"? You didn't even speak Yiddish till you were sixty-five.

Ira takes a small laptop computer out from behind an end table.

FRIEDA I don't need to justify myself to you. It's a miracle your daughter found her faith with you as an example.

MARJORIE Joan is a religious fanatic.

FRIEDA Because she observes the High Holy Days?

MARJORIE She's married to rabbi and lives in Jerusalem.

FRIEDA She's a real estate lawyer who happens to be married to a rabbi.

MARJORIE She wears a sheitel to her condo closings. I'd prefer not to discuss my daughter's beliefs. Before you began your fast, did you eat the meat loaf I made? It was a special recipe from the *Times*.

FRIEDA Marjorie, I told you I had a craving for meat loaf. Just plain meat loaf. I don't ask for much. This had all sorts of dreck in it. Chestnuts and peas and weird spices.

MARJORIE I'm sorry. When I'm feeling better, I'll make you a chicken in a pot exactly the way you like it.

FRIEDA Just don't crap it up.

MARJORIE I won't!

FRIEDA Ira, what are you doing?

MARJORIE He's always at that damn computer. You got one in your den. You have to mess up my living room?

IRA I like the view from here. I'm just trying to catch up.

MARJORIE What do you need to catch up with?

IRA I didn't retire to relax. I retired to teach, to give, to impart.

MARJORIE Are you in one of those chat rooms? What's going on?

FRIEDA Marjorie, don't be a shrike. The world is moving at a clip. The man has to be in constant touch with the scientific community.

IRA The Internet brings me closer to the heartbeat of my patients. Let me read you this E-mail. It's from a young woman. "Dear Dr. Taub, During my entire childhood, I never drew a decent breath. My sinus passages were almost completely blocked. My speech was so nasal that I was severely ridiculed in school and nearly flunked out. When I was fifteen years old, the allergy shot program you prescribed changed my entire life. I graduated summa cum laude at Columbia and placed tenth in the New York Marathon. Because of your inspiration, I have pursued a career helping emotionally disturbed children reclaim their spirits through the circus arts. God bless you, Dr. Taub. Mindy Tannenbaum."

FRIEDA You are quite a man of achievement. In life there are winners and losers. From the word "go," Ira, you are a winner. I am a loser.

IRA You're not feeling well today?

FRIEDA The eternal constipation. Truth to be told, I have not had a satisfactory bowel movement in four years. Ira, I had beautiful BMs. Perfectly formed, always regular. You could set a clock to it. I don't want to discuss it. (*She takes a small box out of the basket attached to the walker.*)

MARJORIE What are you looking for, Mother?

FRIEDA My suppositories. I can't open the wrapper. That's what I came in here for. Not for the scintillating conversation. (*She hands the suppositories to Marjorie.*) Open a bunch of 'em. I tell you, I've had it. Call Dr. Kevorkian.

MARJORIE I've tried. He's in prison.

FRIEDA Just my luck. This isn't a life. Stuck in a craphouse down the hall for everyone's convenience. Oh God, why don't I just give up. I am the loser of the world.

MARJORIE What do you mean, you're the loser of the world?

FRIEDA Do I need to tell you? I lost my husband and firstborn son to heart disease. That's not enough? What should I have expected? As a child I saw my father run down by a milk truck before my very eyes. My mother was insane and went after me with a meat cleaver.

MARJORIE Aunt Shakie says that never happened.

FRIEDA Aunt Shakie is a fucking liar. Except for Papa, they all had it in for me. I am the world's great loser.

MARJORIE (*Trembling with rage.*) Oh no, Mother, you are not the world's greatest loser. Not by a long shot and you know why? Because I am the world's champion loser. Me!

IRA Marjorie—

MARJORIE You say your mother tried to kill you. My mother—my mother did worse. My mother has killed my capacity to dream.

IRA Not again with the competition. It's like a broken record with you two.

MARJORIE Never for a moment has my mother seen anything of value in what I've done.

FRIEDA What have you done?

MARJORIE That's it. Nothing. But maybe I could have. She was always encouraging to Bobby. Sending him for lessons, every kind of lesson. Why not me?

FRIEDA She resents her brother but he was extraordinarily gifted.

MARJORIE She never gave a thought to my needs, my ambitions.

FRIEDA She was a dilettante.

IRA Marjorie, your mother's a fragile, sick, old woman.

MARJORIE She's a knife! A destroyer.

FRIEDA This is not about me. Or your brother.

IRA Marjorie is mourning the loss of her psychiatrist. You have to understand—

FRIEDA This isn't about kooky Reba what's-her-name. You are bored, Marjorie. The girls are grown, live miles away. You are bored. So you go into a store, filled with children, erupt into violence and destroy costly figurines.

MARJORIE This is so simplistic and insulting. You don't know anything about me. We are strangers!

FRIEDA You should get off your duff, get dressed and do some volunteer work. Make yourself useful.

MARJORIE Volunteer work. I should do some volunteer work. I am the queen of volunteer workers, Mother. A brigadier general in the army of volunteers. What do you think I've been doing for the past thirty years? Planned Parenthood, Dance Theatre of Harlem. I gave my life's blood to the Lenox Hill Thrift Shop. Every week, I was in that back room on my hands and knees unpacking every filthy box, sorting through garments stiff from sweat and urine. Every day I saw the other volunteers ransack the shop for any rag with a designer label. Then by chance, buried in a box of moldy paperbacks, I discover a first-edition hardcover English translation of "Siddhartha" in mint condition, still with the original dust jacket, and personally inscribed by Hermann Hesse. I put it aside, making it abundantly clear to everyone that I intended to buy it myself "To buy"—that is the operative phrase here. I come back the next day. "Where's my book? Where is 'Siddhartha'?" The manager, Libby Fleishman, says, "Oh, I'm so sorry. I forgot that you put that aside. I sold it to a dealer." It was an act of deliberate cruelty. I went to the hospital board and exposed Libby's operation of selling directly to antique dealers and getting a personal cut. They demanded proof but none of the other volunteers would back me up. I was humiliated, disgraced and betrayed. So yes, Mother, I have done my share of volunteer work. I have chopped the vegetables, driven the meals on wheels, registered people for the vote, made puppets for the retarded, pushed the hospital cart, stuffed the mailing, licked the envelopes, worked the hot line, sewn the quilt, saved the whales, served everyone's needs but my own. Well, what about my needs, Mother? Who's gonna volunteer to save me?

FRIEDA (*Beat.*) Oy, I feel so bloated.

BLACKOUT

ACT ONE

Scene 2

A few hours later. Marjorie is reclining on the window seat. The doorbell rings.

MARJORIE Who is it?

A woman's voice is heard outside the door.

WOMAN I'm here to see the apartment.

MARJORIE Beg your pardon?

WOMAN I'm here to look at the apartment.

Marjorie opens the door. LEE GREEN *is an energetic, beautifully groomed lady of Marjorie's age, with a very comfortable sense of her own sensuality.*

MARJORIE I think there must be some mistake.

LEE This is 12B?

MARJORIE No. This is 12C. 12B is around the corner.

LEE Please forgive me for disturbing you. (*Peeks her head in.*) Nice place. May I?

MARJORIE I don't know. I'm not dressed.

LEE It looks like such a lovely jewel box of a room. Just for a minute?

MARJORIE All right. Come in. (*She shows Lee into the apartment.*) Please forgive the way I'm dressed. I'm never usually in my robe this late in the—

LEE Don't apologize. Are you having one of those days?

MARJORIE I can't even—

LEE No need to. I've spent whole weeks in bed. And you have a view. Have you lived here long?

MARJORIE Five years. We were around the corner before. I'm sorry. I should introduce myself. I'm Marjorie Taub.

LEE Marjorie. I'm very fond of that name.

MARJORIE Really?

LEE When I was a little girl, I had a best friend named Marjorie. Unfortunately, we moved away when I was ten years old. I never saw her again. Lee Green.

MARJORIE Lee, may I get you something to drink?

LEE Anything sparkling would be wonderful.

MARJORIE Seltzer?

LEE Perfection.

Marjorie goes over to the kitchen area and pours a glass for Lee.

LEE I must say the city has changed since I last lived here.

MARJORIE When was that?

LEE Well, I gave up my apartment in eighty-six but I'm from New York.

MARJORIE I'm a native myself. Where did you grow up?

LEE I'm from decidedly humble origins. The Bronx. Fleetwood.

MARJORIE Isn't that funny? That's where I'm from. We lived in a tiny apartment on Bronx River Road.

LEE Those Tudor buildings? (*Marjorie nods.*) Marjorie, you're not—By any wild coincidence, your maiden name isn't Marjorie Tuchman?

MARJORIE Yes.

LEE Oh my God.

MARJORIE Lillian?

LEE Yes.

MARJORIE Lillian Greenblatt. Oh my God. (*They tearfully embrace.*) I can't believe this.

LEE It's amazing. After all these years. This is too much.

MARJORIE I'm stunned.

LEE The coincidence. I meant it when I said I've often thought of you.

MARJORIE Well, you had a great impact on me. You really did. And your mother. She was so elegant. I can still hear her saying that a lady holds both her teacup and her saucer.

LEE My poor mother. The Duchess of Fleetwood. Now, I'm assuming you're married?

MARJORIE For thirty-two years to Dr. V. Ira Taub. He's an allergist. He retired this year but he remains very active. He's started a free clinic for the homeless.

LEE Admirable. Children?

MARJORIE We have two daughters. Joan and Rochelle. Here they are. (*Marjorie takes a framed photo off a table and hands it to Lee.*)

LEE Very attractive.

MARJORIE Joan is a successful real estate lawyer. Rochelle is a lot slimmer now.

LEE Rochelle. She's the troubled one.

MARJORIE We've had our ups and downs.

LEE Does she live in the city?

MARJORIE Ashland, Oregon. She's a holistic healer. People swear by her. They say she can shrink tumors and cure stuttering.

LEE Was she always interested in alternative medicine?

MARJORIE Two years ago she was in a feminist avocado-farming commune. The year before that she had a cabaret act. I shouldn't be so judgmental. We bring our children into the world to fulfill a fantasy. The creation of the perfect human being. To quote Cocteau, "What are the thoughts of the marble from which a sculptor shapes a masterpiece?" It can't help but resent all the picking and chipping away.

LEE You were always such a voracious reader. I always imagined that you became a writer.

MARJORIE I tried. I wrote a novel. I worked on it for years. It became a joke. Marjorie and her book.

LEE Tell me about it.

MARJORIE I'd rather not.

LEE I've waited forty years to find out.

MARJORIE I don't want to sound pretentious.

LEE I am truly interested. Please.

MARJORIE It was a phantasmagoria. At the time I was heavily influenced by Thomas Pynchon. Some of it was composed as verse drama. There were chapters in various historical periods. Plato and Helen Keller were major characters. Allusions to "Anna Karenina" were woven throughout. I invented an entirely new form of punctuation. I was attempting to break away from conventional narrative structure.

LEE I'd love to read it.

MARJORIE I burned every copy.

LEE Marjorie!

MARJORIE I don't need tangible proof of my own mediocrity.

LEE I'm sure you're being too harsh.

MARJORIE Let's just say that my epic was given the thumbs-down by thirty-two publishers. To be exposed as a sham was devastating.

LEE Tell me, what's with the bandage?

MARJORIE Not what you think. For some unknown reason I went into the Disney Store on Fifth Avenue. I was holding this large figurine and it slipped out of my fingers and smashed on the floor. I was compelled to pick up another. I think it was the Beast, and then it too fell. I couldn't stop. Hercules, Aladdin's genie, the Little Mermaid's father. It looked like a bomb exploded. Ira had to pay a fortune.

LEE I bet that felt good.

MARJORIE Stop that. You're jumping to the wrong conclusion.

LEE I can see with my own eyes that you're tight as a drum with frustration.

MARJORIE My situation is far from grim.

LEE Marjorie, it's perfectly understandable. Don't forget. I know your mother. I remember we put on a performance in the playground with all our little friends, "Pippi Longstocking." All the parents said we were so clever and industrious. Your mother quipped, "This piece of dreck would close in New Haven." My God, with forty more years of that kind of negativity, no wonder you've become a retail terrorist.

MARJORIE (*Emotionally.*) You are most presumptuous. How dare you? You don't know me. You don't know my mother. How dare you? She's endured incredible hardships. She was born into degrading poverty. She saw her father run over by a milk truck. Her mother was insane and went after her with a meat cleaver. We never had any money but she always managed to make us feel we were as good as anyone else. I'll be damned if I'll let anyone put her down!

LEE Stop. I'm sorry. It was inappropriate for me to mouth off like that. I suppose I don't know you. How could I after all these years? It's just that in my mind our relationship has never really ended. I carry the memory of the wondrous, magical child that you were like a talisman. Can we start again? Friends?

MARJORIE Friends. I'm sorry I blew up. Now, it's my turn to be the Grand Inquisitor. I hope you can take it. So Lil, you changed your name?

LEE Lillian Greenblatt wasn't terribly euphonious. It's so—shall we say it? So Jewish. I'm sorry. I just don't identify. Never have. Call me a terrible person. I hope I'm not offending you.

MARJORIE No, I'm with you. I've always sought spirituality on a more individual basis. Joan, my eldest, is deeply religious. She's married to a rabbi and lives in Israel. She calls herself Jonaya Taub-Ben-Shalom. I've just always felt alienated from every group, be it Jewish, American, the West Side Wine Tasters.

LEE I've never even been a part of a couple.

MARJORIE You never married?

LEE Lee has led a totally selfish life, and had a helluva good time.

MARJORIE May I ask what do you do for a living?

LEE Oh gosh, what haven't I done? I've been in public relations. I've been an international food critic. Written a couple of coffee table books. "Balinese Masks." That sort of thing. I worked for several years for Chanel in Paris. For a while I ran a small discotheque in Hong Kong. I helped open a museum of contemporary art in Berlin. And I ran a clam bar outside Mendocino. Now I fund-raise for political organizations.

MARJORIE My, you've really been an adventuress. I would have loved to have traveled more. It's been hard with Ira's practice.

LEE I live for travel. Mainland China, a revelation. Changed my entire perspective of the world, of the very essence of life itself.

MARJORIE Did you go there alone?

LEE No, I went with the Nixons. I was covering the event for a small gourmet food magazine.

MARJORIE Oh my. Did you get to know the Nixons?

LEE Yes, I did. I didn't agree with them politically but I grew very fond of Pat. In fact I was the first person that Pat Nixon phoned after the resignation. I felt as if I was in the midst of a tragedy of Shakespearean proportions.

MARJORIE And you lived in Berlin. That must have been fascinating. I am a great devote of twentieth-century German fiction. My favorite author is Hermann Hesse. My favorite book is "Siddhartha."

LEE I've read every word he wrote. "Demian," "Steppenwolf," "Magister Ludi." The examination of the dark side.

MARJORIE So many people seem to—I don't know—live on the surface. Black is black, white is white. I delve, I reflect, I brood.

LEE You're a figure of shadow and light.

MARJORIE I have also found great solace in the writings of Heinrich Böll, Günter Grass, Thomas Mann.

LEE I had a little affair with Günter Grass.

MARJORIE No.

LEE Very brief but in my safe deposit box, I have some very tender love letters.

MARJORIE Did you ever meet Fassbinder?

LEE Oh, many times. Have you ever seen the film "The Bitter Tears of Petra von Kant"?

MARJORIE Indeed.

LEE In the scene in the bar, I'm the weird chick who looks like she's got a pinata stuck on her head.

MARJORIE My God. What a life you've led.

LEE Well, it's easy in Germany. Never a dull moment. I'll never forget the night the wall fell.

MARJORIE You were there?

LEE Such joy. I was with a group of students from the university. We screamed and shouted and kissed each other, grabbing with our fists great chunks of stone and mortar. By dawn, we were drenched in sweat and cheap champagne.

MARJORIE You certainly know where the action is.

LEE Never intentionally.

MARJORIE (*Embarrassed to ask.*) Did you, um, ever meet Diana?

LEE Oh yes. Lee Green, would you cool it? Marjorie's gonna think you're an obsessive name-dropper.

MARJORIE No, no, no. How'd you meet her?

LEE I met her several times. The most memorable was at a dinner party in London. Diana was seated to my left. She overheard my conversation with Henry Kissinger on the tragic situation of the land mines. She knew nothing about it and was quite fascinated. So I guess in my little way, I helped plant that seed.

MARJORIE Thank God you did.

LEE Now Marjorie, please take note that Lee's life has not been one long ride on the Orient Express. There were also years when she lived in a tiny cold-water flat in the village.

MARJORIE That sounds romantic too.

LEE It wasn't all "La Boheme." That's how I learned the fundamentals of cooking. I grew quite adept at whipping up a creative meal for two dollars. But we did have great fan in those days. Kerouac, Jimmy Baldwin, Andy.

MARJORIE Andy Warhol?

LEE He used to come over and we'd share a can of soup. He got such a kick out of the way I used to pile the empty Campbell soup cans on top of each other. I guess you could say, I planted a little seed.

BLACKOUT

ACT ONE

Scene 3

A week later. Frieda is seated. Ira is trying to open her suppositories.

FRIEDA You're not doing it right. You're gonna smoosh the suppository.

IRA I have no nails. You know, I have a half dozen medical degrees. One would assume I'd have the complex "know-how" required to open one of these things.

FRIEDA Where's Marjorie? Only she has the knack for this.

IRA I've got to get going. I'm being profiled on the radio. The show's called "The Good Walk Among Us." I can't be late.

FRIEDA Ira, I need this suppository and I need it now. You'd think they'd make these things accessible for arthritic fingers. The indignities of old age. Believe me, it stinks. So where is my daughter?

IRA She went out early. She said she had a million things to do.

FRIEDA What does she have to do?

IRA I didn't demand an itinerary. I'm just so relieved to see her out and about.

FRIEDA She's out with that Lee. Lee. Lillian was her name. I'm so tired of hearing about Lee this, Lee that. The woman can do no wrong.

IRA Could you be just a little bit jealous?

FRIEDA No. Concerned, inquisitive, dubious. Marjorie's a fragile creature, a water sprite. An easy target.

IRA But this Lee sounds like a great gal. Been everywhere, done everything. Marjorie says Lee gave Steven Spielberg the idea for "E.T."

FRIEDA I remember her distinctly as a child. There was something funny about her.

IRA How so?

FRIEDA It's hard to explain. But even at ten years old, she'd look down her nose at you and still kiss your ass. And the mother was strange. A British Jew. Queenie Greenblatt. Thought she was better than everyone else.

IRA I just wish we could meet the great mystery woman.

The front door unlocks and Marjorie enters, loaded down with packages. She looks like a completely different woman—vital, energetic.

MARJORIE What a day! I had such a full schedule and I got everything done. (*kisses Ira*) Darling. Hello, Mother. (*She kisses Frieda on the forehead.*)

IRA Whatcha been up to?

MARJORIE Besides buying you the most beautiful Missoni sweater you ever saw, I schlepped all over town until I finally found those leggings for Rochelle. I took a morning yoga class. And I attended at Japan House the most extraordinary seminar given by Kazuo Ohno, the father of modern Bhuto.

FRIEDA Bhuto? What's Bhuto?

MARJORIE It's a form of high performance art and dance developed in Japan as a reaction to the nuclear devastation. The man is amazing. Ninety years old. With one gesture, he can express a world of sorrow and complexity. His is the art of silent poetry.

FRIEDA It doesn't sound for me.

MARJORIE No, Mother, it's not for you.

FRIEDA Did Lee go with you?

MARJORIE No, she had other plans. Why do you ask?

FRIEDA You two have become as thick as thieves.

MARJORIE I have been seeing a lot of Lee. It's so wonderful having a best friend. Did I tell you that she was in the studio when all those rock stars recorded "We Are The World"? She's a close friend of Quincy Jones.

FRIEDA Who's that?

MARJORIE A famous record producer. She met him through Martin Luther King during the March on Washington. (*She exits into the bedroom with her packages.*)

FRIEDA Have you ever heard such dreck? You gotta do something, Ira. I'm very worried.

IRA What am I supposed to do? Forbid her from seeing the woman?

FRIEDA Then I'm going to say something.

IRA Please, Frieda. Don't start up.

FRIEDA What do you mean, start up?

IRA Marjorie is just emerging from a severe depression. Let her be happy.

FRIEDA All right. If you think that's best. You're the doctor.

Marjorie enters again.

FRIEDA Marjorie, are you having a lesbian affair?

IRA Frieda!

MARJORIE Mother, must you poison everything?

FRIEDA I am your mother. I am very concerned about your relationship with Lillian Greenblatt.

MARJORIE I don't know how to answer this. All right, you know what I'm going to say to you. Perhaps I am, perhaps I'm not. (*She turns to Ira and mouths for his benefit, "No, I'm not."*)

FRIEDA Listen, I've been around, These things happen. A woman goes through the menopause. The marriage becomes very, uh, familiar. Forgive me, Ira.

MARJORIE Mother, would you please—

FRIEDA I've never told anyone this but many years ago—

MARJORIE I really don't want to hear this.

FRIEDA You say we don't communicate. Here, I'm trying to communicate. About ten years ago, my neighbor in Schwab House, Rivkie Dubow, put the moves on me.

IRA Rivkie Dubow was a lesbian? She had six grandchildren and wore a hair net.

FRIEDA No. She was not a lesbian. What I'm saying is late in life, she had been widowed for many years, she found herself uncontrollably attracted to me. We were baking hamantaschen in my kitchen. We were folding in the prune butter when she impulsively kissed me on the lips. Oh, she gave me a very difficult time.

MARJORIE Mother, I was joking. Trust me, I am not having an affair with Lee.

IRA I've never quite understood what she does for a living.

MARJORIE She's a fund-raiser for some charity. I don't know. What is this? An investigation? The House Un-American Activities Committee?

FRIEDA We are your family. We are concerned. Within one week, this person has invaded your life and refuses to meet any of us.

MARJORIE It's been my choice. Ira, you have your students and your work. Mother, you have your suppositories. I want something of my own.

IRA You have to understand that when you only hear about a person, they seem very mysterious.

FRIEDA We don't want you to be living a life of illusion like Blanche DuBois.

MARJORIE Maybe this is a good time to bring this up. Lee and I were thinking of taking a trip together.

IRA Where would you go? On a cruise?

MARJORIE I've never been to Germany. We were thinking of taking a boat trip down the Rhine.

FRIEDA You're joking. You've got to be kidding.

MARJORIE Not at all. You know how fascinated I am by German culture. I've studied the language. Why shouldn't I go?

FRIEDA Have you ever heard of a little thing called the Holocaust? Your father's entire family was wiped out in the gas chambers. I can't believe you would set foot on German soil.

MARJORIE Most of the time I'll be on a boat.

FRIEDA Your glib tone fails to amuse.

IRA I'm staying out of this. Listen for me at five-thirty on BAI. I only hope it's not too worshipful. I'll be home by seven the latest. (*Kisses Marjorie.*) Frieda, behave. (*Kisses her and exits.*)

FRIEDA It's that Lee who's put you up to this.

MARJORIE Put me up to what? To take a lovely relaxing trip to Europe?

FRIEDA To go to a country riddled with anti-Semitism, a people who, to this day, are unrepentant. Joan is right. You reject and ridicule your religion's every principle and tradition.

MARJORIE That is not true.

FRIEDA Even as a child, you only wanted to fraternize with Gentiles. You were so impressed with Lillian's mother, Queenie

Greenblatt, because she'd tried to pass as goyim. Let me tell you, she was not your friend.

MARJORIE She couldn't have been nicer to me. And thank God she was, since I got so little affection at home.

FRIEDA She didn't even want you to play with her child. I had to make a big stink about it at your school.

MARJORIE Thank you for telling me that.

FRIEDA You live with rose-colored glasses on. You can't go on being Blanche DuBois.

MARJORIE Enough with the Blanche Dubois! Mother, I am going to Germany. Oh yes. And you know something else? We're gonna hop over to Austria and have tea with Kurt Waldheim.

FRIEDA (*Rising.*) I'm going. You'll do anything to strike back at me. I can hardly walk. I'm in such terrible discomfort.

MARJORIE What's wrong?

FRIEDA (*Bitterly.*) I've got a stabbing pain in my rectum. You know, there's a very strong possibility that I might have cancer of the colon.

MARJORIE (*Not taken in.*) Are you coming over for dinner? I'm making stuffed cabbages.

FRIEDA (*Venomously.*) I don't want your food. You go to Germany, Marjorie. You go to Germany. And I hope you have pleasant dreams while you're sleeping on mattresses filled with Jewish hair!

Frieda exits.

BLACKOUT

ACT ONE

Scene 4

Several days later. Evening. Marjorie has invited Lee to dinner. However, the guest of honor is over an hour late. Ira puts on a CD of Ella Fitzgerald. He hovers over a tray of hors d'oeuvres on the coffee table. He starts to take one but then decides not to disturb the elaborate design of the plate. Marjorie enters.

MARJORIE (*Very tense.*) I don't know what to do. She's nearly two hours late.

IRA You can't call her?

MARJORIE I don't have a phone number. She keeps moving around from friend to friend. Should we be calling hospitals?

IRA No. It's too early for that.

MARJORIE You'd think she'd call. The meat's going to be as dry and tough as leather.

IRA And if she doesn't come, it won't be the end of the world.

MARJORIE If she doesn't come?

IRA It's a possibility. I was so looking forward to finally meeting her.

MARJORIE And she was looking forward to meeting you. I thought a quiet little dinner would be the perfect introduction. What time is it? (*Checks the clock.*) Well, I don't know what to do.

IRA There's nothing you can do.

The doorbell rings.

MARJORIE Oh, thank God.

Ira answers the door. It's Frieda.

FRIEDA Have you sat down to dinner yet?

IRA No, we haven't.

It's clear that Marjorie and her mother haven't spoken since we last saw them.

FRIEDA (*Glancing around the room.*) Where's Lillian? In the bathroom?

IRA She's not here yet.

FRIEDA (*Checking her watch.*) What time's she supposed to be here?

IRA She's late. (*He raises his finger and mouths the word "Don't."*)

FRIEDA Marjorie, I don't like us not speaking.

MARJORIE I'm not angry with you, Mother. You're the one who's angry.

FRIEDA Well, I'm cooling down. Germany is a very emotional subject for me. You've certainly gone all out. This is beautiful. I just wanted to say that I'm okay. Are you okay? (*Beat.*) Okay, I'm leaving.

MARJORIE Mother, sit. Ira, you can stop circling the hors d'oeuvres like a vulture. Eat. You must be starving.

IRA (*Helping himself.*) I've had quite a day. I lectured at NYU. You know, I got a standing ovation. Afterwards, this student, a good-looking kid, came up to me. He said, "Dr. Taub, you are a spellbinder. You radiate a simple goodness that's almost biblical."

FRIEDA He's put his finger on it.

MARJORIE I'm bringing out the bruschetta. (*She goes to the kitchen and takes the bruschetta out and places it on the table.*)

IRA This young man suggested that I compile my lectures into a book.

FRIEDA I'm surprised you haven't thought of that before.

IRA I've had offers, but I wonder if they would translate on the printed page. They might lose something without my timing, my passion, my warmth.

MARJORIE Ira, bruschetta?

IRA Thank you. It looks good. (*Takes a small piece.*)

MARJORIE Mother?

FRIEDA No thank you. The bread looks very hard. You know, my teeth.

Marjorie sits down and starts to eat a piece of the bruschetta.

FRIEDA I haven't eaten much all day. I've had terrible cramps. I may have overdone it with the suppositories. For three days I've had the worst diarrhea. Just light brown liquid.

MARJORIE Mother, you do this on purpose, don't you?

FRIEDA What?

MARJORIE Whenever I'm eating, you always bring up your trouble with your bowels.

FRIEDA That is not true.

MARJORIE No, you do it without fail. It's nauseating. Even when you're not here. You have this sixth sense. I'll be just about to dive into a dish of chocolate mousse and sure enough the phone will ring and it's you talking about the color and texture of your latest BM!

FRIEDA How can you say that?

MARJORIE It's true. It's disgusting.

IRA This is not pleasant table talk.

FRIEDA I'm very sorry. I've just been in terrible discomfort.

IRA When was the last time you spoke to Dr. Finerman?

FRIEDA This morning.

IRA And what did he have to say?

FRIEDA He wants me to come in for another colonoscopy. I don't think I could survive it. You can't eat for twenty-four hours and then the enema and finally that huge thing stuck up you. It's so dehumanizing. I give up. Call Kevorkian. Have him put me out of my misery.

MARJORIE Mother, he's in the slammer, taken down his shingle, out of business.

IRA I think you should have the procedure. They might find the very thing that's giving you this blockage.

FRIEDA They never have before. I've had three in the last six months.

MARJORIE (*On the verge of hysteria.*) This is the limit! Mother, you're not having another colonoscopy.

FRIEDA But Dr. Finerman is insisting on it. In fact, he wants you to call him.

MARJORIE He wants me to call him. Why?

FRIEDA He wants you to convince me to have the procedure.

MARJORIE I'm calling him right now.

She goes to the wall phone in the kitchen and dials the number. It's written on a piece of paper taped to the refrigerator.

IRA Marjorie, I don't think this is the best time for you to be doing this.

MARJORIE I will not have my mother subjected to such abuse! I think he gets off on it.

FRIEDA You think?

IRA He's not in his office at this hour.

MARJORIE I'm calling him at home.

IRA Marjorie, don't.

MARJORIE I've had it!

FRIEDA What's she gonna do?

IRA Marjorie, put down the phone. Marjorie—

MARJORIE Dr. Finerman? Marjorie Taub. I understand you've been advising my mother to have another colonoscopy . . . This is the fourth one in six months. What are looking for, gold? . . . No, you listen to me. That old woman's had more things stuck up her tochis than a gay porn star! If I find out that you've inserted one more probe up my mother's rectum, I will personally come over to your office with my largest pepper mill and buster, you won't be sittin' down for a week!! (*She hangs up, runs out of the room and slams the door.*)

FRIEDA I can't believe she did that. How will I ever face him?

IRA I'm very worried.

FRIEDA I feel sorry for Lee, showing up when she's like this.

IRA I don't think Lee's going to come.

FRIEDA Why? What's happened to her?

IRA Don't you think it's odd that no one has ever seen her?

FRIEDA Marjorie was always very secretive.

The doorbell rings.

FRIEDA That must be her.

IRA No, it's Mohammed, the doorman.

FRIEDA The Arab boy?

Ira opens the front door and it is indeed Mohammed.

IRA Mohammed, please come in.

MOHAMMED I can only stay but for a few minutes. Hello, Mrs. Tuchman.

IRA Please, sit down. (*Mohammed sits on the sofa.*) Mohammed, you've worked a lot in the past week.

MOHAMMED Every day. I've been filling in for Felix. He fell off his bike and hurt his knee.

IRA Yes, I gave him the name of an excellent orthopedist. I told him I'd pick up the tab. Don't spread it around. If my wife had any visitors, it's a good chance you'd have seen them. Right?

MOHAMMED I should think so.

IRA Has my wife had any visitors in the afternoon?

MOHAMMED None that I am aware of, Dr. Taub.

FRIEDA Then you've never seen Lillian Greenblatt?

MOHAMMED Who is that?

IRA Mrs. Taub's friend.

MOHAMMED I suppose I haven't.

FRIEDA What does this mean?

IRA She's a phantom.

FRIEDA You're upsetting me, Ira.

IRA It's very upsetting. You know how a lonely child will invent an imaginary friend? I think that's what Marjorie's done.

FRIEDA Don't say such a thing.

IRA I know it seems inconceivable.

MOHAMMED I should be going. This is a private matter.

IRA If you could stay for a few more minutes. I know how fond Mrs. Taub is of you.

FRIEDA But all the things she's told us. The stories, the travels. It's all ephemera?

IRA I don't know what else to believe. Of course, it's my fault. I'm never around. My children suffered from my absence. I slave for the needy, for the disenfranchised, but am oblivious to my own wife's torments.

FRIEDA Stop it. You're the greatest husband and father in the entire world. My poor Marjorie. You really think she's invented this Lee out of thin air?

IRA The human mind protects us from trauma. Marjorie was so devastated by the loss of her therapist Reba Fabrikant that she created the fantasy figure of a beloved childhood friend, a friend who's led the romantic, adventurous life that Marjorie wished she had.

FRIEDA My mind is agog.

IRA It's all somehow connected to her frustration with her intellectual limitations.

FRIEDA (*Indignantly.*) Limitations? What limitations? She has no limitations.

IRA She needs our help. Can I count on you?

FRIEDA I must find the physical wherewithal. You know I'd kill for my daughter. I'd kill for her. With my bare hands I'd kill for her.

Ira crosses to the bedroom door.

IRA Marjorie! Are you okay? Marjorie?

Marjorie enters wearing lounging pajamas. She's trying to put on a brave face.

IRA You've changed.

MARJORIE The Vera Wang was depressing me. I think we should eat. Mohammed?

FRIEDA He was looking for me. He's installing new handrails for my toilet.

MARJORIE Would you like something to eat? We've plenty of food.

MOHAMMED Oh yes. I adore bruschetta. When I was a child, we had a summer villa in Tuscany.

IRA Please. (*Beat.*) Marjorie—

MARJORIE What is it, sweetie?

IRA I feel I've led you astray.

MARJORIE That sounds very melodramatic. Don't you want to eat? I thought you were hungry.

IRA A marriage is a partnership and in incalculable ways I've let you down.

MARJORIE Ira, you are who you are. Now please, let's just eat. Mohammed, have another.

IRA Loneliness can make us play all sorts of funny tricks on ourselves. Invent things, create fantasies.

MARJORIE Invent? Create? What are you talking about?

IRA Lee.

MARJORIE What about Lee?

IRA I think you wanted a friend so desperately that you made her up.

MARJORIE Made her up? What are you saying?

IRA It's perfectly understandable why you would do this.

MARJORIE Ira, if you're putting me on, this is a very sick joke.

IRA Darling, I love you so much. There is no Lee.

MARJORIE Are you saying that she's a figment of my imagination? That I've flipped out?

IRA Please, don't put it that way.

MARJORIE I don't know how else to put it. That you would even think that I would do such a thing. I am not crazy.

IRA Nobody's saying you're crazy.

MARJORIE I'm telling you, I've seen the woman. I talk to her. Every day.

FRIEDA Darling, I talk to your Aunt Minna every day and she's been dead for forty years. It's not all that different.

MARJORIE You and Aunt Minna don't go to the Film Forum to see a Werner Herzog revival.

IRA So you've been to the movies with Lee?

MARJORIE Yes. Well no. At the last minute, Lee couldn't make it. Something came up. No big deal. I went by myself. (*The awful truth's beginning to dawn on her.*) And then we were supposed to see that Korean cellist at Merkin Hall. Lee canceled out of that too. And the matinee of the Folklórico Ballet of Mexico.

IRA But surely you've gone out to lunch with her. You've walked down the street with her.

MARJORIE She never shows up whenever we have plans outside the apartment. That's so weird. It's never occurred to me. Has anyone else ever seen her? Mohammed, you let her in every day. You see her go out.

MOHAMMED Mrs. Taub, I have never seen her.

MARJORIE A woman my age. Very attractive, tall. (*He shakes his head.*) She wears a gold ladybug on her coat. You've never seen her because she never buzzes up. She just appears at the door. Like a ghost. Oh my God. Oh my God. (*She bursts into tears and is unable to talk.*)

IRA Take a deep breath.

MARJORIE I've lost my mind.

FRIEDA (*Starting to cry.*) You haven't lost your mind. Don't say that. My beautiful baby. (*Desperately.*) Oh my, look. Look who's here. Lee. You look wonderful. How's Queenie?

IRA Frieda, stop it.

FRIEDA (*Sobbing.*) I don't know what to do! Tell me what to do.

MOHAMMED I should go. This is no place for me. Mrs. Taub, if there is anything I can do for you.

IRA Thank you, Mohammed.

Ira opens the door and Mohammed exits.

MARJORIE Mohammed's never seen her. Call Bellevue. Commit me. Put me in one those tubs with the canvas zippered up.

IRA I would never do such a thing. We need to find you a new therapist.

MARJORIE Somewhere along the line, I've tipped into madness.

IRA You need a tranquilizer.

MARJORIE No. I want to hold on to whatever lucidity I have left.

FRIEDA Marjorie, please, you're upsetting me.

MARJORIE All those years I spent poring over the letters and diaries of Anne Sexton and Sylvia Plath, Virginia Woolf, I never thought I'd end up the same way. An imaginary secret friend. It's like something out of Kafka. A candle flickering in the bleak darkness.

IRA I'm getting you a tranquilizer. (*Ira runs into the bathroom.*)

MARJORIE No, it's not Kafka at all. What am I talking about? Only Thomas Mann could do justice to this situation. I'm Aschenbach in "Death in Venice"—aging, pathetic, in tragic pursuit of a dream of beauty.

FRIEDA I need the tranquilizer. I'm going to have another stroke.

MARJORIE No, no, no, no, no.

FRIEDA What is it, Marjorie?

MARJORIE I'm Siddhartha.

FRIEDA Who?

MARJORIE Siddhartha, from the masterwork by Hermann Hesse. Siddhartha, a young Indian Brahmin, in quest of the great Buddha. Only this majestic figure can provide him with the nirvana he so desperately seeks. Lillian Greenblatt is my Buddha.

FRIEDA So you're saying she's real?

MARJORIE (*With great ferocity.*) Mother, must you be so literal? No, she's not flesh and blood. I have created this illusion to bring my mind and soul closer to spiritual purification.

The doorbell rings. Ira runs on holding the bottle of tranquilizers. He answers the door. It's Lee, holding two suitcases.

LEE I am so sorry I'm late. I had this forcockta Indian cabdriver who took me all the way across the river.

BLACKOUT

END OF ACT ONE

ACT TWO

Scene 1

Two days later. Early evening. Lee is in the kitchen, with Marjorie assisting her. Ira is reading a magazine. Frieda scrutinizes them all.

LEE I'm making such a mess. I hope the dinner's worth it.

MARJORIE It's been fascinating. I'm so grateful you brought along your wok.

LEE I always travel with a wok and three pairs of false eyelashes. Darling, slice up some of those scallions. But never, and I mean NEVER, attempt a paella in a wok.

MARJORIE Bad news, huh?

LEE Just ask Placido Domingo. He'll never let me forget it.

FRIEDA How many more nights do you think you'll be shacking up here?

MARJORIE As long as she wants.

LEE You are a true friend. This couple I was staying with used to be so hip and lively. What happens to people when they get older? Somewhere along the line, they turned into right-wing zombies. I had to hotfoot it out of there before we killed each other.

MARJORIE Put it all behind you. You're safe now.

IRA So, um, what are we having for dinner? It seems very complicated.

MARJORIE Don't interrogate her. Let it be a surprise.

LEE It's a crazy quilt of a Chinese meal. Stir-fried clams in a black bean sauce, Peking duck, ants climbing a tree.

FRIEDA What the hell's that?

LEE You're supposed to visualize the minced pork over the cellophane noodles as ants climbing up a tree. It's the whimsical Szechwan sense of humor.

FRIEDA I don't eat pork.

MARJORIE Since when? You, the queen of the BLT.

LEE I'm making a lovely vegetable medley called a rainbow salad.

IRA That has a healthy ring to it.

MARJORIE Everything Lee cooks is healthy.

LEE Frieda, the three of us had so much fun this afternoon in Chinatown. I wish you could have joined us.

MARJORIE You should have heard Lee speaking Chinese to all the vendors.

IRA You would have thought she was Madame Chiang Kai-shek.

MARJORIE Was that meant to be sarcastic?

IRA Stop snapping at me.

LEE Margie, slice up the cucumber and carrots into very thin slices. I love having you as my sous-chef. (*She kisses her on the cheek.*)

IRA You gotta teach me a little of that Chinese. I have two students from Beijing.

LEE Ira, my darling, any time. (*She tosses off a sentence in Chinese.*)

IRA Is that from Column A or Column B?

FRIEDA My dentist, Dr. Ling, is Chinese. Tell me how to say 'I'm not sitting in this waiting room one more minute, Dr. Fuck Face."

LEE I think that's a little beyond the linguistic capabilities of an imaginary friend.

MARJORIE You are real, aren't you? I'm not making up these last few days.

LEE This phantom is so real, she's even got a bunion.

IRA Okay, make fun of me. Somehow it all added up.

LEE It was because you cared.

MARJORIE It's because I'm such a pathetic figure. How could I ever have a fabulous friend such as you.

IRA Stop that, Marjorie.

MARJORIE Poor Mohammed thought he was protecting me. That's why he lied. He thought I had a secret lover. Boy, I really thought I was losing it.

LEE Have you told them the big news?

IRA What news?

LEE Marjorie's writing a new book.

MARJORIE The silence is broken. At last, I feel free to create.

IRA What's the book about?

MARJORIE I really shouldn't discuss it at this early stage of gestation. All I'll say is the protagonist is a cloistured nun in nineteenth-century Munich. The book is a response to Schopenhauer's treatise "The World as Will and Idea."

FRIEDA Marjorie, write about what you know.

MARJORIE (*To Lee.*) You see what I'm dealing with here? The anti-intellectualism.

IRA But isn't there a limited audience for this sort of endeavor?

MARJORIE Don't say that to me now when the juices are flowing.

IRA I'm just saying, would you buy a book like that?

MARJORIE I would find it very stimulating. Yes. Ira, why must everything be an entertainment? If you want that, go to the circus. Watch a plate spinner. Must everything be dumbed down to the lowest common denominator? The highest goal a writer can attain is creating something that challenges the reader's perceptions.

IRA If they can stay awake. I see you dozing at some of the oddball things you drag us to.

MARJORIE I am not perfect. Sometimes I don't get it. Goes right over my head. Doesn't matter. I am there.

IRA But Marjorie, that's like a punishment.

MARJORIE (*Tensely.*) Ira, please, this is not your metier.

IRA Maybe I'm not expressing myself clearly.

LEE What I think Ira is trying to say is that depth should not be measured by obfuscation. There is, after all, the profundity of the simple. The innate mystery found in ... orange, a persimmon.

IRA Thank you. That's precisely my point.

MARJORIE All right! All right! Just say it. Say it! I'm a pretentious, bourgeois cow! I want to write something that I would hate! Is that what you're saying?

IRA Honey, I'm not trying to upset you—

MARJORIE End of discussion. This summer I'm going to reread all of Rilke.

LEE Marjorie, while we're in Europe, we should go to Switzerland and visit Rilke's grave. It's remarkable the sense of peace that washes over you. And in Zurich, I have a friend you've got to meet. Fabulous woman. She's a mute but she conducts the symphony. She lives in the most—

FRIEDA (*Interrupting*) You know what I got in the mail today? A letter requesting a donation to the United Negro College Fund signed by Jesse Jackson. I wrote him some letter back.

MARJORIE Mother, what did you say?

FRIEDA I wrote "Dear Mr. Jackson, I wouldn't give you a red cent after the vile and irresponsible ways the leaders of the black community have fanned the flames of anti-Semitism in this city.

As far as I'm concerned, you and your buddies, Farrakhan and Khalid Muhammed, go flick yourselves with a kosher salami." And I signed it "Hymie from Hymietown."

MARJORIE Mother, I am appalled.

IRA So what else is new? She wrote the same thing to Jesse Helms, the president of Sony and her old hairdresser. She's an equal opportunity fuck you-er.

LEE Frieda, I don't want to get into a heated discussion over racism with you. However, if you feel threatened by disempowered people of color, you can make a difference by giving money for education.

FRIEDA I give money to Israel.

Lee carries out a plate of dumplings.

MARJORIE (*Uncomfortable*) Very good. Now, let's eat. My, this is really a Babette's feast.

IRA Mmmm. Smells great.

LEE Now be very careful. These dumplings are hot. Plunk it in the dipping sauce. I intentionally left a bit of the soup in the dumpling so you have the sensation of it bursting in your mouth. It's spicy.

Marjorie and Ira each take a dumpling.

MARJORIE Mother, you want me to cut one up for you?

FRIEDA I don't think so. I like my food bland.

MARJORIE Oh, it's marvelous. Bursts in your mouth, just like you said.

IRA You're some gourmet. You really should try one, Frieda.

FRIEDA My digestive system is so out of whack. I've still got the worst cramps and diarrhea.

MARJORIE Mother, please.

FRIEDA Dear merciful God, every morning I sit on the toilet in such agony. It would be a mitzvah if you could just kill me. Call Dr. Kevorkian.

MARJORIE You want to die, Mother? You really want to die? Well, I would like very much to oblige you with that gift. (*She goes over to Ira's laptop computer.*)

IRA What are you doing?

MARJORIE Show me how this thing works. I want to go online. Now that Kevorkian's in prison, there's got to be others who are providing this service. I am going to find this person. I am determined to find this person!

IRA Get away from that computer. You'll break it.

MARJORIE Don't tell me what to do and don't patronize me.

FRIEDA The man's a saint to put up with you.

MARJORIE A saint to a homeless person with a stuffed nose but not to me. Dr. Taub, I'm suffocating in here. You don't know me. The real me. How could you? You see only the surface of things. I have ambiguities you can't even begin to fathom. How do you turn this goddam thing on?

IRA Why are you doing this?

MARJORIE Oh, look, I did it. I'm not such an idiot. Ira, show me how to get on the World Wide Web. Isn't that what it's called? The superhighway? I'm going to search and find someone out there in cyberspace who will kill my mother! And I will pay. I will pay top dollar for this service. And pronto. Wednesday soon enough? Tuesday? Monday? You're history. Say your prayers 'cause you're going down.

LEE (*Shutting the laptop.*) Stop it! You hear me! Stop it!

MARJORIE I can't take it! I can't take any more!

FRIEDA No sympathy, no compassion, no rachmones for anyone but herself.

LEE Enough out of you. Two grown women carrying on like infants. This is the time in your lives when you should make peace with each other.

MARJORIE It's impossible.

IRA Lee, this goes on five shows a day.

LEE Come with me. I want you to sit next to Frieda. (*Lee leads Marjorie over to the divan where Frieda is sitting.*) I want you to sit on the arm of the chair.

MARJORIE What are you doing?

LEE Frieda, take her hands.

FRIEDA This is ludicrous.

IRA Frieda, do as she says. I want to see this.

LEE You both love to view yourselves as victims. All the awful cards that have been dealt you. Well, you can't both be victims all the time. One of you occasionally has to be the perpetrator. Got me?

FRIEDA I have never done anything to intentionally hurt my daughter.

LEE But unintentionally you've hurt her many times. And you, Marjorie, you make no allowances for other people's tsuris. Maybe your mother is particularly bitchy today because she's terrified of death. And seeing us all laughing and running around and having a great time is a grim reminder of her bleak future. Frieda, I want you to say to Marjorie, "Yes, there have been times when I have been a complete and utter asshole."

FRIEDA What?

LEE Say it.

IRA Frieda, this is the sort of thing Rochelle does for a living. You heard the lady. Say the magic words.

FRIEDA Yes, there have been times when I have been a complete and utter asshole. Now, it's her turn.

LEE Marjorie?

MARJORIE Mother, yes, there have been times when I have been a complete and utter asshole.

LEE Now kiss and make nice.

Marjorie and Frieda do a perfunctory "air kiss" and separate.

MARJORIE (*Forced to laugh.*) This is the nuttiest therapy I've ever heard of.

IRA I've got to remember this at the next AMA conference.

FRIEDA (*Unrelenting.*) I want to go home and stretch out on the bed.

MARJORIE You're not staying for dinner?

FRIEDA I don't want to wreck up anyone's good time.

MARJORIE (*Onto her mother.*) What are you going to eat?

FRIEDA (*Pointedly.*) I've got an Omaha steak in the freezer. I can pan-fry it in all of five minutes.

MARJORIE Then I'll walk you down the hall.

Marjorie helps her mother get to the door.

LEE Good night, Frieda

MARJORIE I'll be right back. Hold the dumplings. (*She rolls her eyes when her mother isn't looking. They exit. Outside in the hall, we hear Marjorie shout,* "Give me your hands!!")

IRA You should be a diplomat.

LEE It'll last ten minutes.

IRA Five. Lee, you're a very special woman.

LEE I know I can be obnoxious when I get on my soapbox.

IRA I admire your activism. I've had to fight a lot of battles to get my clinic going. Last week I treated a young black man, a sidewalk portrait artist, nearly suicidal from pounding sinus headaches. No insurance. Could I abandon him to fate? Some cortisone spray and I saved that man's life.

LEE If we had a national health care system, he'd have full medical coverage. The *New England Journal of Medicine* wrote that African-American males in Harlem have the same mortality rate as people in Bangladesh. "Lee Green, stop it. You're starting up again."

IRA It's all right.

LEE I guess I'm just a passionate pain in the ass. We're two of a kind, aren't we? Ira, one question. You're such a firebrand. Why early retirement? It doesn't jibe.

IRA I shall hereby dispel the mystery for you. Being trapped in that office six days a week—and I was there six days a week, sometimes seven, ask Marjorie—it left me with the sense that I was limited in my efforts to ease human suffering. I felt that there was an entire world out there that could benefit from everything that I had gleaned from my years of study and application. This decision has given me the renewed vigor and idealism of a first-year grad student.

LEE That's so inspiring. Have another dumpling before they get cold. (*She takes a dumpling and feeds him.*) I think you've got a little on your fly but you'll have to wipe that off. We don't want Marjorie finding us in a compromising position.

IRA Reminds me of an old joke. A man is walking down the street with his little boy. On the way to the park, they see two dogs having sex on the pavement. The little boy says, "Daddy, what are those dogs doing?" The man says, "Don't look over there." They keep walking but the little boy can't get his eyes off the two dogs. Again he asks, "Daddy, what are they doing?" The man says, "It doesn't matter. Let's go." A third time the little boy asks, "Daddy, what are those dogs doing on the sidewalk?" Finally, the father says, "Son, I'll tell you what they're doing. One dog is sick and the other one is pushing her to Mount Sinai." Corny old joke.

LEE Very funny.

IRA Marjorie hates my jokes.

LEE I'm sure she just says she does. You remind me of a friend of mine. He passed away a long time ago. He could always make me laugh. His name was Lenny Bruce.

IRA I remind you of Lenny Bruce?

LEE Lenny had the same charm and quiet sense of danger.

IRA I'm flattered but I'm hardly dangerous.

LEE No?

IRA I drink very moderately, rarely lose my temper and I've never been unfaithful to my wife in thirty-two years.

LEE Man, you must be one of a kind. My life has been littered with nogoodniks.

IRA Men have treated you badly?

LEE When it comes to true love, I'm quite the virgin.

IRA Your first lover wasn't tender and romantic?

LEE My first lover was my father. Just kidding. Sort of. He wasn't physically abusive but rather emotionally seductive. To maintain his interest, Lee became quite the accomplished femme fatale by the age of six. She'd sing songs, do imitations of Jimmy Durante, scratch his back for hours. Evidently her kindergarten set of feminine wiles weren't enough. One night he went out to buy some tonic water and never came back. Daddy's early sayonara taught Lee the power of the elusive. For all you know, I might still be a ghost. Try putting your hand through me.

Drawn like a moth to a flame, Ira hesitantly moves his hand toward her chest. Marjorie enters in the nick of time.

MARJORIE I want to apologize for that scene you just witnessed. Ira, I'm sorry I snapped at you.

IRA Apology accepted.

LEE Your mother's a lot to handle. You do very well, Marjorie.

MARJORIE I get so full of frustration. I just have to lash out.

LEE That's why I vent my rage in activism. Getting involved with the Universal Human Rights Coalition was the best thing that ever happened to Lee Green—and her ulcer.

IRA This is the group you raise money for?

LEE Uh-huh.

IRA You really haven't talked much about what exactly this group does.

LEE We're an international relief organization. We give aid wherever help is needed, regardless of politics. I feel funny talking about this. I don't want you to think I'm pressuring you into making a donation.

MARJORIE I know you're not. But we do make donations to a large number of charitable organizations. Simon Wiesenthal, Equity Fights AIDS, the Roundabout.

IRA How much are you looking to raise?

LEE A hundred and fifty thousand dollars by next Tuesday.

IRA A hundred and fifty thousand. Whew.

LEE It all goes literally into putting food in babies' mouths, vaccines. Sometimes a little cash can bribe a firing squad from shooting an innocent political prisoner. I have actually witnessed that.

MARJORIE You've been to executions?

LEE I have seen political prisoners fall into open graves. Yes.

MARJORIE Well, we'll have to, um—

IRA —think about this. If you have any brochures or, um—

MARJORIE —literature. I mean, is it tax-deductible?

LEE I can get you some literature right away. You're both so adorable. I love the way you finish each other's sentences.

MARJORIE Do we?

IRA Really?

LEE I'm going to say something very shocking.

MARJORIE Lee, we're sophisticated people. Go ahead. Shock us.

LEE I can't decide which of you I'm more attracted to.

MARJORIE Lee!

LEE Now Marjorie, don't get all fartootst. You can't tell me you've never had a crush on a woman.

MARJORIE A schoolteacher, a playmate, the girl who runs the Clinique counter at Saks.

IRA Marjorie?

MARJORIE I just like looking at her. She has a very aristocratic neck. Does that make me a lesbian?

LEE Marjorie, I'm astonished at you. Tell me you're just putting on this bourgeois conservative act.

MARJORIE No, I'm really at heart a very conservative person.

LEE You can't love Hesse's work and be so judgmental of human sexuality.

MARJORIE What are you talking about?

LEE Demian. The relationship between Sinclair and Demian is very homoerotic.

IRA Who are they?

MARJORIE Two male characters in a book by Hermann Hesse. Lee, they were best friends. Sinclair was in love with Demian's mother.

LEE Because Demian's mother looked just like Demian. The whole book was a celebration of a kind of divine pansexuality.

MARJORIE Lee, are you telling me you're a pansexual?

LEE I don't believe in labels. I'm sensual. I'm a sensual being. I love touching and being touched. Haven't you ever wanted to move closer to that salesgirl at Saks and stroke that beautiful neck?

MARJORIE It never occurred to me. I just ask for the astringent.

LEE You're blushing.

MARJORIE Yes, I'm blushing. You're outrageous.

LEE You're blushing because you're intrigued and titillated.

MARJORIE Ira, you haven't said anything for a long time.

IRA I'm staying out of it.

LEE I love seeing the two of you squirm like horny teenagers.

MARJORIE We are merely amused by your shenanigans. You're just teasing us.

IRA You don't really believe in all this mishegoss.

LEE You know what I did this morning? I took a bath and turned on the Jacuzzi. It was fantastic. I'd like to get the two of you into that absurd marble tub and bathe and perfume you and pamper you like spoiled courtesans in a seraglio.

IRA We both have allergic reactions to many floral scents.

Lee starts to unbutton her blouse.

MARJORIE What are you doing?

LEE Getting comfortable.

MARJORIE Well, be uncomfortable.

LEE I love you like this. You've become a young girl again.

IRA Well, I think this kooky conversation has gone on far too long.

LEE Oh Ira, you're a doctor. You can't be afraid of nudity.

IRA My own, yes.

LEE You shouldn't be. I opened the bathroom door a crack when you were taking a shower this morning. You've got nothing to be ashamed of.

MARJORIE (*Aghast.*) Lee, you are talking about my husband.

LEE Lucky lady. (*She gives Marjorie a sudden kiss on the lips.*) Yum yum. (*She kisses Ira.*) Tasty.

MARJORIE I think you've got the wrong idea about us. We are not swingers.

IRA Shouldn't we finish getting dinner ready?

LEE The duck needs to soak in the marinade for at least an hour. I've got an idea. Be right back. (*She dashes off into the bedroom.*)

MARJORIE She's outrageous. A ménage à trois. Could you?

IRA I don't know. You're both very attractive ladies.

MARJORIE Ira, you're not serious.

IRA Probably not. When she gets back, we'll tell her to cool it.

MARJORIE I don't know. Maybe we should have the experience. You find her sexy?

IRA Honestly?

MARJORIE Be honest.

IRA Yes, I do. You know why? Because she reminds me of you.

MARJORIE (*Rolling her eyes.*) That's very sweet. (*She pats his hand.*)

Lee returns with a hash pipe and a plastic bag filled with "something."

IRA That's not tobacco.

LEE Nope. And it ain't marijuana.

MARJORIE Thank God for that.

LEE It's hash.

MARJORIE You've brought hashish into our home?

LEE Darling, if we were in Tangiers, before and after dinner we'd all get blissfully stoned.

MARJORIE Well, we're not in Tangiers. We're on Riverside Drive. They'll smell it down the hall. My mother will have a fit.

IRA Come on, Lee. Put it away.

LEE Now you both think I'm a bad girl.

MARJORIE A very bad girl. I'm having another cocktail. (*She gets up and goes to the kitchen.*)

Lee takes Ira's hand and begins kissing his fingers.

MARJORIE (*Not seeing them.*) Honestly, Lee, I'm more intrigued by bisexuality on an intellectual plane. In theory. Vita and Virginia, Colette and Missy. We're more Ethel and Lucy.

She looks out from the kitchen and sees Lee kissing Ira. Marjorie feels a pang of jealousy but is not sure over whom. She leaves the kitchen and returns to the living room.

After a difficult decision, Marjorie takes Ira away from Lee and gives him a long, sensuous kiss. Ira bends Marjorie back. Lee uses this opportunity to take Marjorie's head in her hands and kisses her deeply.

IRA I feel like I'm in the middle of a *Playboy* spread.

The three of them laugh and move closer together, and the nocturnal revels begin.

BLACKOUT

ACT TWO

Scene 2

The following evening. Ira and Frieda are seated at the dining room table, finishing their profiteroles.

IRA You're getting the early bird special. We're finished and you can still watch *Jeopardy*. Happy?

FRIEDA You're eating early because you're going to a Broadway show.

IRA We're going to BAM to see an experimental all male Irish Oresteia. Marjorie says the director is a twenty-five year old international wunderkind.

FRIEDA She's making you schlep all the way out to Brooklyn. Dear merciful God.

IRA It doesn't take long on the subway.

FRIEDA You should get the Nobel Prize for what you endure.

IRA It's supposed to be very innovative. Epic. Marjorie! We really should get going!

FRIEDA I wish you wouldn't. I'm feeling so shaky.

IRA I'll have my cell phone with me. You can reach us anytime.

FRIEDA I don't understand all that crap. Where were you late last night?

IRA We were home. We ate our Chinese food and we digested it. Where else would we be?

FRIEDA Around one in the morning, I tried calling and no one answered. I stayed up all night worrying about the two of you. Today I can hardly walk.

IRA You must've dialed a wrong number.

FRIEDA I left a message on your answering machine, "chochem" (*Trans. Wiseguy*).

IRA Frieda, you're far too clever for me. You want the truth? We're selling you to white slavers in Singapore.

Lee enters.

LEE We're doing great on time. Ira, how cute you look. So toasty and cuddly. I could take a great big bite out of you.

IRA (*Very uncomfortable.*) Thank you.

LEE I sure hope this Oresteia's livelier than dinner.

IRA I'm sorry. I guess Marjorie and I both had very long days.

LEE I didn't mean to sound critical. I just missed seeing you guys all day. And you both seemed a little down at dinner. Well, as of this moment, please meet the self-appointed vice-president of Good Times. Margie's still dressing?

IRA She can never make up her mind.

LEE But when she's finished, it's certainly worth the wait.

IRA So Lee, you seem like a lady with a lot of plans. What's next for you? I can't imagine you staying put in one place too long.

LEE I'm kind of playing it by ear. It's rather fun not knowing where I'll be next month.

IRA Next month? So you think you'll be leaving New York in a few weeks?

LEE I honestly can't say, sweetie. Miss Lee Green has rekindled her love affair with Manhattan. I adore every smelly block of it.

FRIEDA Oy, I'm so stuffed up. I need a tissue. (*Frieda clears her throat and crosses to the downstage table to take a tissue out of a box. She blows her nose and sits.*)

LEE Frieda, your shoe is untied. Let me fix it before you trip. My mother drilled into me that a good houseguest should make herself indispensable.

Lee bends down in front of Frieda to tie her lace.

FRIEDA Let Marjorie do it. There's a special way.

Marjorie enters from the bedroom. From her angle, it looks like Lee is performing an intimate sexual act upon the elderly Frieda.

FRIEDA It's too tight. Leave it alone!

MARJORIE (*Horror struck.*) Mother!!!!

Lee moves away and Marjorie, embarrassed, sees how innocent it all is.

FRIEDA What's wrong with you?

MARJORIE I'm sorry. I don't know what I was thinking. (*She takes Frieda's plate into the kitchen.*)

LEE So what are we three musketeers going to do tomorrow? I am dying to see the Francis Bacon retrospective at the Guggenheim.

IRA Oh, tomorrow's bad. I have to be at the clinic. I have a welfare mom coming in with phlegm as thick as rubber cement.

MARJORIE Tomorrow I promised I'd go shopping with my friend Paula Zaback. It's her youngest daughter's wedding.

LEE That actually sounds like fun. May I join?

MARJORIE You'd be miserable. Paula's such a bore. I only hang out with her because she gets me free tickets to the lectures at the Ninety-Second Street Y.

LEE Let's skip it. It's just as well. I should catch up on some of my phone calls. Your guestroom is so comfy. It's like a warm, little cocoon.

IRA Lee, I'm glad you feel so at home. But it really is a rather small apartment. That's why we rarely have houseguests for more than a weekend.

LEE Okay. Say no more. Your darling husband's been dropping hints like grenades.

IRA Actually, what I was trying to say was . . .

LEE It's the phone, isn't it? I feel terribly guilty making so many calls. You know, the answer is to have another line installed in the guest room. Don't worry. I'll order it the first thing in the morning. Now, not another word about it.

IRA Actually, what I wanted to say was—

FRIEDA (*Interrupting.*) I have to go to the bathroom. (*Sarcastically.*) Marjorie, if it's not too much trouble?

LEE I'll take you. Marjorie, sit.

FRIEDA Let Marjorie do it. You have to stand outside until I finish.

LEE Don't worry. I won't go away.

Lee insists on helping. Frieda moves towards the bathroom down the hall. Lee walks behind her.

FRIEDA Don't touch me or I'll fall and break my hip again.

LEE I promise I won't. I was briefly a nurse in Sarajevo. (*They exit.*)

IRA Marjorie, I can hardly look you in the eye. I cannot believe what we did last night.

MARJORIE I know. How do you think I feel? I was a daughter of Sappho.

IRA You didn't do anything to be ashamed of.

MARJORIE I lay there and allowed myself to be—pleasured by another woman. I have to be held accountable. What does this say about us?

IRA Nothing. It was just one of those crazy things. We mustn't blow it out of proportion. She has some chutzpah suggesting we put in another phone line.

MARJORIE She does have chutzpah. But we must be egging her on.

IRA Egging her on? About the telephone?

MARJORIE I'm talking about last night. The menage. I can't even say it. We must have sent out some sort of a smoke signal. We let her feel that we were available.

IRA In what way did we do this?

MARJORIE I don't know. Body language. We projected an easy sexuality. It's not a conscious thing, Ira. And out of these subliminal erotic thoughts, we created a rampaging golem.

IRA A what?

MARJORIE A golem. In Jewish folklore. It's sort of a yiddishe Frankenstein monster. It's sculpted out of mud, and acts out its master's most secret wishes. Perhaps we created this golem out of our hidden sexual desires. And now the creature is running amuck.

IRA Well, let's stop the creature before it calls A, T & T.

MARJORIE She's gotten me all confused. I can't express it. I never imagined that I could allow another woman to make love to me. Maybe there are other experiences I need to open myself up to.

IRA What experiences? Bestiality? Necrophilia?

MARJORIE Darling, I'm asking you to be a little sensitive here. Really listen to me. Maybe our marriage is something we need to discuss.

IRA I didn't know our marriage was in trouble.

MARJORIE I'm not saying that. Oh God, I don't know what I'm saying. I just don't want us to be complacent or stagnant. I don't want us to be afraid of self-reflection. A painter like Rembrant revisited the same subject time after time and always with a very different take on it.

IRA I buy that. A nose and throat man examines the same asthmatic patient several times a year. The condition is the same but the bronchial obstruction is ever changeable. However, with careful monitoring, breathing can be restored to normalcy.

MARJORIE Something has happened Ira. For weeks, months really, I lay on this sofa, feeling a kind of blankness. Just this queasy terror of the unknown.

IRA And now it's different?

MARJORIE Yes, I do feel something. I feel the need to question. What do I want? What do I need? What do I believe in? What do I want to believe in? Which questions are mere vanity?

IRA But you were always asking yourself questions? You're a questioning individual.

MARJORIE They were the wrong questions. And they weren't truly questions of the soul. They were intellectual calisthenics.

IRA I know one thing. I want Lee out of here. And soon.

MARJORIE And where's she going to go at such short notice?

IRA She has to leave some time. Doesn't she?

MARJORIE I hate kicking her out because we're so uptight.

IRA Trust me, we're not so uptight. Last night I was like a man possessed. Going back and forth between the two of you. That wasn't Dr. V. Ira Taub. That sex-crazed madman was a stranger.

MARJORIE What if she expects a second performance? We both can't feign a headache.

IRA It probably won't happen again. Last night for her was more about the conquest. We were forbidden fruit.

MARJORIE You think she just wanted us once and that was it?

IRA You want more?

MARJORIE (*With mounting indignation.*) No. I just hate being tossed aside like an old cabbage at the Fairway. Really, the more I think about it, we were, in a sense, raped.

IRA (*Dubious.*) Well—

MARJORIE No, Ira. It was date rape. We said no and she persisted.

Frieda enters, followed by Lee.

FRIEDA It was nearly a catastrophe. I fell.

MARJORIE Oh my God.

IRA Are you all right?

LEE She's fine.

FRIEDA I fell trying to sit on the toilet. Lee came in and picked me off the floor. She's really something. Do you know she's friends with Andy Griffith?

IRA Look at the time. We should get going.

MARJORIE Mother, I'll walk you back.

LEE I'll take her. You know, darlings, I woke up with a touch of bursitis in my shoulder. Too much fun and games last night. Do you guys really want to go to this thing? I mean, it is five hours long and mostly in Gaelic. Maybe we should stay in, relax, put on some cool jazz, open a bottle of wine and just, you know, party.

Ira and Marjorie know exactly what she means by "party" and they definitely don't want to stick around for round two.

IRA I gotta confess. I was really set on that Oresteia. I am a major Greek theater buff from way back. (*Ira grabs their coats out of the closet.*)

MARJORIE And this production is supposed to be revelatory. I understand for the first time they've really mined the bitter humor in Aeschylus. You stay home and nurse that shoulder. And go to bed early. That's an order.

IRA And when we get back we should have a talk. A real talk.

LEE As long as you don't mind talking in front of Raffi.

IRA Who's Raffi?

MARJORIE You invited someone over?

LEE He's a good pal. Teaches movement over at HB Studios in the Village. He's just a frisky, androgynous free spirit. Ira, I think you'll get a real kick out of him.

IRA (*Freaked.*) Marjorie, the golem is out of control.

MARJORIE We've really got to go. You get a good night's sleep. Take an Ambien. Take Two.

Ira pushes her out the door. We can hear them talking in the hall.

IRA Marjorie, ring for the elevator.

Lee and Frieda are left alone.

LEE What's s a golem?

BLACKOUT

ACT TWO

Scene 3

The following day. Afternoon. Ira and Mohammed are in deep conversation.

IRA Now this is coming from personal experience? Not just heresay?

MOHAMMED Well, if it is the same group, I believe my cousin was involved with them in Baghdad. Powerful American people help finance this organization. Only they don't know what it really is.

IRA So you're telling me the Universal Human Rights Coalition is dangerous?

MOHAMMED I will merely tell you this. If one attempts to break away from them, one is never heard from again. We have not seen my cousin in over a year. Is Mrs. Taub mixed in with them?

IRA A friend of hers.

MOHAMMED Miss Green.

IRA How did you know?

MOHAMMED I have always had strange feelings about the lady. I do not like her.

The front door opens and Marjorie and Frieda enter.

MARJORIE Okay, we're all gathered here. So what's the big megillah?

IRA Ladies, sit down.

MARJORIE Why is Mohammed here? Is this another intervention to tell me I'm crazy?

IRA Marjorie, do you know when Lee will be back?

MARJORIE She said late afternoon. She wants to take us to a party tonight. I asked her if it was dressy and the only thing she'd say is that there'd be costumes waiting for us. We may be in over our heads.

IRA Lee really has to go.

MARJORIE On the other hand, perhaps exposure to this decadent netherworld could fuel my craft.

IRA Listen to what you're saying. You're swinging back and forth like a pendulum.

MARJORIE You think I don't know? I am ravaged by ambivalence. Look, my eye is twitching.

IRA Can't you see you're drawn to this woman like a moth to a flame?

MARJORIE She has this mesmerizing power over my mind and spirit. She is like a Rasputin.

IRA The spell may be broken after what I have to say.

MARJORIE What's wrong? What's happened?

IRA This morning I was paying bills. And, as you know, part of my monthly routine is balancing Frieda's checkbook. Frieda, two days ago did you write out a check to the Universal Human Rights Coalition?

FRIEDA (*Defensively.*) I don't know. I might have. Yeah.

MARJORIE That's Lee's group. Mother, that was very generous of you.

IRA It was for five thousand dollars.

MARJORIE (*Screams.*) Mother, are you crazy?

FRIEDA I don't have to fucking answer to any of you.

IRA Calm down, both of you. Frieda, do you remember writing this check?

FRIEDA I don't know. Yes. I suppose I did.

MARJORIE What possessed you?

FRIEDA You both left me to see that goddam piece of crap in Brooklyn, left me in the clutches of that phony. Oh, she was so lovey dovey. My best friend in the world.

MARJORIE She wouldn't do something like this. Tell us exactly what went on.

FRIEDA She took me back to my place. I was showing her photographs of your father and then I don't know what happened.

IRA Don't get upset.

MARJORIE Could you have misunderstood her? (*To Ira.*) She can barely hear out of her left ear.

FRIEDA Next thing I'm seated at the desk, she's hovering over me and I'm writing out a check. It was for five thousand dollars? I must have shit for brains.

MARJORIE I'm in such shock.

FRIEDA (*Desperately.*) You gotta cancel that check, Ira. Is it too late?

IRA It's been cashed.

MARJORIE Well, we've got to get the money back from them.

MOHAMMED No, Mrs. Taub. These are dangerous people.

MARJORIE What?

IRA I asked Mohammed up here because I had a hunch coming from Iraq, he might know something about the Universal Human Rights Coalition. Mohammed, you have the floor.

MOHAMMED Thank you, Dr. Taub. I do not wish to alarm but it is my understanding that this is a group who believes in action at any cost. Some of their ideas are noble in theory but they will stop at nothing to achieve their goals. They are fanatics.

MARJORIE This is a nightmare. They advocate violence?

MOHAMMED I can only tell you what I've heard. My friend's uncle's business partner had an associate who was in disagreement with them and they chopped up a tiger's whiskers into a fine powder and sprinkled it in his hummos. The sharp hairs perforated holes throughout his um . . .

FRIEDA Intestines and lower bowel?

MOHAMMED Yes and he, forgive my vulgarity, he shit himself to death.

FRIEDA Really?

MARJORIE (*Noticing her mother's rapt attention.*) Well, you certainly know your audience. This is the limit, Ira. This is the limit. This cannot go on.

IRA You really mean it? You're not going to waffle?

MARJORIE I feel so utterly betrayed. To raise cash for her crackpot group, she plied money out of the arthritic hands of my aged mother. And it's not even the money that's the issue. She kissed my ass and I fell for it. I'm such an idiot.

IRA We have to forge a plan. Tonight we tell her we've got family coming for a visit and we need the guestroom.

FRIEDA Who's coming? Uncle Izzie Hecht from Jacksonville? Why the hell'd you invite him?

MARJORIE Nobody's coming. It's a ruse!

They hear the front door unlocking. Lee enters carrying groceries.

LEE Hello, darlings.

MARJORIE I thought you were going to be out all day.

LEE My meeting ended sooner than I expected.

FRIEDA Was it a good meeting? You got something big planned?

LEE A celebrity auction and although I'm dying to tell you all about it, I'm sworn to secrecy. Marjorie, I found us the most divine hair conditioner. I know you're an Herbal Essence girl from way back but any hair stylist will tell you, you got to switch products now and then. Trust me on this. I'm a licensed beautician. Mohammed, have you come to fix the sink?

IRA Lee, we need to have a little talk. I understand that Frieda wrote you a check for five thousand dollars as a donation to your group.

LEE Yes, she did and everyone was so grateful.

IRA She thought she was writing it out for fifty dollars not five thousand. She'd like to write you out a new check.

FRIEDA No fucking way am I giving fifty dollars to those madmen.

LEE What did you tell them, Mohammed?

MOHAMMED You killed my cousin Achmed.

LEE Look, if we're going to eat at a decent hour, I'd better hustle. Tonight we're dining on Persian cuisine. Kashmiri lamb kebabs with an apricot dipping sauce.

FRIEDA Don't try anything funny. We know all about the tiger whiskers in the hummos trick.

LEE You've really lost me. What exactly am I being accused of?

MARJORIE I think you know.

LEE Believe me, I don't have a clue.

MARJORIE Then I'll spell it out for you. Acts of international terrorism will not be tolerated in this household.

LEE Let me get this straight. You think I'm some sort of a mishuganuh terrorist? How? Why?

IRA We've pieced it together. We know all about your organization. What they stand for and what they've done.

MARJORIE And Lil, I have to say, I am horrified beyond words.

LEE Margie, listen to me. Candace Bergen has donated a pair of De La Renta Gaucho pants for our spring auction. She is not by definition a terrorist.

FRIEDA An innocent dupe.

LEE This is patently absurd. This fantasy construct. First you guys think I'm invisible, now you got me blowing up Zabar's.

MARJORIE Mohammed's from Iraq. He knows from what he speaks.

LEE I am your friend. You're gonna listen to him? You're gonna listen to the doorman?

MARJORIE We trust Mohammed.

LEE And you don't trust me?

MARJORIE Mohammed didn't bilk my mother out of five thousand smackers.

LEE She made that donation out of her own free will.

FRIEDA Is she saying I'm gaga? I'll sue her ass in court.

MARJORIE How could you do this to us? You betrayed our trust.

LEE I was always very upfront. I told you I was fundraising.

MARJORIE From my mother? For all she knows, she could be signing the Camp David Accords. Was everything a lie? Are you really some sort of fanatic?

LEE Your definition of "fanatic" may be very different from mine.

IRA I think you've quite tested our friendship and generosity and patience.

LEE Oh, the saint feels used.

MARJORIE Lee!

IRA Let her denigrate me if it gives her satisfaction.

LEE You devote so many hours to your allergy clinic for the homeless. How about attacking the institutional structures that make such a clinic necessary? The environment that's strangling the breath out of us. But no, that won't provide the ego fix that the great man requires. It's not about helping people. It's just another tribute to the saintly Dr. Taub.

IRA Fuck off! Fuck you!

MARJORIE How dare you talk to my husband that way. Ira grew up as underprivileged as the lowest untouchable in India. My husband, who's never turned any patient away, who goes into the worst neighborhoods in Harlem on his day off to help the needy. I deeply resent this indictment.

LEE You should defend him. You're the perfect couple. He loves to see himself as the great man, and you love being the pathetic loser. Poor Marjorie. Poor pitiful Pearl.

MARJORIE I don't need to hear this. I'm going out.

IRA Where are you going?

MARJORIE To a movie. A museum. Anywhere to get away from her.

LEE Don't you get tired of spending your whole life in museums and dark screening rooms?

IRA My wife is an intellectual.

LEE That's great if she gained something from it. You read all these wonderful books but you learn nothing from them. All you get is another chance to brood and bitch that you've done nothing with your life. Don't you see, it's just cultural masturbation?

MARJORIE That's disgusting. I brought you into this house when you stranded out in the cold, without a—without a "blechel to your lechel". (*Trans: a penny piece in your ass.*) Is that good Yiddish, Mama?

FRIEDA Something like that.

MARJORIE And you've done nothing but exploit and swindle us. And now you mask it by pretending to shine the light of truth on our sad, deluded lives. You are a terrorist of the heart, of the soul. You go back to your group and tell them you failed in your mission to blow up this house, Mrs. Saddam Hussein.

LEE Turn me into whatever you need me to be. Identify me with any cause. I really don't care.

MARJORIE You know, Lil, at the moment, I'm identifying quite strongly with the State of Israel. My borders feel threatened and I'm getting very angry.

LEE Well, the other night the State of Israel didn't seem to mind its multiple orgasms.

IRA Lee, for God's sake, not in front of uh Mohammed.

MOHAMMED I'm perfectly fine, Dr. Taub. I know that terrorists will employ any weapon in their arsenal.

LEE Suddenly you're all so obsessed with terrorism. Are you aware that most terrorism in the world is financed by the United States?

IRA We don't want to get into a political debate with you.

LEE I can give you a list of U.S. financed Israeli atrocities against the Palestinians.

FRIEDA Lee, are you a Jew for Jesus?

MARJORIE Mother, please. Lee, are you anti-Israel?

LEE I am not anti-Israel. I believe in the dignity of all peoples.

IRA Cut the bull. Give us a straight answer. What is your involvement with the Universal Human Rights Coalition? The truth.

LEE The real truth is that Marjorie's upset because of the unexplored feelings I've stirred in her.

FRIEDA What feelings?

LEE You don't give a damn if Golda Meir was a world class terrorist. The truth of the matter is you can't face your bi-sexuality, your sterile, joyless marriage to this ego-maniac, your warped children who can't stand the sight of you and your inability to free yourself from your monster of a mother.

MARJORIE Golda Meir was a terrorist? That wonderful old woman who lived a life of heroism? You are sick. You are a sicko. I bet you're one of those kooks who go around saying the Holocaust never happened.

LEE That's not fair. I have never said that. You cannot accuse me of that.

MARJORIE Get out! Out! Out of my house!

LEE Marjorie, don't be childish.

MARJORIE I want you out of this house this minute.

IRA I'll get you your coat. (*He gets her coat from the closet.*)

LEE But my things.

MARJORIE You can pick 'em up with the doorman. Go!

LEE Marjorie, open your eyes. You're desperately inventing some excuse to get rid of me.

MARJORIE No, you are the one who must open her eyes. You look at us and only see hand puppets easy to manipulate. But you know what you are really looking at? A family, a unit, a small army and this nine hundred thousand-dollar co-op is a fortress unconquerable.

LEE Marjorie—

MARJORIE You infiltrated our home with the modus operandi of exploitation and Lillian, I condemn you for it. My little army has had its insurrections, true, our inner rebellions. Yes. Bitter rage over past injustices but we know where to draw the line. Blood is never shed in apartment 12C. Your presence has changed us irreparably but not the way you intended. We have traveled a mountainous road full of land mines. But we will endure and you know why? You know why? Because love triumphs. Love, acceptance, faith and forgiveness, my little partisan army has all of that in abundance. Now get your controlling, manipulative, self-hating, pretentious, anti-Semitic ass out of here!

Ira hands Lee her coat. With quiet dignity, she takes the Taub's house keys out of her bag and hands them to Marjorie.

LEE Marjorie, here are your keys. I think you've figured out which doors to open.

MARJORIE Where will you go? Do you want to pack your things?

Lee crosses to the door. Mohammed opens it for her. She pauses in the doorway with an enigmatic smile on her face.

LEE You can leave them downstairs. I guess I'll head for Monaco sooner than I expected. Long ago, I promised Grace that I'd keep an eye on the children. Au revoir.

She exits. Mohammed closes the door behind her.

IRA You sure gave it to her. Like Sonny Liston, right in the chops.

FRIEDA You were magnificent. Like Judith or Ruth in the bible. I'm so proud of you.

MARJORIE I'm glad I could make you both proud but it's a very sad situation.

IRA Our home is our own again. You did good. (*He kisses her.*)

MARJORIE I still feel unsettled.

FRIEDA Here she goes.

MARJORIE Lee. She's an enigma. A sphinx. Was it an accident that she just happened to knock on our door or did she plan it? Was everything from the beginning a scheme to exploit us?

IRA Why? You think the other night? Everything. You think she wasn't attracted to—

MARJORIE Ira. (*She indicates that he should ixnay about the threeway.*)

IRA She is an enigma. She is a sphinx.

MARJORIE To begin to understand her, one would have to read the entire collected works of Schnitzler. Perhaps Lee left us with a special gift. Perhaps inadvertently, she gave us all a sense of—

IRA (*Interrupting her.*) Look at the time. I was due at NYU over a half-hour ago.

MARJORIE When will you be home?

IRA I promised I'd have coffee with some of my students at five.

MARJORIE You have to?

IRA I can't let 'em down. I've been out of touch the last few days. My kids say they need their weekly fix of Dr. Taub.

MARJORIE Then you must.

IRA I feel crummy running out on you like this. Maybe I can leave a message at the Student Union and tell them I can't make it.

MARJORIE It's fine. Really. You shouldn't let them down. Those kids are crazy about you, and why shouldn't they be?

FRIEDA Ira, walk me back. If I hurry I can still catch that *Matlock* rerun.

Ira walks Frieda to the door.

IRA Marge, you're really something.

FRIEDA Ira, you exposed that woman for what she is. Don't give Marjorie all the credit.

MARJORIE Mother, I noticed a small tear in the carpet in the hall. Watch where you're going and don't trip.

FRIEDA Wouldn't that be the clincher?

IRA I'll be back before you know it.

They exit.

MOHAMMED Mrs. Taub, will you be all right?

MARJORIE What an interesting question? Yes. I think I'm think I'm going to be fine.

MOHAMMED Oh, I finally read your favorite book *Siddhartha.*

MARJORIE You did? And?

MOHAMMED I liked it very much. So deceptively simple. After his long spiritual quest, Siddhartha discovers that the Buddha he seeks is within himself.

MARJORIE And he derives great comfort from communing with a ferryman. How perfect. Yes? A man who shuttles people across the river on his boat. His work provides him with a unique insight into the human comedy.

MOHAMMED Rather like a doorman.

MARJORIE Very much so.

She studies his face for a moment and then gets a new inspiration.

MARJORIE Are you hungry?

MOHAMMED I forgot to eat lunch.

MARJORIE I'm famished. Starving like a prisoner escaped from

Devil's Island. How about I fix us a snack? And nothing too fussy or frou frou. I have a craving for something simple and basic. Bread, coarse peasant bread with seeds and grain, a sharp Vermont cheddar, and a thick juicy beefsteak tomato. Sound good and hearty?

MOHAMMED Sounds wonderful. May I help?

MARJORIE You'll be my sous-chef. Come into the kitchen.

Marjorie and Mohammed move toward the kitchen. She throws an apron at him. He ties it around his waist.

MARJORIE I've got a jar of fantastic marinated olives. You can start chopping them up and I'll throw together some sort of spread. It'll be Heaven. Don't worry, I'll show you how to do it.

MOHAMMED I'd love to learn how to cook, Mrs. Taub, but I've always been a little afraid of the kitchen.

MARJORIE There's absolutely nothing to be afraid of, Mohammed. It's just another room filled with infinite possibilities. I'll show you how to make a perfect Bernaise. There's a secret tip I wormed out of Julia Child.

MOHAMMED (*impressed*) Julia Child? You know her?

MARJORIE No. She was signing books at Barnes and Noble, but I got it out of her.

MOHAMMED A Bernaise sauce. It sounds very difficult.

MARJORIE It's both simple and difficult, Mohammed. Like so much in life.

The two of them begin to prepare their small feast and gab about food and books and a million things as music rises and our tale comes to an end.

END OF PLAY